Making
Connections
That Work

Making Connections That Work

A Biblical Guide to Building and Maintaining Godly Relationships

Robert Fergusson

Sovereign World

Sovereign World Ltd
PO Box 777
Tonbridge
Kent TN11 0ZS
England

Email: info@sovereign-world.com
Website: www.sovereign-world.com

All Scripture quotations are taken from the New International Version unless otherwise stated. Copyright © 1973, 1978 International Bible Society. Published by Hodder & Stoughton.

ISBN 1 85240 341 1

Cover photo and internal photos provided courtesy of Don Cooper-Williams
Cover design by CCD, www.ccdgroup.co.uk
Typeset by CRB Associates, Reepham, Norfolk
Printed in the United States of America

Contents

Acknowledgments

How can I possibly thank all the people who have inspired, encouraged and influenced me over the years? This book is simply a by-product of all the grace shown to me by others and all the lessons taught me by often older, usually wiser and mostly better people! Nonetheless, I would especially like to thank . . .

My wonderful wife and best friend Amanda who has taught me grace and without whose unfailing support, practical wisdom and persistent prayers I wouldn't have been able to write.

My children, Catherine and son-in-law David, Andrew and Eleanor, who are all a constant source of inexpressible joy.

My family in England who has taught me so much and is always there for me.

My wonderful friends and family at Hillsong Church in Australia with whom I share my life and who have accepted me with all my idiosyncrasies! Words cannot express what they mean to me.

The Lord Jesus Christ who gave His life for me. I am eternally grateful. What more can I say?

Foreword

If there is one book that my husband Mark and I have been waiting for, it is this one. Robert Fergusson, our dear friend and one of our treasured pastors, lives a life worthy of being called a 'minister of the gospel' and is one of those Bible teachers that you wish would never finish preaching! He has an ability to communicate the Word of God with such precision and fervency. Every sentence is, without fail, carefully and prayerfully constructed, jam packed with anecdotes, historical facts, insight and revelation, not to mention accompanied by some of the funniest true stories you've ever heard!

When I started to read the book, the Holy Spirit started speaking to my heart so powerfully, as many years ago, when talking to my Lord about my mission in life, He gently but powerfully spoke into the core of my being, that I was to be a bridge ... face down, allowing my life to be used to 'provide passage'. For many years I never understood what this meant, but I did start to feel the Master's hand working in my life, a process that is still very much 'in motion', to cause me to be emotionally, relationally and spiritually strong in life, that as the winds of life started to blow, this bridge would remain strong and secure. It is indeed a journey, and one that takes time, energy, focus, passion, commitment and confidence, *'that he who began a good work in you will carry it on to completion until the day of Christ Jesus'* (Philippians 1:6).

As you read this magnificent book, you will begin to see that unless you begin to apply these eternal principles to your own existence, a life rich in relationship will always be out of your reach, bringing much disappointment and heartache. Humanity was never designed to exist void of connection, but *was* designed for relationship and community, honesty and hope.

I pray that as you read your heart is challenged and inspired to pursue a life of truthful connection and bountiful community.

Be blessed, dear friends,

Darlene Zschech

Introduction

It was a typically grey autumn day when I first walked over the Millennium Bridge in London. Two years before, in the summer of 2000, a drama was played out there: a drama that is the central theme of this book. Amid great self-congratulation, the first bridge to be built in London for over one hundred years was opened. The Millennium Bridge, designed by Sir Norman Foster, stretches, in his words, like a 'slender blade across the Thames'.[1] The costly aluminium and stainless steel footbridge links the old St Paul's Cathedral with the new Tate Modern Art Gallery. The city required a new twenty-first-century icon, a symbol of achievement, a sign of a bright and cultured future, with which the despondent could enliven their hopes. And so it built itself a bridge.

A similar project had been completed in France a year before. This time the Pont Solférino footbridge was built in Paris to link the old Tuileries Gardens on the Right Bank of the River Seine with the new Musée d'Orsay Art Gallery. Once again, a city was looking for more than a thoroughfare. Yet, despite its promise, Paris' new bridge was closed as soon as it opened. There were concerns about it swaying in the wind. After the event, Marcus Binney, the architecture correspondent for *The Times* newspaper in England, in an article entitled 'Troubled Bridge Over the Water', wrote, 'A bouncing bridge across the Seine is a warning to our own Millennium footbridge'.[2] As anticipated, London's Millennium Bridge was also closed on the day of its official opening, after an estimated 100,000 people had crossed it! People complained of seasickness as the bridge swayed dramatically. The experts were called in to stabilize both bridges.

Predictably, the failure of the bridges elicited a great deal of comment and provoked a number of questions. In London the media ridiculed the planners. Many thought it was indicative of the state of the nation. The design, testing procedures and the huge costs involved were all challenged. Was it safe? Should the number of pedestrians be

limited? How was it going to be fixed? Did we need a bridge anyway
when there are other worthier causes? And so the drama continued!
I was in England when the Millennium Bridge was opened and the
debate hit the headlines. As I read about the demise of the bridge,
I concluded that I was not observing a play so much as reading a
parable, a parable about our society.

The idea was highlighted to me a number of years earlier during a
trip to Tasmania, Australia, a trip that proved to be the inspiration for
this book. I was visiting the picturesque town of Richmond with some
friends. Richmond is famous for being one of the earliest European
settlements in Australia and infamous for its jail. The Coal River flows
through the town and in an area of parkland is crossed by a small stone
bridge on which is inscribed 1823, the date in which it was built.
Richmond Bridge is considered the oldest in Australia. Constructions
such as these were not part of Australia's ancient history.

Standing just next to the bridge is St John's Church, built in 1836
amidst a time of conflict and hardship. It is the oldest Catholic Church
in Australia. I walked past the bridge and on into the church where I
picked up the small guidebook. In it I read the following statement,
'There is an affinity between bridges and churches – one taking you
safely over its span to the bank on the opposite side; the other taking
you safely over the span of life, from birth to eternity'.[3] Though a
simple and well-worn illustration, it struck me with an unusual
freshness.

It occurred to me at the time that my life as a minister was
inextricably involved with the building of bridges: bridges between
God and humankind and bridges between humankind and itself. I
was, in fact, called to build relationships and that if I was serious about
my life and future, I needed to give some time to the study of bridges!
Over the last few years as I have done so, the truths that I have learned
have greatly helped my own relationships and have also enabled me to
assist others more effectively. Thus the brief incident in Tasmania not
only challenged me to grow personally, but also inspired me to write
this book so that others may apply the same truths.

In the light of this, the stories of the Solférino and Millennium
bridges may well have some lessons that can be practically applied to
all of our lives. As our decaying, yet strangely expectant world starts a
new century, it is looking for symbols of hope. It is not surprising that
two of its key cities built a bridge that connects the old with the new.
Communities need to make these connections. They require bridges.

They are prepared to pay a high price for them and subsequently are shocked at their failure. Their designers are questioned and their need challenged, but thousands want to experience them. The same could be said of our relationships. Despite our circumstances, the high price involved and the current crop of failures we can and must build successful relationships: 'life bridges'. That is the subject of this book.

Notes

1. Sir Norman Foster. Quoted by Marcus Binney, *The Times*, Monday 12 June 2000.
2. Binney, *The Times*, Monday 12 June 2000.
3. Guidebook, St John's Church, Richmond, Tasmania, Australia.

PART 1

The Theory of Building 'Life Bridges'

Chapter 1

Civil Engineering

A Bridge Defined

Bridge. n. **1**. A structure that crosses over or spans an obstacle such as a road, railway, river or harbour and provides passage over that obstacle. E.g. The Sydney Harbour Bridge. n. **2**. Something that resembles this span, either in shape or function. E.g. A relationship between two people.

To an engineer, they were two, twin tandem compound steam engines built by Armstrong, Mitchell & Co. of Newcastle, England: Numbers 608 and 609. To me they were dragons! They towered above me, a glistening and scaly green, belching steam and menacing energy. The image is still vivid in my mind! I was staring at the heart of a bridge. I was around ten years old and my mother had somehow arranged a trip to visit the bowels of the great Tower Bridge in London, the steam engines that then raised the roadway for the ships to pass. I am sure that there were other people there but I don't remember them. It was just me and the engines! Maybe it was then that I learned to love bridges. Or maybe it was a few years later on the 2000-year-old Pont du Gard in the south of France. Either way it was my mother's fault! This time I clambered, much to her consternation, along the top of the crumbling, 47-metre-high Roman aqueduct and imagined the glories of Rome. Whether consciously or not, I don't know, my mother was instilling a passion in me.

With definite intention, when my daughter was eighteen, I took her to Istanbul and we stood on the walls of the Topkapi Palace and looked out over the Bosphorus, the historical stretch of water that flows from the Black Sea to the Sea of Marmara and divides the city. I wanted her to see the Bosphorus Bridge which connects Europe with Asia. I don't know whether my daughter was impressed or not, but I was doing what a friend of mine says is one of the main responsibilities of parenthood, to build memories. In the same year I revisited my own memories on another trip to Tower Bridge. I discovered my childhood 'dragons' in a museum, quiet and sadly impotent. In 1976, they were replaced with more modern and efficient electric motors. Nonetheless, the bridge itself still possessed a magical quality: a quality that I find in all bridges.

Evidently, I am not on my own in my fascination with bridges. Whenever friends arrive in my hometown of Sydney for a visit, I take them over the Sydney Harbour Bridge on the way home from the airport. It's not a particularly convenient route for me but it's worth it to see their face and hear their comments. 'It's massive!' 'What an amazing piece of engineering!' 'When was it built?' 'In the depression – amazing!' Many of them want to walk across it on foot or even climb it. There is no doubt that bridges of all types possess a great power to instill wonder.

The construction and sometimes destruction of natural bridges have proved to be an inspiration not only to my friends and me but also to generations of poets, writers and film makers. The poet Lord Byron wrote about the famous Venetian bridge, the 'Bridge of Sighs', in his poem 'Childe Harold's Pilgrimage'. Award-winning books and films, such as *The Bridge of San Luis Rey* by Thornton Wilder, and Pierre Boulle's book, *Bridge over the River Kwai*, which was later turned into a popular movie, have captivated readers and audiences. Yet it has not been only natural bridges that have motivated communicators but also metaphorical ones. Simon and Garfunkel's 'Bridge over Troubled Water' remains one of the top-selling music albums of all time.

In the English language the word 'bridge' refers to a whole variety of connections and there are numerous expressions that use the picture of a bridge. Idioms commonly used are 'to burn one's bridges' and 'to cross a bridge when one comes to it'. Rarer ones include 'beside the bridge' which means to have gone astray, or 'a silver bridge' which refers to an attractive way of escape. Yet it is the use of the term 'bridge' as a form of relationship that particularly concerns me here. For instance, we can 'bridge the gap' between separated communities or 'build bridges' with new acquaintances. The word 'bridge-builder' is often used of those accomplished in the art of making or mending relationships.

The Church regularly uses this image of bridge-building. Yet it is a strange image to use since it is not one that is mentioned in the Bible. Though various significant rivers meander their way through the chapters of the Bible, it rarely refers to the regular crossing of those rivers. Moses, of course, crossed the Red Sea and his servant Joshua crossed the Jordon, but neither of them used bridges! We do know that bridges existed in ancient Israel and were used extensively by the Romans. American Professor of Religion Roger S. Boraas writes that, 'Archaeological remains and literary texts show use of such devices in the biblical period both in and out of Palestine',[1] yet the term 'bridge' itself, apart from an inconclusive reference in the Apocrypha, is not used as such in the Bible. Nonetheless, if I were to describe the Bible to someone who has never read it I would call it a 'book of bridges'.

The Bible is about relationships: the covenant between God and the nation of Israel, the marriage between Jesus Christ and His Church, the reconciliation between God the Father and any one of us who will return to Him and become His children. In each of these cases, love is the common link. We know that it also connects us as people. It enables us to share what we have and establishes communication between us. It removes the obstructions that so often separate us. God-given love is, therefore, perhaps the greatest and most profound bridge of all. Jesus Christ Himself said that all the Law and the Prophets, that is the entire Bible, can be summed up in the two phrases, 'Love God' and 'Love your neighbour' (Matthew 22:34–40). So it is accurate to describe the Bible as a book of bridges and reasonable to use its wisdom as a basis for this book. The purpose of the book, therefore, is to use the truths of the Bible to demonstrate why we all need these bridges in our lives and to illustrate how we can build them successfully.

What is a bridge?

The English word 'bridge', as I have already suggested, has a multi-plicity of meanings that range from a wooden support on a violin to a passage in a song that connects two verses. It is a term that is used in sport, electronics and even dentistry! However, all of the various uses of the word can be reduced to two basic meanings. Either a bridge is a structure that spans an obstacle or it is something that resembles such a span.

In this book, I am going to compare the attributes of the structures that span roads, railways or rivers to the various relationships in our lives that resemble these structures. Civil engineers are concerned with the design, building and maintenance of the first category of bridges. They are called 'civil' engineers because their work is concerned with the 'ordinary life of citizens'. The second category of bridge is the domain of what I call 'relational engineers'! They are equally involved in serving the community by building strong and positive relationships. It is my contention that we should all be 'relational engineers' and though we may never be civil engineers as such, as those committed to the formation and health of 'bridges', we can all learn a great deal from them.

For instance, I would like to suggest that the building of a 'relational bridge' has the same purposes and is established on the same premises as that of a civil bridge. The two purposes give us a simple working definition of a bridge. The three premises give us the essential theory that will be the foundation stone for the practical skills taught later.

If we are to embark on any building project it is essential that we first determine the purpose behind our work. One of my ancestors, George Edward Gavey, was a civil engineer in the nineteenth century and was involved in the building of railways in various countries including Russia, Spain and Venezuela. Between the years 1846 and 1856 his responsibilities comprised of supervising works in central and southern England. It was a time of burgeoning industrial growth. The pressure to transport goods across the country would have been enormous, and many relied on him to do so. The work, in common with all engineering projects, had many challenges, but none more so than the building of bridges over the numerous valleys, gullies and streams that crisscross the country. He would have had to draw on the expertise of his supervisor, one of the greatest bridge-builders of his day, Isembard Kingdom Brunel. Gavey's purpose was simply to overcome these obstacles in order to transport goods. This simple conclusion gives us the purposes behind all bridge-building, whether civil or relational.

All bridges are required to span a gap between two separated 'bodies' in order to provide some sort of passage between them. They therefore have two definite purposes. Firstly, a bridge is built in order to span a barrier or an obstacle. In other words, it overcomes or removes a 'negative'. Secondly, a bridge is built in order to provide passage or communication. In other words, it creates or provides 'a positive'.

It is very important for us to understand both what I have called the negative and the positive purposes of bridge-building. A great engineer, like Brunel, who built the Clifton Suspension Bridge in Bristol, England in 1864, had carefully to balance these two purposes when building a bridge. On the one hand, he had gracefully, safely and defiantly to span a deep valley. On the other hand, he had carefully and pragmatically to meet the transport needs of the community. The danger of just concentrating on the first purpose is that the bridge would be safe but useless! The danger of just concentrating on the second purpose is that the bridge would be useful but unsafe!

The same is true of relational engineers. We must balance the negatives and the positives. If we unrealistically attempt to create a totally 'safe relationship', our focus will be solely to overcome obstacles. All our time will be taken up dealing with the negatives so that we have little time for positive communication. The end result will be a useless relic! Conversely, if we concentrate on all the benefits of the relationship and yet fail to deal with the evident problems, it will end in collapse and tragedy.

At this point you may be asking, which comes first, the removal of the negative or the addition of the positive? In reality, they often occur at the same time. Nonetheless, if we are building a bridge, we cannot provide passage until the barrier has been overcome. In other words, the negative must be tackled initially. Imagine a young man who has been brought up to be racially prejudiced. Despite this curse, he falls in love with someone from another culture. They are both attracted to one another and they communicate readily and positively. It seems to be a blessed relationship until the curse of prejudice rises to the surface. The woman is made to feel inferior and undervalued. It becomes obvious that the blessing cannot continue until the curse has first been removed. Sooner or later the obstacles will come to light.

Paul the apostle gives some good advice to his friends in Ephesus when he tells them that in order to change for the better they need both to 'put off' the negatives and 'put on' the positives. He wrote,

> *'You were taught, with regard to your former way of life, to put off your old self, which is being corrupted by its deceitful desires; to be made new in the attitude of your minds; and to put on the new self, created to be like God in true righteousness and holiness.'* (Ephesians 4:22–24)

His logic was very simple. If we long for the freedom that truth brings, we must first stop being a liar and then be honest. If we desire to remove the devil from our homes, we should first rid ourselves of our anger and then be gentle. If we want to be a 'giver' we must first stop being a 'taker'. If we want to be encouraging we must first stop being insulting. In other words, beneficial growth always involves both subtraction and addition. To use a different image, a snake cannot enjoy a new skin until it has removed the old one.

As I explained earlier, an understanding of the two purposes of a bridge, the removal of a negative and the creation of a positive, now gives us a clearer working definition of either a civil or relational bridge:

▶ *A bridge both overcomes barriers and provides communication between two separated entities.*

However, our understanding of the two purposes not only gives us this definition, it also gives us inspiration. The force that has driven man to build bridges for thousands of years has been the God-given passion to overcome obstacles and also the craving to communicate. These same desires should compel us to build bridges of relationships.

The three premises on which a bridge is built

Having established the purposes of bridge-building, we now need to turn our attention to another fundamental principle. I have already mentioned that both civil and relational bridges are built on the same three premises. They are simple observations but vital to the application of the lessons that are taught later. The three 'premises' are the bedrock from which the bridge gains support.

Most of us have the tendency to neglect the theory and cut straight to the practice. We then wonder why we are having such difficulty applying the steps that we have learned. The second half of the book of Ephesians, from which I have already quoted, contains some excellent guidelines for relationships. However, the first half is more theoretical, more principle based. I don't think this was an accident. Paul understood that principles are foundational to practice. In this book, I am starting with definitions, purposes and premises for the same reason.

Bridges are necessary

We might expect that the first of the foundational principles or premises on which a bridge is built to be wonderfully profound. Well, it isn't! We simply need to believe that bridges are necessary. We need to have faith that 'parties' need joining and without a bridge they would be incomplete. Our faith in their necessity demands their building and fuels their maintenance. A bridge requires a huge amount of time and resources both initially to build and then to service. We must therefore believe that our investment will bear fruit.

In the case of a river, there may be technical, economic or even political reasons why a bridge is not built. The community may determine that transport or communication can occur without the aid of a bridge. After all, obstacles can be crossed in a number of ways. Merchandise can be transported by ferry. Information can be carried electronically. However, there comes a point when the requirements of the community to convey goods outweigh the difficulties and a bridge is planned. Nonetheless, the question must still be asked, 'Is the bridge really necessary?' This is not just a question of necessity, it is a question of faith. The community must believe that the bridge is necessary or they won't use it. On 17 July 1981 the Humber Estuary Bridge was opened in Yorkshire, England. At the time it was built it had the longest span of any cable-suspension bridge in the world. It was an astounding piece of engineering but it soon became apparent that the traffic flow was way below expectation. In other words, much of the community did not believe that it was necessary and chose not to use it. The critics called it 'the bridge from nowhere to nowhere'!

This line of argument can readily be applied to the formation of relationships. If we are going to be successful in their creation we must believe that they are really essential or they will go nowhere! Their formation and maintenance also takes a great deal of sacrifice. We must believe that it is worth it! If we don't fully grasp the necessity of a relationship, it will quickly become obsolete in our thinking and we will abandon it. The exact reasons for their necessity will become evident later in the book. However, it would be profitable at this stage to highlight the questions that we must honestly ask ourselves:

- Do I believe that relationships in general are really necessary?
- Do I believe that my current relationships are necessary?
- Am I prepared to pay the price for building new relationships?
- Am I prepared to pay the price for growing my old relationships?
- Have I ever abandoned a relationship because I didn't believe in it?
- Am I prepared to re-establish a relationship if my faith is restored?

Bridges overcome obstacles

In some quarters engineers might be accused by some of being boring, surrounded, as they are, by the mundane and the measurable. However, in reality, the great engineers are visionaries, seeing what others have only glimpsed and achieving what many have not even dreamed. They often build bridges that are later described in the newspapers as a 'masterpiece of modern engineering' or a 'triumph of contemporary design'! The reason they can do this is because they genuinely believe the second premise of bridge-building, namely that bridges overcome obstacles. This second premise is drawn from the 'negative' purpose of building bridges, the overcoming of barriers. However, the second premise, like the first, is an issue of faith. It is what might be termed a scientific faith. The engineer has to believe that the bridge has the power to span the barrier facing him. He has to believe in what is often the unknown surveyor, the untried design, the unproven materials and his own ability to master them all with his already stretched expertise! No one has built this bridge before and he has to convince his backers that all is well.

Although the American president, John F. Kennedy, was not an engineer, his vision of sending man to the moon illustrates my point. In 1962, he had to convince his backers, the American public that the 'divide' that he was proposing to cross was not only necessary but also possible. His speech delivered at Rice University, Houston, Texas on 12 September 1962 still inspires. In it he said,

> 'We choose to go to the moon in this decade and do the other things, not because they are easy, but because they are hard ... we shall send to the moon, 240,000 miles away ... a giant rocket more than 300 feet tall ... made of new metal alloys, some of which have not yet been invented, capable of standing heat and stresses several times more than have ever been experienced, fitted together with a precision better than the finest watch, carrying all the equipment needed for propulsion, guidance, control, communications, food and survival, on an untried mission, to an unknown celestial body, and then return it safely to earth, re-entering the atmosphere at speeds of over 25,000 miles per hour, causing heat about half that of the temperature of the sun ... And therefore, as we set sail we ask God's blessing on the most hazardous and dangerous and greatest adventure on which man has ever embarked.'[2]

There is no doubt that he believed that the 'bridge' that he was proposing to build could overcome all obstacles.

It is this type of measured yet visionary faith that we need when we propose to embark on the adventure of building relationships. If we are getting married, we are facing the unknown! Whether we like it or not, there are massive differences between us. So we draw strength from the faith that our commitment to each other will bridge the gap that separates us. We don't ignore the problems. We know that there are genuine difficulties, yet we believe that the bridge has the power to overcome them. If we do not believe in the power of the relationship, then the obstacles will grow in our minds, undermine the very foundation of the bridge and eventually sweep it away. It might be helpful at this stage to ask ourselves some more questions:

- Do I believe that one of the purposes of building relationships is to overcome problems?
- Do I believe that I need faith in order to overcome relational problems?
- Do I have faith in the power of relationships?
- Am I prepared to take the risks that are necessary to build bridges?

Bridges provide passage

The third and final premise on which a bridge is built is that it must be believed that the bridge being built will provide a passage between the two 'parties'. This premise is taken from the 'positive' side of bridge-building, the provision of communication. Once again, the engineer must build on a premise of faith. He must have no doubt that successful communication will not only be possible but will be constantly improved.

In many modern cities the building of a bridge is often accompanied by a vast array of criticism from all quarters. The 'city fathers' complain about the ugliness of the design, the taxpayers argue about the prodigious cost, and of course the local residents remonstrate about the inconvenience of the building work and the changes in traffic flow. Amid this barrage of negative comment, when the innocent engineers often have to read insulting newspaper articles and possibly even negotiate aggressive picketers or demonstrators, their faith has to be maintained. They have to believe that they are doing the right thing. Their constant theme during this time is, 'Wait and see. It will improve. Mark my words!' Of course, the opening of the bridge is accompanied by fanfare but still the hecklers curse the new toll and mumble that they will refuse to use the bridge! Six months pass, however, and faith prevails. It is evident that communication in the city is improved. Thousands now praise the new landmark. Inhabitants boast of the achievements of their city. The critics are strangely silent or perhaps turn their attention to another new project. The engineers continue to believe, their faith rewarded.

This story may seem far removed from the subject of relationships until one is involved, as I am, in promoting them. I have extolled the virtues and benefits of marriage only to be rounded on at the end of the talk by those opposed to its 'design'. I have challenged people to make friends only to be told that it takes too much time and effort. I have tried to persuade a couple to get married after years of double-minded engagement and have heard the words, 'But I am worried about all the changes that will be required'. It is amazing how negative we can be about what is so essentially good. Through it all I have tried to remain positive because I fundamentally believe relationships are the right thing and will provide powerful and vital communication. Of course, the critics change their tune when they begin to reap the benefits of the relational bridge. Even my own mother was initially highly critical of my proposed marriage, saying on one occasion, 'I will only give you two years'! She eventually became one of our greatest supporters. She began to believe. Nonetheless, even many years later, if we do not determine to work consistently at the 'positive purpose' of bridge-building, and believe in the premise that the marriage does 'provide passage', then the relationship could collapse through neglect and decay. Once again, some questions will enable us to focus our thinking:

- Do I believe that communication can be both positive and powerful?
- Do I believe that good relationships release the power of communication?
- Do I believe in the concept of marriage?
- Am I prepared to accept the changes that new relationships will bring?
- Am I prepared to remain positive about relationships despite the critics?

If we return to the book of Ephesians, we see that these same three premises are beautifully illustrated for us. Paul encourages us that, though we used to be separate from God and His promises, we are now reconciled to Him. He uses the image of the Ephesians, as Gentiles, being historically barred from God's blessing of Israel. Initially, he establishes the first premise of bridge-building: bridges are necessary. Notice the language he uses:

> '... *remember that at that time you were* **separate** *from Christ, excluded from citizenship in Israel and foreigners to the covenants of the promise, without hope and without God in the world.'*
>
> (Ephesians 2:12, emphasis mine)

Without a 'Life Bridge' we are distant and alienated from God. We have no future, promise of blessing or power to change. A bridge to God is vital.

Paul then establishes the second premise of bridge-building: Bridges overcome obstacles. Once again notice the language:

> *'But now in Christ Jesus you who once were far away have been brought near through the blood of Christ. For he himself is our peace, who has made the two one and has destroyed the barrier, the dividing wall of hostility, by abolishing in his flesh the law with its commandments and regulations. His purpose was to create in himself one new man out of the two, thus making peace, and in this one body to reconcile both of them to God through the cross, by which he put to death their hostility. He came and preached peace to you who were far away and peace to those who were near.'*
>
> (Ephesians 2:13–17)

There was a barrier, a wall that divided God and humankind. Yet, through Christ's death on the cross, the two totally separate sides were connected. A 'Life Bridge' had overcome all known obstacles.

He continues by describing the third premise of bridge-building: bridges provide passage,

> *'For through him we both have* **access** *to the Father by one Spirit.'*
>
> (Ephesians 2:18, emphasis mine)

Once the barriers have been overcome, transport can take place. We have access to God through the blood of Christ. We can communicate with each other freely. The 'Life Bridge' has fulfilled its purpose. At no point has Paul mentioned the word 'bridge' and yet he doesn't need to. The principles of 'relational engineering' are established, the foundations built.

In this chapter, I have given a definition of a 'bridge' based on its two fundamental purposes. I have also described three premises of bridge-building that are rooted in the two purposes. We need to be aware at this stage that we will never tackle the all-too-often complex and painful task of building and rebuilding relationships until we fully grasp these principles, which is why the first half of this book is devoted to them. However, if we do master the knowledge, belief and determination on which a bridge is supported, and if we do effectively apply the simple skills of 'civil engineering', then there are no boundaries to the success we will achieve or the fulfilment we will experience in our various acquaintances, friendships and marriages.

Summary and advice

1. **Bridges are an essential part of our history and our language.** We need to study and learn from them.

2. **The Bible is a 'book of bridges'.** We should read it in order to learn how to connect with God and relate with people.

3. **We are all 'relational engineers'.** We therefore have a responsibility to build bridges of relationships.

4. **There are two purposes of a bridge.** A bridge has a negative purpose and a positive one. Firstly, a bridge overcomes barriers and, secondly, it provides communication. In order to create the positive in our lives we need first to eliminate the negative.

5. **There are three premises on which bridges are built.** These premises are issues of faith.

6. **Premise 1: Bridges are necessary.** We must believe that relationships are a necessity in our lives.

7. **Premise 2: Bridges will overcome obstacles.** We must believe that relationships have the power to overcome the difficulties that oppose them.

8. **Premise 3: Bridges will provide passage.** We must believe that relationships provide powerful and vital communication.

9. **It is essential to understand the theory before we attempt the practice**. Too many people have tried to build relational bridges without a clear purpose or any foundational faith in the principles of bridge-building.

Notes

1. Roger Boraas. Quoted in *Harper's Bible Dictionary*, ed. Paul J. Achtemier (Harper & Row, 1985).
2. John F. Kennedy. *The Greatest Speeches of President John F. Kennedy* (Titan Publishing, 2000).

THE FIRST
PREMISE

*Bridges
Are Necessary*

Chapter 2

The Reason for Rialto

Why We Build Bridges

It is no coincidence that the Sydney Harbour Bridge and the Empire State Building were opened within a year of one another. Sydney Harbour Bridge, perhaps the most famous and significant landmark in Sydney, Australia and at the time the longest single-arch span bridge in the world, was opened on Saturday 19 March 1932. The Empire State Building in New York, the tallest building in the world at the time, was officially opened by President Hoover a few months previously, on 1 May 1931. They were both built in the 'Depression' when people needed to build impossible dreams. They both remain icons today. Civil engineering is not simply practical, it is sometimes prophetic.

In a television interview to mark his seventieth year, Billy Graham, perhaps one of the world's most respected preachers, was asked a revealing question by the interviewer: 'If there was one problem in the world that you had the power to eradicate, which one would it be?' Dr Graham replied without hesitation. 'Race,' he said, 'the race problem.' When I heard his response I have to admit to being somewhat surprised, not only at the speed of the obviously well-thought-out reply but the answer itself. However, on reflection, I tend to agree. After all, his birthplace, the United States of America, has been seriously scarred by racial tension over the years, a tension that inspired Martin Luther King Jr to give one of the greatest speeches of the twentieth century. It was delivered, appropriately, on the steps of the Lincoln Memorial in Washington, DC on 28 August 1963. It was a dream, an impassioned plea for racial harmony.

However, it is not just America that has been affected by race-inspired conflict but virtually every nation on earth to some degree or another. In the last few years we have witnessed genocide, apartheid and what is repulsively called 'ethnic cleansing' in a wide variety of countries and situations. Even in the seemingly tranquil and idyllic Pacific Islands there has been race-inspired conflict. So it is no surprise to find similar, though thankfully less volatile, prejudice where I live in Australia. This friction inspired not a speech but a march that took place in Sydney on 28 May 2000. An estimated 250,000 people petitioned for unity. The word 'sorry' was written in the sky above the masses, as a reminder of the injustices of the past. The site chosen for the march was not a stadium, a church or a sacred site but the Sydney Harbour Bridge, the two flags of the separated communities flying together on a bridge of reconciliation.

The reason that I am writing of these two events is not for political comment but simply to point out that our communities regularly use symbols in order to communicate deep-felt needs. Martin Luther King knew that the Lincoln Memorial, for Americans, represents the declaration of equality enshrined in the constitution of the United States. For Australians, Sydney Harbour Bridge has become a national icon and, in common with numerous other bridges around the world, a symbol of togetherness. A little further down the river, the Anzac Bridge flies the flags of two nations, Australia and New Zealand, to remind the world that they fought together. These bridges, in a deeply significant way, are necessary for the community. They symbolize what we feel and, as we shall see, they represent the passions that motivate us.

Humanity is triggered and sometimes driven by deep-seated desires. It is these that, usually unconsciously, compel us not only to build civil bridges in a city but also to build relational bridges with others in the community. It was to these desires that Martin Luther King was appealing in his speech. He wanted the community to act. He wanted them to be motivated to build a uniting bridge to 'the other side'. He wanted them to be together. Listen to his words: 'With this faith we will be able to work together, to pray together, to struggle together, to go to jail together, to stand up for freedom together . . .'.[1] His message was togetherness. But what are the driving forces which his words were addressing that will cause us to make the effort to build bridges together?

In his book on public speaking, Waldo Braden suggests that in order to motivate people we need to understand their human 'drives'. He gives a number of, what he calls, 'motive appeals'[2] which are self-preservation, self-esteem, acquisitiveness, belongingness, social approval, exploration and aesthetic enjoyment. These are the target of the orator. Of course, they should not be used manipulatively, but the speaker knows that the audience will only act if motivated by these deep-felt desires. All speakers, including Billy Graham, Martin Luther King and even the Lord Jesus Christ Himself, want their audiences to act and therefore appeal to their motives. When they tell us to 'shun hell' they are appealing to our desire for self-preservation. When they tell us to 'possess the land' they are appealing to our desire for exploration. When they tell us to become part of the 'Body of Christ' they are appealing to our desire for belonging. Of course, these are not the only motives in our lives but they serve as a good platform to illustrate what compels a community to build bridges and what prompts us to make friendships. If we can understand and harness them, we will all reach out to others.

Many pragmatists would argue that bridges are built solely for practical reasons. They tell us, 'It is because we need them', 'They enable us to get places'. However, let me take the Rialto Bridge in Venice as an example of a typical bridge. If we ask the locals, 'Why was the Rialto Bridge built?' we are unlikely to hear the simple reply, 'To get to the other side'! The reasons are much more complex.

Bridges provide a sign of devotion

One of the motives that Braden failed to highlight was our God-planted need for devotion. Every one of us longs for a spiritual experience. Legend tells us that in 1177 a shepherd in the south of France by the name of Bénézet had such an encounter. A voice from heaven told him to build a bridge across the River Rhône. The bridge was to link the communities of Avignon and Villeneuve. It is this bridge that became famous through the traditional French folk song, 'Sur le pont d'Avignon, on y danse, on y danse' ('On the bridge of Avignon everyone is dancing'). Apparently the bridge was built with the help of the 'brotherhood of bridge-builders', the 'Frères Pontifes'. This concept may seem strange to us now but it was relatively common in the Middle Ages. For instance, some years later, 'The brotherhood of the Holy Spirit, founded in 1265, was responsible for the construction of the Bridge of the Holy Spirit over the Rhône, not completed until 1307'.[3] The town of Pont St Esprit takes its name from the bridge. The reason that these bridges were built by the friars was because bridges were considered to be spiritual places, which explains why a shrine or chapel was often built mid-way along the span.

The clergy have, in fact, always been associated with the building of bridges. 'In antiquity, the construction of bridges was accompanied by religious rites performed by priests. The Middle Ages respected this tradition, and examples abound of members of the clergy encouraging the construction of a bridge, invoking the assistance of the Almighty or his saints. An ancient tradition held that bridges were often the work of the devil or resulted from divine intervention'.[4] Even today the Pope is still referred to as the 'Pontiff', a title meaning 'bridge maker', which was taken from the term used of the head of the Sacred College of ancient Rome, 'Pontifex Maximus', and was later assumed by the Roman emperors. This all may seem terribly removed from our situations today and yet, when a new bridge is opened in this twenty-first century, the clergy are still often asked to give a blessing!

It is this same instinct for spiritual devotion that causes us to seek out friendships and partners. God designed us with a need and desire for connection and therefore we are spiritually incomplete without it. I use the word 'instinct' because that is how many people view it. They believe that, since we have evolved from lower animals, it is some base animal drive that pushes us to reproduce, a chemically inspired conditioned reflex that causes us to salivate at the sight of the opposite sex! We may well salivate but it is not just hormones! We are the cherished product of divine choice with a spirit and a destiny, not a haphazard product of chance without hope or God in this world. Relationships are a part of that destiny and while we have breath in our bodies we will continue to seek out the company and fellowship of others.

The Bible makes it clear that there is a spiritual side to marriage. God not only instituted it but put His stamp of approval on sex within it by equating the physical union of husband and wife to the union of Christ and His Church (Ephesians 5:31–32). There is no doubt that the bridge of marriage is a sign of devotion and fulfils a profound longing in the human heart. In the Western world, where the institution of marriage has become less popular, thousands who don't even believe in God still ask priests and ministers to bless their union. People rarely turn down an opportunity to be prospered! However, we would all be wise to learn from the French shepherd Bénézet and seek an encounter with God, and then ask God's people to help us and bless us as we endeavour to reach out and relate to other people. In this way we will unite the community in which God has placed us. As the Bible and the *Book of Common Prayer* tell us, the divine institution of marriage was not created just for our personal wellbeing but also for the 'good of society'.

Bridges provide a place of exchange

The Ponte Vecchio, or Old Bridge, in Florence in Italy, is the only one in the city to have survived the Second World War. When it was built in 1345, it soon became a market, occupied by butchers, tanners and blacksmiths. Unfortunately, however, they used the river as a rubbish tip and eventually the stench became so great that in 1593 the ruler of the city, Duke Ferdinando I, evicted them and the workshops were rebuilt for the cleaner and quieter goldsmiths and jewellers who, apart from a brief respite in the seventeenth century, have traded there to this day. The Rialto Bridge in Venice, along with many other bridges around the world, is similarly lined by market stalls. In its heyday the Old London Bridge, too, was festooned with rickety shops and stalls and crowded with hawkers of every conceivable kind until it was cleared in the middle of the eighteenth century. Nowadays, the increasing traffic flow in our cities means that modern bridges can no longer accommodate these traders but, nonetheless, the trucks and trains that daily cross them identify them as routes of commerce, places of exchange.

Humankind's passion for trade is driven by our desire for acquisition. This desire for possession and ownership has in some quarters received a bad press. After all, many wars have been fuelled by voracious motives, the strong overtaking the weak and the rich oppressing the poor. However, the motivating desires that we all have are God-given. God always wanted the children of Israel to possess the land. He wanted every one of them to live in safety, *'each man under his own vine and fig-tree'* (1 Kings 4:25). It is only when we twist and corrupt the desires that they become dangerous. It is only when we attempt to possess and own something that God has not given us that everything goes wrong. It was therefore in humankind's godly nature to build bridges where exchange and acquisition could take place and in humankind's sinful nature to pollute them.

It is one thing, however, to own land and goods and quite another to own people. In our modern world we are repulsed by the concept of being owned. It reminds us of the horrors of slavery. Yet the Bible says that as Christians, we are slaves of righteousness. We belong to Him. He bought us and then released us so that we could willingly choose to become His bond-slaves, His possession. It is only in this place of commitment that true exchange can take place. I completely give myself to Him and He completely gives Himself to me.

This process also takes place to a lesser extent in a marriage. We have a desire to acquire and so we want to build a bridge, a place of exchange. After the marriage ceremony, when we have given ourselves to each other, we want to say, 'This is *my* wife', 'This is *my* husband'. There is a sense in which we want to 'own' and be 'owned'! We want to 'possess' and be 'possessed'! Of course, this does not involve either unwillingness or total ownership, but it does involve a deep commitment that includes the idea of belonging. As the Bible says,

> *'The wife's body does not belong to her alone but also to her husband. In the same way, the husband's body does not belong to him alone but also to his wife.'*   (1 Corinthians 7:4)

Once we belong to one another, we can and must release each other so that we can willingly submit to one another. In a similar way to our relationship with God, it is only then that genuine sharing and exchange can take place.

One of the reasons why some people are reticent to marry is that their selfish independence refuses to be 'possessed'. They will not allow themselves to be 'owned'. They don't want to belong. They therefore cannot commit to the relationship. By making this choice, however, they rob themselves of the delight of genuine exchange.

Bridges provide an object of beauty

A number of years ago, I watched the film *The Double Helix*, about the lives of Watson and Crick, the scientists who discovered DNA, the molecule of life. In it, they were portrayed as doggedly searching for a structure that 'worked'. It not only had to fulfil all the chemical criteria and expectations, it also had to be aesthetically pleasing! They instinctively knew that something as profound as this would be exquisite. Life and truth are meant to be beautiful! Their search encapsulates what we are all doing. Although they may not have attributed their discovery or their search to God, it is nonetheless God who is the Author of life, truth and beauty and gives humankind the desire to search for it. One of the reasons that we build bridges is simply that we need and like beautiful things. This is the motive of aesthetic enjoyment. Some of the most awe-inspiring, graceful and elegant man-made structures in the world are bridges. Whether we look at a humble concrete bridge or the magnificent Golden Gate Bridge in San Francisco, we can see that the architects and engineers have attempted to create something beautiful. They desired it and the community demanded it. It was important for them.

When we look for a friend or a marriage partner one of the criteria in our choice is beauty. Not, as many people make the mistake of thinking, solely in the person but in the relationship itself. We are looking for a beautiful friendship! The bridge itself must be beautiful. Many of us simply look for a handsome husband or a pretty wife and are disappointed to discover that not only is the partnership increasingly ugly but our partner's good looks are also fading!

The reason that beauty is so essential in the building of relationships is that we value it enormously. The value of a work of art is determined by the price that someone is willing to pay for it. We may not find a Van Gogh painting remotely attractive and so would be reticent to pay even $20 for a cheap print. Yet other people are prepared to pay over $50 million. Then how much is the painting worth? The answer, of course, is $50 million. If they find it beautiful, they value it, and if they value it they will pay for it. If they pay for it they consider it worth it!

We will commit to that which we love, act on that which we believe, but we will invest in that which we value. If we love our marriage we will make the necessary sacrifices to ensure its success. If we believe in it we will take the required actions to improve it and if necessary restore it. If we consider our relationship to be an object of beauty we will invest in it. Sadly, there are many couples who don't believe in the sanctity of the relationship. Instead they cheapen it in their conversations, undermine it in their thoughts and destroy it with their actions. Although they all desire beauty, they won't really search for it, and if they discover it, they won't pay the price for it. I find it strange that people the world over will give their lives in order to build a relatively temporary stone bridge because they consider it beautiful and yet others fail to invest in their eternal relationships. Forty men died during the construction of London Bridge in the 1830s. The Brotherhood of the Holy Spirit took forty years to build the Pont St Esprit. Yet so many abandon their friendships and even their marriages after a few months because the price is too great, it costs too much. True beauty is of eternal worth and it's worth paying a high price for.

Bridges provide a point of defence

According to zoologists and ethologists, we all have an effective 'fight or flight' mechanism that is part of our drive for self-protection. In order to preserve our safety, we either run toward the threat to conquer it, or run away and hide from it. In some cases it is better to be aggressive and in others it is wiser to be defensive. This mechanism is fuelled by the adrenaline that increases our heart rate to prepare us for either eventuality. This is why our heart races both when we are angry and when we are frightened. Once again we have been reduced by some to a series of chemical responses! However, this idea does reveal an interesting dilemma between two God-given passions in our life: the desire for self-protection and the desire for exploration. The first causes us to find a place of safety and retreat to it in times of danger. The second demands that we move out from our comfortable havens in order to discover new things. This, of course, makes us highly vulnerable and we may need to retreat once again. Our personalities tend to favour one or the other, yet we are all caught between these two choices.

This choice was illustrated for me at school. One of my favourite subjects was geography and one of my favourite topics was 'settlement patterns'! Rather strangely, I remember being fascinated by the question, 'Where is the best place to start a town?' Is the best choice high ground that can be easily defended or the plains that are rich in food and water? In the first century the Zealots chose the mountain of Masada by the Dead Sea and successfully defended themselves for years against the Roman army. Yet in order to do this they had to have extensive stores of food and a complex system of reservoirs for their water. Others, like those who built near the coast in Israel on the Via Maris (the sea road), on the other hand, have discovered that such locations have the advantage of plenty of food and water and the opportunity to explore and expand, while exposing the community to crushing attack by every passing army. The best solution, we were told, was found in the early Anglo-Saxon settlements which were established in the loop of a river. In this way, they had food and water and also the river afforded them a measure of defence. They did have one problem, however. In order to fulfil their desire to explore and expand they had to build a bridge across the river, and this bridge made them vulnerable again. The bridge also became a focus for them. It was both an outlet for exploration and a point of defence. It allowed them to reach out and to retreat. The town, therefore, defended it with vigour.

The application for our lives today is obvious. We have a desire to explore and so we make contacts and build bridges with other people. These relationships make us vulnerable. Every enemy knows that the best way to break someone is by attacking those closest to them. In order to protect ourselves from these attacks we tend to avoid building bridges and so lose the joy of expansion: hence our dilemma. The extroverts among us tend to build too many bridges and get hurt. The introverts tend to build too few bridges and fail to grow. The answer, of course, is to build the right number of bridges with others but then defend them with our lives! Before I discuss the merits of exploration I want to draw two conclusions about defence: firstly, the Bible and history tell us that our bridges are highly vulnerable and, secondly, the Bible and history challenge us to fight for them.

If we study any military campaign, whether it is the Spanish conquest of Mexico or the early Greek wars, we will find that bridges are strategic in war. All commanders know this and therefore the defence or destruction of a key bridge is high on their tactical agenda. This was clearly evident in the Second World War. On 17 September 1944 nearly 35,000 airborne troops took off to execute Field-Marshall Montgomery's 'Operation Market-Garden', with its objective of taking five bridges in Holland. This campaign prompted Lieutenant-General Browning to make his now famous remark reportedly describing the fifth, in Arnhem, as 'a bridge too far'. This, in fact, proved to be the case. However, at the time the army strategists considered the attempt was worth the risk because of the distinct advantage every army gains by the possession of a key bridge. Our spiritual enemy Satan knows this and constantly attacks our relationships in order to get the upper hand in his war against the Church. His primary objectives are the most significant 'bridges', the relationships of the leaders. He is well aware of the old proverb, '... *strike the shepherd, and the sheep of the flock will be scattered*' (Matthew 26:31). It is the leaders who are going to be required to explore and take territory and it is therefore the leaders' bridges that are at greatest risk.

The answer, as I have said, is to defend them at all costs. Many old bridges bear the evidence of this policy of defence. The Valentré Bridge over the River Lot in Cahors in the south of France was built between 1308 and 1380 and boasts three towers that are part of the extensive fortifications of the town. The Manelli Tower has defended the already mentioned Ponte Vecchio in Florence for hundreds of years. The Manelli family refused to demolish it when, in 1565, the ruling Medici family wanted to build themselves a convenient corridor over the bridge so that they could walk between their two palaces without mixing with the people. The defence of the bridge, however, was more important to the Manellis and they were prepared to fight for it. This is the kind of attitude that we need in our relationships.

We have seen that we build bridges to others because we want devotion, exchange and beauty, but we also want something to fight for! We want to believe in something that is worth defending. As John Eldredge puts it, 'In the heart of every man is a desperate desire for a battle to fight, an adventure to live and a beauty to rescue'.[5] We shouldn't just want to preserve ourselves, we should want to protect those closest to us. In the Old Testament we find God blessing Abraham for defending his family vigorously after they were captured in the battle of the nine kings (cf. Genesis 14:14ff.) and we hear Nehemiah encouraging the people of Israel to defend themselves against the aggressors and fight for their families (Nehemiah 4:14). In the New Testament, we read Paul's instructions to the Ephesian church on the subject of relationships and his challenge to them to fight against the devil and his strategies (Ephesians 6:10ff.). Tragically, the reason that so many abandon their relationships without fighting for them is that they only want them as a convenient corridor for their selfish ends and not a point of defence for the good of the community.

Bridges provide an outlet for exploration

Rome was and still is bridgy. Six of the eight bridges that the Romans built over the River Tiber between 200 BC and 260 AD are still there! The ancient Romans had an expansionist policy. They had a passion for the exploration and possession of new territory. In order for their imperialistic desires to succeed it was necessary for them to develop a large network of communications that extended throughout the Mediterranean region. They understood both the necessity and the power of good communication. This is clearly evident if one studies the amazing growth of the Roman Empire in the centuries before and after the birth of Christ. By the second century AD this network of roads exceeded 100,000 kilometres and covered an area of more than 5 million square kilometres, from Scotland in the north to the Sahara in the south. 'In this way, innumerable small and distant townships, by means of roads, bridges, ports and aqueducts, kept in touch with a distant capital'.[6] Hence the expression, 'All roads lead to Rome'. The Pont du Gard, the 275-metre-long bridge that still stands over the River Gard, near Nimes in the south of France, gives us both an insight into the Romans' extraordinary engineering achievements and also the necessity of bridges for their communication and exploration.

For a natural kingdom, like Rome, to achieve its objectives of geographical expansion, economic increase and worldwide power, it had to maintain its communication and the strength of its unity by the building of bridges. Equally for a spiritual kingdom, for instance the Church, to achieve its objectives of spiritual enlargement, numerical growth and worldwide influence, it has to build and maintain bridges of relationships. The same is true of a company that wants to widen its market, grow the business and multiply its worldwide influence. Of course, because we are human, we often want to expand for the wrong reasons and achieve growth, like the Romans, at someone else's expense. As a result, growth, especially in some circles in the Church, has a bad name! This is a ridiculous argument since it is evidently part of our God-blessed destiny.

The desire for exploration and expansion is birthed and fostered by God and planted in the human heart. God is a God of increase and multiplication. This was His plan for humankind from the beginning. The Bible says,

> 'God blessed them and said to them, "Be fruitful and increase in number; fill the earth and subdue it. Rule over the fish of the sea and the birds of the air and over every living creature that moves on the ground."' (Genesis 1:28)

He wants each one of us to expand and grow as individuals. He is a God 'who makes things grow' (1 Corinthians 3:7). He wants us to be enlarged and stretched: as He said to Israel,

> 'Enlarge the place of your tent,
>   stretch your tent curtains wide,
>   do not hold back;

> *lengthen your cords,*
>   *strengthen your stakes.'*   (Isaiah 54:2)

Enlargement for us means exploring and possessing new territory; doing things that we have never done before. Stretching means achieving our potential. Using what we already possess to accomplish more. The reason that we build relationships is because we want to do just that.

New contacts, acquaintances, friends or a marriage all fulfil our desire to explore and communicate and in some basic way to rule. We are looking for synergy, with all its benefits, where the two become one. On the other hand, those who retreat from these opportunities and challenges and burn their bridges are not only robbed of an exciting destiny but are also sentenced to a life of diminishment and mediocrity.

Bridges provide a mark of social approval

Recently, a woman approached me and introduced herself as coming from Arizona. I gave what I thought was a polite response and then was taken aback by her reply. She immediately started telling me all about Lake Havasu, the town in Arizona that bought London Bridge in 1968. Maybe I didn't look interested enough in Arizona, or maybe it was because I was from England; whatever the reason, the dream of Mr Robert Paxton McCulloch, the American entrepreneur and millionaire, who bought the bridge, had been realized. He bought it in order to put Lake Havasu on the map, and here we were in Australia talking about it. McCulloch had a plan to build a city in the Sonora Desert. He began to purchase land in 1958 next to a lake that had been formed by the Parker Dam. However, as Terry Gwynn-Jones wrote in an article entitled 'The Town London Bridge Built', 'McCulloch's dream city was in danger of stalling'[7] until he purchased the bridge and rebuilt it stone by stone in 1971. The town is now a thriving tourist centre with a population of around 60,000. The bridge had given the community the credibility it desired.

There is no doubt that a bridge can bring a community acceptance and social approval. In relational terms, 'it's not what you know but who you know' that will put a person on the map! Although we know this to be true, we may dislike this concept because it speaks of exclusivity and social privilege. Yet, the phrase is not quite as objectionable as it first appears. After all, the Bible says that in the end we will be judged on the basis of whether we know God or not. There is no doubt that building a bridge with Christ brings God's approval:

> *'God is just ... He will punish those who do not know God and do not obey the gospel of our Lord Jesus. They will be punished with everlasting destruction and shut out from the presence of the Lord and from the majesty of his power.'* (2 Thessalonians 1:6, 8–9)

This may seem unfair to us but, since we each have an opportunity to know God within our lifetime, it is perfectly just. In the same way that knowing God benefits our lives, is it also true to say that knowing the right people brings success on earth? Does building a bridge with the right people bring God's approval? In order to answer this I would like to ask three more questions!

- Is it important to have the right social connections?
- Is it important to make the right business contacts?
- Is it important to keep the right company?

In some elitist circles one's social connections are considered import-ant: 'Do you know him?' 'Are you related to her?' 'Are you in with them?' These kinds of questions come across as condescending. It is communication that divides rather than connects. God is not a respecter of persons and neither should we be. In some business communities, it is not so much 'connections' as 'contacts' that are promoted. Some time ago, I attended a Christian businesspersons' conference. At the required lunch I was saddened and somewhat disillusioned. There had been a great deal of motivational talk, product-boasting, backslapping and card-swapping. Yet, despite being a conference full of committed Christians, I left with many contacts but no relationships. It seemed as if the conversations were shallow, competitive and motivated by selfishness. I made a decision that day that I wouldn't look for good contacts but good company.

We all desire social approval and all know that bridges provide it. We all want to be accepted and credible in the society in which we live and so there is no harm in building relationships to fulfil that God-given desire. However, in doing so we should avoid arrogance and selfishness. Ultimately it is not human approval that will bring us success on earth, but God's approval. However, His method is people and success on earth depends on relating to the right ones, keeping the right company. He encouraged us that, *'He who walks with the wise grows wise, but a companion of fools suffers harm'* (Proverbs 13:20) and warned us that, *'Bad company corrupts good character'* (1 Corinthians 15:33). It was in the company of the prophets that King David found refuge, King Saul found hope and the prophet Elisha found his destiny.

Bridges provide a symbol of identity

The reason that Mr McCulloch wanted London Bridge for his city was not just to provide social approval but also to provide a focus around which the city could grow. As Judith Dupré argues, 'The relocation of the London Bridge was ingenious, granting an unknown desert oasis an instant cultural identity and conferring immortality on an other-wise architecturally ordinary bridge'.[8] Whether he initially appreciated the power of such an icon I don't know, but it seems that he wanted more than just a landmark, he wanted a 'soul' for the city from which the population could draw a sense of identity and belonging. Certainly many cities, including London, have grown up with a bridge as a focus. So, when the bridge is destroyed it creates a deep sense of loss in the community, an emotion that no doubt accompanied the writing of the ancient nursery rhyme, 'London Bridge is falling down'. In fact, I still remember the disquiet in England when the later London Bridge went on the market, as though somehow we were going to lose something of our personality.

Individuals as well as communities search for this 'belongingness', as Braden calls it, and we often discover it by associating with others, by building a bridge. As one who has the opportunity and privilege to conduct weddings, I have often introduced the newly married couple to the congregation at the end of the service by announcing, 'I would like to present to you Mr and Mrs ...!' Before I do, however, I ask the couple how they would like to be addressed. The custom both in England and in Australia, where I have been involved in wedding ceremonies, is that the bride takes on the surname of the bridegroom. Usually this custom is followed. By changing her name, the bride is identifying herself with all that the bridegroom's name signifies: his ancestry, his character and his allegiances. She is becoming one with him. My wife's maiden name was Preston but by changing her name to the Scottish name of Fergusson when we married, my wife is welcomed by the clan, even though she has no Scottish heritage. The change of name is a sign of belonging, a symbol of identity.

The Scottish clan societies are a thriving concern. Thousands from all over the world contact them in order to discover their possible ancestors. Their search is not just born out of a love for Scotland, despite what the Scots think: they are driven by something much more basic; they want to belong to something. They want to own the badge and to wear the tartan. They want to meet with people who share their name, who come from the same family, however far removed. It is the same passion that makes genealogy searches one of the most popular 'hits' on the Internet. It is what makes people join clubs, societies, associations and even churches. We want to wear the T-shirt or the scarf. We want to have a letterhead, with a name on it that identifies us.

God understands this, of course, because He came up with the idea! The Old Testament is filled with references to various tribes and clans. God's heart, however, is that we belong to His family. That is why He wants us to bear His Name (cf. Acts 15:17) and expected Paul the apostle both to carry it and suffer for it:

> *'This man is my chosen instrument to carry my name before the Gentiles and their kings and before the people of Israel. I will show him how much he must suffer for my name.'* (Acts 9:15–16)

We don't find Paul complaining or shirking from the responsibility because that is what he had always wanted. He had found a focus around which to build, a bridge that identified him. He soon found himself in Antioch with others of like mind, and it was there that *'The disciples were called Christians'* (Acts 11:26) because they belonged to Christ.

Bridges provide a feeling of self-esteem

The early 1930s in Australia, in common with numerous other nations around the world, were a time of depression. The numbers of jobless in Sydney grew daily. As Manning Clark put it, 'Unemployment increased sharply: by 1933 nearly one third of the breadwinners were unemployed. In all the capital cities the unemployed clamoured for work or relief'.[9] As a result, many people suffered extreme hardships. These, however, were only the external physical symptoms. The depression was also a time of disillusionment, anguish and hopelessness. The people began to lose faith in the major institutions such as the banks and the government to provide a solution. The gap between rich and poor widened and an atmosphere of bitterness, distrust and uncertainty pervaded the city. In answer, while the employers demanded greater sacrifice, the clergy preached inevitable judgment and the politicians offered empty theories, the civil engineers built a bridge!

Of course, the planners and contractors of Sydney Harbour Bridge had no idea that the opening would occur at such a critical time for the city. Nonetheless, the public response at the time was staggering. In a world awash with broken oaths and unrealizable dreams, here at last was something real and tangible. Some estimates suggest that, on that momentous weekend in March 1932, as many as three-quarters of a million people gathered in Sydney in order to watch the opening ceremony. For them the bridge meant jobs, hope, pride, a sense of identity, a feeling of self-esteem and the promise of connection in a divided city.

It is interesting to note that it was on the same bridge nearly seventy years later, as we saw at the beginning of the chapter, that another crowd gathered, this time to march for reconciliation. Some would say that march was politically motivated, some that it was a cry for justice. No doubt, both are true. Yet, I personally think that some of it was inspired by a simple desire for self-esteem. The alienated members of the community were asking for the self-respect and self-esteem that come from normal healthy relationships. Others were demonstrating because they felt that Australia itself was in danger of losing something of its esteem in the eyes of the world. In times of depression, countries and individuals build bridges! It's the sensible thing to do. It's the wise thing to do. It's the right thing to do.

Bridges provide a means of transport

So far, all of the reasons I have listed for building civil and relational bridges may seem a little philosophical and yet they are all a fundamental part of our make-up and need to be appreciated. If our aim in forming relationships is purely practical we are going to have very empty friendships and colourless marriages. Nonetheless, the list would not be complete if we didn't add that bridges are built to 'get to the other side'! We do build them to provide a means of transport over an obstacle. However, even this logical solution to a problem is stimulated by a need to communicate that is in-built in all of us. It is a need that demands a chapter of its own!

Summary and advice

1. **Natural bridges are symbolic**. They can teach us practical principles for our relational bridges.

2. **We build bridges out of deep-felt needs**. If we don't understand these motivations we will not act appropriately or build them successfully.

3. **Bridges provide a sign of devotion**. It is not just emotional requirement or physical attraction that inspires marriage but a need for spiritual intimacy.

4. **Bridges provide a place of exchange**. We all desire to 'possess' and be 'possessed'. It is only in this place of loving commitment that true sharing can take place.

5. **Bridges provide an object of beauty**. Relationships themselves are beautiful. We consider beauty to be valuable and we will invest in that which we value.

6. **Bridges provide a point of defence**. Building bridges makes us vulnerable so some refuse to build them. However, we need vulnerability and we need something to fight for. Relationships create an outlet for both these desires.

7. **Bridges provide an outlet for exploration**. All of need us to reach out and explore in order to fulfil God's will for increase and enlargement in our lives.

8. **Bridges provide a mark of social approval**. It does matter whom we know. We should keep good company rather than have good connections or make good contacts.

9. **Bridges provide a symbol of identity**. It is important to belong to a clan. We need to identify with something of worth.

10. **Bridges provide a feeling of self-esteem**. Depression robs us of this essential quality. Connection and reconciliation restores it.

11. **Bridges provide a means of transport**. Every one of us has a 'down to earth' desire to communicate, a practical need to 'get to the other side'.

Notes

1. Dr Martin Luther King Jr, speech delivered in Washington, DC, 28 August 1963. Quoted in Clayborne Carson and Kris Shephard (eds.), *A Call to Conscience* (Warner Books, 2001).

2. Waldo W. Braden, *Public Speaking: The Essentials* (Harper & Row, 1966).
3. The World Atlas of Architecture, ed. Mitchell Beazley (Reed International Books Limited, 1984).
4. Ibid.
5. John Eldredge, *Wild at Heart* (Thomas Nelson, 2000).
6. The World Atlas of Architecture, ed. Mitchell Beazley.
7. Terry Gwynn-Jones, 'The Town London Bridge Built', *The Australian Way*, Qantas (April 1997).
8. Judith Dupré, *Bridges* (Könemann, 1998).
9. Manning Clark, *A Short History of Australia* (Penguin, 1987).

Chapter 3

The Ministry of Transport

Why We Need Communication

Sydney Harbour, the mouth of the Parramatta River, divides the present-day city of Sydney, Australia. The first European settlement in 1788 was on the southern bank of the harbour. In 1794 there was an initial attempt to expand to the north shore that resulted in some isolated settlements. In 1815 Francis Greenway, an architect and ex-convict, in a report to the governor of the colony, was the first person seriously to propose a link between the south and north shores. In 1817 'Billy Blue', also an emancipated convict, started the first ferry service across the harbour, transporting goods and passengers in his rowing boat. It is interesting to note that both of these pioneers were once prisoners. Their passion for communication was perhaps an expression of their freedom.

Much of the success of a town is determined by its ability to communicate. A bridge can readily provide that communication. The town of Hobart in the south of the island of Tasmania is bisected by the River Derwent. A ferry trip between the west and east shores is two kilometres long while a round trip by car from one side of the town to the other is eighty kilometres. A floating bridge built in 1943 proved inadequate for the ever-increasing transport needs, and so it wasn't until the completion of a graceful high-level concrete bridge in 1964 that the town was truly united. Nonetheless, the importance of that bridge was probably not truly appreciated until eleven years later.

On Sunday night 5 January 1975 an 11,000-tonne bulk carrier *Lake Illawarra* steered off course and struck one of the pylons of the bridge, causing a large portion of the bridge to collapse. The tragedy, which many people thought was inevitable, killed twelve people, sank the ship and devastated the city. 'Suddenly, Hobart was a divided city. With one third of its population – about 140,000 at the time – living on the eastern shore, the fast developing eastern suburbs were in one stroke isolated from their hospital, their shops, their jobs'.[1] Every one of the inhabitants of the city was affected by this loss in some way. Transport between the sides of the city reverted back to the lengthy road trip or the crowded ferries. This situation continued for over two years until the Tasman Bridge was re-opened on 8 October 1977, but with a warning by the Government that the bridge remained 'extremely vulnerable'.

We can draw a number of conclusions from the Hobart tragedy, each of which can be applied either to civil or relational bridges. The first is that humankind has a need and a desire to communicate; this desire is so great that a community will always build bridges, despite the obstacles, effort, cost or warnings. Second, a community is both adversely and seriously affected by the destruction of key bridges, because much of its perceived success is connected with them. Third, bridges are always vulnerable. In 1979 the Australian Minister of Transport warned the House of Representatives that the new Tasman Bridge had a 'one in three' chance of being struck a second time in ten years. Thankfully, this did not happen, but it is a warning that is worth heeding whether one is building a bridge or contemplating marriage, especially since the statistics are similar.

The purpose of this chapter is to endeavour to explain the fundamental reasons behind the first of these conclusions. Why should we communicate? Why does humankind have a passion for transport? Why is it that we build so many bridges when we know that they are so vulnerable? Why is it that communication is so important to us? Unlike the last chapter where I gave general reasons for building both civil and relational bridges, the following reasons for communicating refer primarily to relationships.

God's character demands our communication

Catherine of Siena lived as a nun in Italy in the fourteenth century. She describes a dialogue with God in which God spoke to her soul and said, ' . . . my only begotten Son is a bridge, as you see he is, joining the most high with the most lowly'.[2] The author C.S. Lewis used the same image in his classic Narnia books. In them, he portrays a magical kingdom in which good triumphs over evil. In the allegory, the king, the lion Aslan, represents the 'Christ figure'. At one point the children ask Aslan how they can get to his country, to which he replies, 'I will not tell you how long or short the way will be; only that it lies across a river. But do not fear that, for I am the great Bridge-Builder'.[3]

This picture of God as a builder of bridges came to me with great clarity on a trip to Israel. I found myself on my own, in an open courtyard in Bethlehem. My attention was drawn to a small inscription on a pillar in the corner of the courtyard. I walked over to look. It simply said, *'And the Word was made flesh, and dwelt among us'* (John 1:14).[4] Suddenly it dawned on me that I was standing in the place where Christ was born and the place where God's bridge reached the earth. I have stood in wonder and admired many man-made bridges around the world, but that day I was admiring a divine and indescribable bridge of immense stature and beauty. In that second I caught something of God's heart for communication: His passion to provide a way. I saw what Catherine of Siena saw. This is the reason we communicate with others. This is the reason we try to build bridges because God Himself is a Bridge-builder and we are made in His image.

Even though I am fully aware of my failings as a parent, I still instinctively want to pass on to my children the good characteristics that I do have. So it is not surprising to discover that God, like any good father, wants His children to embrace His character. He is holy and so He wants us to be holy. He is Truth and so expects us to be truthful. He builds bridges and so wants us to do the same. He also has the qualities necessary for the building of bridges and wants to pass them on as well. For instance, He is one and He longs for us to share this unity. In fact, it was the statement, *'The* LORD *our God, the* LORD *is one. Love the* LORD *your God with all your heart and with all your soul and with all your strength'* (Deuteronomy 6:4–5), that became the 'Shema' or creed of the children of Israel. Every Israelite was required to live it, write it on their houses and impress it on their children. It was also for unity that Jesus cried to God on our behalf,

> ' . . . *that they may be one as we are one: I in them and you in me. May they be brought to complete unity to let the world know that you sent me and have loved them even as you have loved me.'* (John 17:22–23)

God is the embodiment of love, unity and fellowship. He possesses all the attributes of successful communication. He is both the inspiration and the wherewithal to build relationships.

Life contains an instinct for communication

God created Life with a 'language'. In every chromosome, in every nucleus, in every cell of every human being there is an in-built desire to communicate. Every cell that we have has a desire to reproduce, to replicate itself. In order to do this effectively it has to have a chemical language with which it can communicate all the information necessary for the new cell to form properly. This was the code that Watson and Crick were trying to interpret when they discovered DNA. In the book *The Language of Life*, George and Muriel Beadle write that, 'The deciphering of the DNA code has revealed our possession of a language much older than hieroglyphics, a language as old as life itself, a language that is the most living language of all – even if its letters are invisible and its words buried deep in the cells of our bodies'.[5] It is therefore beyond our ability to prevent communication, even if we had a desire to do so. It is ingrained in our make-up. Those who shun the company of others are not only rebelling against God but are also fighting against their own nature.

As I have already suggested, it is one of the traits of parenting to desire to pass on that which we have. It is also in the nature of human beings to communicate that which we know. One of the pains of childlessness comes from an inability to replicate oneself, a powerlessness to communicate to the next generation. The book of Proverbs describes the 'barren womb' as 'never satisfied', never saying 'Enough!' (Proverbs 30:15–16) and explains Rachel's desperation when she cries out to her husband Jacob, *'Give me children, or I'll die'* (Genesis 30:1). The ability to have children and communicate with them should be considered one of the greatest joys. It is an indication of life. Equally, for the disciples of Jesus it would be a violation of nature to refuse to carry out the Great Commission He has given us and communicate the truths that He has taught us.

Creation demonstrates communication

Some years ago, I had the opportunity and privilege to assist a group of scientists from Oxford University who introduced me to a world of communication. They were studying animal behaviour on an island in the north-west of England and the subject of their studies was the language of gulls! There were 100,000 gulls on the island and it soon became apparent that for the colony to thrive the gulls needed to have a complex system of communication. The language consisted of a number of different signals, which included sounds, movement and even coloured markings. Once one had interpreted the language it became possible to predict how they would behave. The professor of the group, a man by the name of Niko Tinbergen, had written a book about them entitled *Signals for Survival*.[6] The gulls were often violent (as I found out to my cost) and so the colony was a dangerous place, especially since some of the gulls were cannibals. Thus their language wasn't just for show, it was for survival, a concept that we would do well to learn ourselves!

God has created a world of communicators and communication. Every species of animal and even plant has an ability to communicate in some way. They communicate for a variety of reasons that include the purpose of feeding, defence, courtship, health and wellbeing. God has planned this for the survival and success of His creation. In the case of humans, the language is more complex. For instance, spoken symbolic language, that is, the use of words that can represent objects even if they are not present, is a uniquely human trait. Yet the foundational principle is the same. We all have a creative desire and ability to communicate and the way that we do will determine not only our effectiveness and the fruit of our lives but will also decide our fate. Unlike the gulls, we are unlikely to be eaten if we communicate inappropriately! Nonetheless, Jesus taught us a sobering principle when He said,

> *'men will have to give account on the day of judgment for every careless word they have spoken. For by your words you will be acquitted, and by your words you will be condemned.'*   (Matthew 12:36–37)

Common sense suggests that we take notice!

Human beings were created for communication

When I was younger I used to ask the question, 'Why did God create the earth?' The usual answer that I was given, by some intelligent-looking Christian, was, 'Because He is love and wanted to have a relationship with human beings with whom He could share that love'. In my view, a better answer would be, 'I have no idea!' The reality is that this is an impossible question to answer since we are not God and we weren't there! However, if I was also to hazard a guess, I would add to the first answer and also say, 'Because He is a Creator and therefore has to create and is a Communicator and therefore longs to communicate'. Of course, I am using the word 'communicate' here with all its potency.

If we read the book of Genesis through the eyes of the latter explanation, it reads something like this: God created the world for communication and through communication. He spoke it into existence and now sustains it *'by his powerful word'* (Hebrews 1:3). The first human beings, Adam and Eve, walked and talked with God and each other. They enjoyed all the fruits and benefits of good relationship and communication, until their 'Eden' was shattered by one malicious conversation. Satan questioned God's communication when he tempted Eve by saying, *'Did God say ... ?'* (Genesis 3:1). It was through this 'miscommunication' that humankind was separated from God. A gulf was fixed between them. They began to die when their communication with God and each other was destroyed. Humankind attempted to restore the principle and power of communication by building a tower, but this only resulted in greater miscommunication (cf. Genesis 11). So, God built a bridge of communication to humankind by sending His Word, the Lord Jesus Christ, to earth (cf. John 1:14), and it is only through His life, substitutionary death and example that our communication with God is restored.

Whether you agree or disagree with my answer to 'Why did God create the earth?' does not take away from the fact that God did create us with a capacity to communicate with Him and each other. Subsequently, humankind has a craving to communicate: an insatiable desire for contact and communication. Denial of such a crucial truth robs us of an essential part of our humanity. Failure to act on it deprives us of a fundamental part of our destiny. Today, if we fail to pray to God or communicate lovingly with our friends or partners we are in danger of being 'disconnected' and so powerless. Relational bridges provide essential communication and communication is essential for our temporal and eternal wellbeing.

The life of Christ exemplifies the benefits of communication

We all respond to heroes. When a champion tennis player, runner or swimmer appears out of nowhere in a particular nation it inspires a

crop of new talent in that nation that then dominates the world scene
for a few years. The motivation seems to be, 'If he or she can do it then
so can we!' The performances, however, tend to diminish gradually
until a new hero emerges. As a result, sporting prowess in a country
seems to come in waves. I believe that God understands this need for
motivation. The fact that God is a Communicator and we were created
to communicate should be enough motivation for us. After all, we
know that once human beings communicated perfectly and we have
been restored to that destiny. But that doesn't seem quite enough! We
need to see it working. We need a template, a model, a standard at
which we can aim, a hero to which we can aspire. God, therefore, sent
Jesus, not only to restore to us the possibility of true communication,
but also to show us what it looks like. Even in a world that often
ignores Him, Christ remains the benchmark.

Jesus Christ was completely successful in His communication and
there are two primary ways in which He exemplifies this. He was
perfect in relation to both His human and His divine communication.
I would like to illustrate this with two events in the life of Jesus, one at
a well and one at a pool! In the first case, Jesus stopped at a well while
His disciples went to buy some food. While there, He spoke to a sinful
Samaritan woman. This shocked His returning disciples since Jesus was
a righteous Jewish man and, on top of that, He was speaking to her
alone: good reasons why they wouldn't have talked to her! In this
situation Christ's compassion and method of questioning were
remarkable. He asked one question, *'Will you give me a drink?'* (John
4:7) and her entire life story tumbled out! To which, of course, He
responded with the answers. His extraordinary communication
method is repeated in incident after incident. Eddie Gibbs was
evidently impressed when he wrote, 'when we begin to focus on the
method as well as the message we soon find that God is a master
communicator. He is the enthralling story-teller, the exquisite artist,
the atmosphere-creating dramatist, the popular broadcaster, the mem-
ory-engraver, the penetrating interviewer and the tough instructor
who pushes his team to the very limit'.[7]

Many people have attempted to describe the essential ingredients of
Jesus' method of communication. Roy Zuck identified four elements
when he concluded that, 'Jesus used a number of teaching tools to
make people eager for the truth, desirous to learn, hungry for his
teaching. Four elements in his ministry – motivation, variation,
participation, and visualization – enabled him to interest his students

in what he taught'.[8] These are, of course, all true and well observed. Yet for me, there is only one reason for His successful communication and Jesus Himself gave the answer when He said,

> *'For I did not speak of my own accord, but the Father who sent me commanded me what to say and how to say it. I know that his command leads to eternal life. So whatever I say is just what the Father has told me to say.'*   (John 12:49–50)

Thus the secret of His human communication was His divine communication. This is further illustrated for us at the Pool of Bethesda.

Jesus went to the Pool during a visit to a feast in Jerusalem. It was famous for attracting invalids who were looking for a cure. Jesus prayed for one man only, a man who had been crippled for thirty-eight years, and he was healed. Had I been there, I would have asked the question, 'Why did You not heal them all?' Others may have questioned His choice of invalid. Why that one? The Jews, however, wanted to know why He was healing on the Sabbath. The response that He gave answers us all. He said,

> *'I tell you the truth, the Son can do nothing by himself; he can do only what he sees his Father doing, because whatever the Father does the Son also does.'*   (John 5:19)

His successful ministry was based on a perfect relationship with His Father. He spoke what He heard in prayer and acted on what He saw. We may be left with many questions about healing but we are left in no doubt about the method and benefits of Jesus' communication. Such perfect communication, like the performances of a great athlete, can either depress or motivate us! As for me, I want to say, 'If He can do it, then by His grace, so can I!'

The message of the gospel commands communication

When you mention the phrase 'preaching the gospel' to some people it provokes a highly negative response. To them it connotes judgmental finger pointing, lifeless religion and a boring, irrelevant message that repels any reasonable person. Sadly in some cases this is only too true! However, preaching the gospel simply means 'heralding the good news'. It should not create barriers but rather bridge them. This is a concept that John Stott discusses in his book entitled *I Believe in Preaching*. He suggests that preaching is 'the conveying of a God-given message to living people who need to hear it'. However, the message is contained in a book, the Bible, that is hundreds of years old. So 'Christian communicators', he goes on to say, 'have to throw bridges' between the old and the new. 'Our task', Stott continues, 'is to enable God's revealed truth to flow out of the Scriptures into the lives of the men and women of today'.[9] Karl Barth, the German theologian, also understood the need to bridge the gap between the ancient and the modern. When someone asked him how he prepared his sermons, he replied, 'I take the Bible in one hand and the daily newspaper in the other.'[10] Such an attitude embraces the relevance that the gospel demands. This, however, is not just the domain of the preacher: it is the responsibility of every Christian.

The Bible says that every Christian is required to communicate the gospel. This Good News commands relevant communication. Our role in life is to build bridges between God and our fellow human beings, to provide passage between the eternal and the temporal, the old and the new so that 'holy transport' can take place! We are all ministers of transport with a ministry of reconciliation. Paul taught this concept in his second letter to the Corinthians. To summarize his teaching:

- Why should we build bridges? – Christ's love compels us (5:14).
- What is the bridge? – The message of reconciliation (5:19).
- Who should build bridges? – We are Christ's ambassadors (5:20).
- How should we build bridges? – Preaching the gospel (5:20).
- To whom should we build bridges? – Those that need to be reconciled (5:20).

On my wall at home I have a picture of my daughter, complete with black French beret, standing on the banks of the River Seine in Paris, looking dreamily at the famous Pont Neuf. Every time I look at it, apart from my obvious parental warmth, I am reminded of our responsibility to preach the gospel! The Pont Neuf (New Bridge) was built between 1578 and 1609. Henry IV of France, who oversaw its completion, wanted to restore a war-torn Paris. 'The Pont Neuf was built to connect the two halves of Paris with its original core, the Île de la Cité'.[11] The bridge is in two halves. One half connects the Right Bank of the Seine with the Island of the City and the other connects the Island with the

Left Bank. On the island, in the heart of the city, is the Cathedral of Notre Dame. For me it is a parable. The Church has a responsibility to build a bridge to God (the Bible) on the one hand and the world (the newspaper) on the other. If it fails to build a bridge to the Word of God it has nothing to offer the world. If it fails to build a bridge to the world it has nothing to offer God. If it builds neither bridge, it remains an irrelevant and disconnected island. If it builds both it takes its place at the core of the city. This, it seems to me, is the ministry of the Church.

Cultures value communication

Every country has its greeting ceremonies. These range from the simple 'G'day' in Australia to a complex dialogue in some countries in Africa. They include stylized body language such as bowing, hand clasping or nose rubbing and often involve recognition of authority and therefore a display of submissive behaviour by one or other of those involved. They are a vital part of our culture or as a friend of mine put it, 'The way we do things around here'! The interesting thing about many of these ceremonies is that they are not taught so much as learned by observation. We simply pick them up as we go along. Some years ago I was invited into a house in what was then Yugoslavia. Without explanation I was presented with a glass of water, a pot of jam and a spoon! Everybody waited expectantly and silently. Apparently I was meant to do something! With a little prompting I ate a teaspoon of jam, drank the water and placed the spoon in the empty glass. They were cleared away in silence with no explanation given! I was now welcomed!

These sometimes curious ceremonies, along with thousands of others, are established for the good order of the society in which we live. They are vital for courtship, self-protection and successful trade. They determine friend or foe and therefore are essential for the defence of the community. In every case the cultural requirements have to be communicated to the next generation. Anthropologists Carol and Melvin Ember write that, 'All people known to anthropologists, regardless of their kind of society, have had a highly complex system of spoken, symbolic communication that we call language. Language is symbolic in that a word or phrase can represent what it stands for whether or not that thing is present. This symbolic quality of language has tremendous implications for the transmission of culture'.[12] Our cultures, therefore, not only value language and communication but also require them for successful transmission. This takes place with what the Bible describes as word, deed and sign.

Paul, a Jew, wanted to preach the gospel to the Gentiles. However, he didn't want to impose his national customs, as so many missionaries have been accused of doing, nor did he want to communicate his religious traditions, as so many ministers do today, but he did want to transmit a 'culture': a Christian culture, not a national one, concerning the way we live, the way we should do things! This he did, through what he said (word), the way he lived (deed) and the miracles (sign) that he performed. In explaining this to the Romans he said,

> *'I will not venture to speak of anything except what Christ has accomplished through me in leading the Gentiles to obey God by what I have said and done – by the power of signs and miracles, through the power of the Spirit. So from Jerusalem all the way around to Illyricum, I have fully proclaimed the gospel of Christ.'* (Romans 15:18–19)

This is not only why but how we should communicate the gospel. Anything less than this and the good news has not been 'fully proclaimed'.

Leadership requires communication

The American President Harry Truman once defined leadership as 'a person who has the ability to get others to do what they do not want to do, and like it!'[13] Although perhaps too cynical a definition, there is no doubt that in order for leaders to influence others toward a goal they have first to have a vision and then be able to communicate that vision persuasively. Thus, every successful leader, whether in a religious, social, business or political arena, will tell you that their success rests not just on the quality of their vision but also on their ability to communicate that vision effectively. James Humes, a highly experienced presidential speechwriter, put it like this: 'The difference between mere management and leadership is communication. And that art of communication is the language of leadership'.[14] Since we all have some responsibility to lead and influence others for good, whether through a specific role of leadership, or as parents or disciple makers, it follows that we all must learn to communicate. One of the main reasons we do communicate as leaders is that it is communication that gets the job done!

When Jesus challenged His disciples to *'make disciples'* (Matthew 28:19), He told them to teach and preach, in other words inform and persuade, the two ways with which a leader communicates vision. In the case of information, leaders need to bridge the gap of misunderstanding between what they are seeing and what their followers are doing. John Haggai writes, 'Since the leader transfers his thoughts to his group through communication, it follows that only effective communication can make clear to the group their real needs and move them toward the appropriate goals to fulfil their needs. Effective communication, through speech and writing, is possibly their leader's most valuable asset'.[15] Most of this teaching is done through personal communication such as private conversation, informal corridor talk or more formal written instructions. Thomas Jefferson, the third President of the United States and author of the Declaration of American Independence, once said that if leaders do not inform their followers effectively they will get one of three responses, 'rumour, apathy or revolution'![16] The Bible says that lack of knowledge brings destruction (Hosea 4:6). Reason enough to communicate!

As for persuasion, much of this is done in an inspirational public arena. Leaders have to convince the listeners that the road they are proposing is the right one and persuade them to take it. Jack Valenti, another presidential speechwriter and so obviously committed to the need for oratory, wrote, 'The role of communication has become dominant in the careers of anyone who must try to convince others'.[17] In this case, the gulf that needs to be bridged between the vision of the leader and the actions of the followers is not misunderstanding so much as lack of passion. The leader has the power to communicate that passion. The statesman and orator Winston Churchill wrote in 1897, 'Of all the talents bestowed upon men, none is so precious as the gift of oratory ... Abandoned by his party, betrayed by his friends, stripped of his offices, whoever can command this power is still formidable'.[18]

We may not all be leaders but there is no doubting that every one of us is called to the role of discipling others. This involves a measure of leadership and influence. In order to do this effectively we need to be committed to teaching and preaching, informing and persuading, private and public communication. This is not just the role of the professionals, it is the responsibility of every one. We all need to bridge the gap of misunderstanding and apathy and learn to communicate a vision.

Relationships necessitate communication

It may seem wholly unnecessary to have to state that positive communication and successful relationships go hand in hand. Nonetheless, with the relational turmoil in our society, it is an essential reminder. Where communication breaks down the relationship will stumble. When a relationship has broken down communication has already broken down. They are inseparable. Equally, if we desire to build or maintain a relationship we do so through communication. Human beings need relationships in order to survive; therefore the reason that we communicate is because we have to. This is not a philosophical motivation it is purely a pragmatic one.

Like all bridges, every relationship needs to be built. They don't just appear. They take energy, effort, thought and commitment. The nature of the relationship will determine the design, the cost, the time taken and the manner in which it is built. However, as we shall see later in the book, one of the tools used is the same for all bridge-building exercises. The tongue! As the Bible says,

> *'Do not let any unwholesome talk come out of your mouths, but only what is helpful for building others up according to their needs, that it may benefit those who listen.'* (Ephesians 4:29)

The original Greek word for 'unwholesome' here is *sapros* which means 'rotten'. It is often used in the context of decaying and mouldy fruit. In other words wholesome, helpful, selfless and beneficial words build others up whereas rotten words destroy them. Whether we are building acquaintances, friendships or marriages, we have to use positive communication.

Communication is essential for our wellbeing

Since we are made in the image of the 'Communicator', we 'cannot not communicate', and so our communication both with God, others and ourselves fulfils our God-given destiny and thus determines our wellbeing. In order to understand how this operates we need to know what we need! The psychologist Abraham H. Maslow concluded that humans have five basic needs. These are physiological, safety, love and belonging, esteem and self-actualization needs.[19] He suggested that each of these needs must be satisfied in the order in which they are listed before we concern ourselves with the next one. Thus we are unconcerned about our safety if our basic physiological needs, such as air and food, are not met. Whether Maslow is completely accurate is open to debate. However, it is clear that we do all have specific needs in our life. In Chapter 2 I have already described a number of our deep-felt desires that motivate us to build bridges. Here I want simply to categorize our needs as physical, emotional, social and spiritual and begin to show how communication is often necessary to fulfil them.

Although some people require more personal contact than others do, we all need satisfying personal relationships and the essential communication within those relationships. This communication is obviously indispensable for the physical needs of our safety, self-preservation and reproduction. But there is also evidence to suggest that communication is necessary for our physical health. Lynch's research into the medical consequences of loneliness is summarized by Ronald Adler and George Rodman: 'Divorced men (before aged seventy) die from heart disease, cancer, and strokes at double the rate of married men. Three times as many die from hypertension; five times as many commit suicide; seven times as many die from cirrhosis of the liver; and ten times as many die from tuberculosis. The rate of all types of cancer is as much as five times higher for divorced men and women, compared to their single counterparts'.[20] Positive 'bridge-building' is evidently healthy and the destruction of an established 'bridge' between two people can even jeopardize their lives. This observation would not have been lost on Adam and Eve who were separated from the 'Tree of Life' due to their sinful and broken relationship with God and each other (Genesis 3:22–24).

If some of our physical needs are met by communication, what about our emotional ones? We have observed that numerous stone bridges were built in Rome in order to fulfil its citizens' desire for exploration and acquisition. They were essential means of communication if the Empire was to expand and develop new markets. At the same time these beautiful structures must have given an enormous degree of satisfaction, not only to the builders but also to the general citizens of Rome. Almost unconsciously, the bridges were meeting the emotional needs of the whole community. The Romans, in common with all of us, had in-built passions for, among other things, discovery, 'ownership', wellbeing and beauty, and the building of bridges fulfilled them. These four passions seem unrelated to communication within interpersonal relationships until we translate them into a simple conversation. We can easily imagine a young man returning to his family and saying, 'I am feeling wonderful [wellbeing], I have found [discovery] a beautiful woman [beauty] and I have asked her to be mine [ownership]!' The act of building a bridge with another had met his deep emotional longings.

Thomas Mann wrote, 'Speech is civilization itself. The word, even the most contradictory word, preserves contact – it is silence which isolates'.[21] We have all felt the pain of a harsh word but, as Mann suggests, the agony of silence is sometimes greater. In fact, it is often only during the absence of something, in this case communication, that we fully appreciate how much we need it. The situation is perfectly illustrated in the well-documented true story of the 'Wild Boy of Aveyron'.[22] This boy was discovered in a French vegetable garden in 1800! Apparently, his lack of contact with human beings had left him with an inability to communicate, a complete lack of social skills and a total loss of identity as a human being. More recently, in 1994, a movie which explored the subject of communication was *Nell*, starring Jodie Foster. This film portrayed a woman isolated from the community and was interpreted by some as containing the message of the 'need for silence'. However, as in all of these illustrations, it led me to the inescapable conclusion that we don't so much need silence as each other!

Moreover, it is not just our obvious social needs that are met by communication but our less apparent spiritual ones too. On a trip to China in the eighties, I was struck by the spiritual awareness of a group of young people to whom a friend and I were teaching English. They asked us, 'What exactly do you do for a living?' Aware of their non-religious background, we replied with another question, 'Of the body, soul and spirit, which is the most important?' To my surprise, they instantly replied, 'The spirit.' We then explained that our 'job' was to address the spiritual health and wellbeing of the community. However, the conversation convinced me again of the observation that everyone in the world, whatever their background, is aware of a 'God-shaped space' that needs to be filled. Our various spiritual journeys in life strive to fill the vacuum. We all have a longing for spiritual communication: 'holy transport'. Some try to pray to stone images. Some get involved in astral travel. Some attempt to contact the dead! Some, as we have seen, build natural bridges, possibly unaware of their spiritual significance. Even if we remain unconvinced of our need for spiritual conversation, most of us still invest in relationships because we instinctively know that the formation of beneficial relationships partially fills the vacuum. It is a vacuum that exists because we were created with an unquenchable thirst for the giving and receiving of love. Whether we appreciate it or not, our deep-seated spiritual needs are temporarily met by communication. It is only God who meets them eternally.

It should be evident that at every level of our lives we were built to communicate. We are all ministers of transport, servants of communication. Yet even if that is the destiny of the human race, there remain many who seem strangely unaware of it. It would profit us to look further into the constructiveness of connection and the destructiveness of isolation.

Summary and advice

1. **The construction and destruction of bridges reveals our need for communication**. It is often not until we lose a relationship that we discover its true value.

2. **Relationships like bridges are both vital and vulnerable**. The pain of rebuilding a bridge is far greater than the cost of protecting one.

3. **God's character demands our communication**. The coming of Christ to earth reflects God's heart to build bridges and inspires and empowers us to do the same.

4. **Life contains an instinct for communication**. We have an inbuilt desire to replicate ourselves; to pass on who we are, what we have and what we know.

5. **Creation demonstrates communication**. In common with the animal kingdom, the survival of humanity is dependent on its ability to communicate effectively.

6. **Human beings were created for communication**. Much of our continued miscommunication comes from our failure to understand our origins.

7. **The life of Christ exemplifies the benefits of communication**. Jesus Christ is the ultimate model of successful human and divine communication.

8. **The message of the gospel commands communication.** All preachers have a responsibility to build a bridge between the Word of God and the world of the human race.

9. **Cultures value communication.** Language, and its successful transmission, is essential to the health and survival of a culture.

10. **Leadership requires communication.** Leaders must have vision and the ability to communicate that vision. Eyes without a mouth see no followers!

11. **Relationships necessitate communication.** The tongue is one of our greatest bridge-building tools. Conversely, rotten words destroy healthy relationships.

12. **Communication is essential for our wellbeing.** Our physical, emotional, social and spiritual needs are all met by positive communication.

Notes

1. Ian Mackay, *Great Australian Disasters* (Rigby Publishers Ltd, 1982).
2. Catherine of Siena. Quoted in Richard J. Foster and James Bryan Smith (eds.), *Devotional Classics* (Hodder & Stoughton, 1993).
3. C.S. Lewis, *The Voyage of the Dawn Treader* (Puffin Books, 1965).
4. The King James Version (Cambridge, 1769).
5. George and Muriel Beadle, *The Language of Life* (Doubleday, 1966). Quoted in Carol and Melvin Ember, *Anthropology* (5th edn, Prentice Hall, 1988).
6. Niko Tinbergen and Hugh Falkus (Clarendon Press, 1970).
7. E. Gibbs, *The God Who Communicates* (Hodder & Stoughton, 1985).
8. Roy B. Zuck, *Teaching as Jesus Taught* (Baker Books, 1995).
9. John Stott, *I Believe in Preaching* (Hodder & Stoughton, 1983).
10. Ibid.
11. Judith Dupré, *Bridges* (Könemann, 1998).
12. Ember, *Anthropology*.
13. H. Truman. Quoted in J. Oswald Sanders, *Spiritual Leadership* (Marshall, Morgan & Scott, 1967).
14. James C. Humes, *The Language of Leadership* (The Business Library, 1991).
15. John Haggai, *Lead On* (Word (UK) Ltd, 1986).
16. Thomas Jefferson. Quoted in Malcolm Gray, *Public Speaking* (Schwartz & Wilkinson, 1991).
17. J. Valenti. Quoted in Gray, *Public Speaking*.
18. Winston Churchill, *Epigraph from Comp.* Vol. I, Part 1. Quoted in Steven Hayward, *Churchill on Leadership* (Forum, 1997).
19. Abraham H. Maslow, *Toward a Psychology of Being* (Van Nostrand Reinhold, 1968).

20. Ronald B. Adler and George Rodman, *Understanding Human Communication* (Holt, Rinehart & Winston, Inc. 1988). From J. Lynch, *The Broken Heart: The Medical Consequences of Loneliness* (Basic Books, 1977).
21. Thomas Mann, *The Magic Mountain.* Quoted in Adler and Rodman, *Understanding Human Communication.*
22. R. Shattuck, *The Forbidden Experiment: The Story of the Wild Boy of Aveyron* (Farrar, Straus & Giroux, 1980).

Chapter 4

The Promise of Connection

Our Need for Relationships

The middle of the nineteenth century saw the suburbs on the north shore of Sydney Harbour growing substantially, necessitating a regular steam-driven ferry service from Dawes' Point on the South shore. By the 1890s the ferries were carrying more than five million passengers annually, not to mention the thousands of vehicles and horses. In 1890, £48,000 was paid for this service. By 1928, the ferry passengers had increased to an amazing forty-six million. It was evident that a bridge across the harbour was vitally necessary. The city demanded a more permanent connection.

There is no doubt that I was brought up to honour God but I don't remember thinking that I needed Him. My home was loving and secure and God was definitely a part of it but not, it seemed, a fundamentally vital part of it. The reason for this lack of spiritual hunger on my part was, ironically, the very love and security with which God had blessed us. I had become self-reliant. I was, in fact, blind to this blessing and blind to God's plans and purpose for my family and myself. I was ungrateful to God, unconcerned about my future and completely unaware of my plight. In common with many others, it wasn't until I became discontented with the direction of my life and honestly faced the dissatisfaction and emptiness within that my situation began to change.

On 14 March 1974, I read a booklet entitled *The Bridge of Life* that I had been given by a friend. It suggested that the cross of Christ, spanning the divide between sinful humanity and a holy God, was the greatest bridge of all. For the first time in my life I realized that I needed a personal encounter with the Lord Jesus Christ. I needed to invite Him into my life and ask Him to forgive me. I needed to reach out to Him. I needed to cross the bridge. It was by far the best, the most significant and the most life-changing decision that I have ever taken. Not only was it the right thing to do, it has also opened up previously unimaginable blessings and opportunities. It is my firm conviction that every one of us must have this God-designed bridge in our life.

It was not long after this encounter that I had another momentous decision to make. This time it concerned another person, my girlfriend Amanda. The bridge that I was proposing to cross was marriage. Again my background nearly proved to be my downfall. My boarding school, though exceptionally privileged, taught me the twin 'evils' of independence and self-sufficiency. I was conditioned to believe that it was a sign of weakness to really need other people. So, especially since my father died when I was eight, I was hurting but I couldn't show it, fearful but unable to admit it, longing for love but struggling to ask for it. It was not a good combination for an open relationship.

What I have discovered in a remarkable marriage is that I do need my wife but not in that sentimental and selfish way that stifles so many relationships. I have come to admit freely that the love and security that have liberated me and enlarged me to begin to become the transparent person that I am meant to be, are essential. I needed to reach out. I needed to cross that bridge. It has therefore become apparent in my life that relationships are imperative. I must learn the art, science and gift of bridge-building if I am going to fulfil my God-given potential.

In Chapter 1 I suggested that the first of the foundational premises on which all bridges are built is the understanding that they are necessary. In Chapter 2, I started to assess this premise by looking at why we build bridges. Yet, I wonder, do we really understand the importance of these relational bridges in our lives? It might seem unnecessary to have to answer this question. However, sadly, my experience tells me otherwise.

Numerous vulnerable and rejected people have come to my office trying to excuse their solitary lifestyle by saying that they don't need relationships. The reality is that we all need these God-given bridges. In order to establish this, however, I need to explain two truths: firstly, that withdrawing into isolation is a harmful choice and, secondly, that reaching out to others is a beneficial one.

Isolation is destructive

The forces that motivate a town to grow are for the most part positive. All living things grow. A vital and vibrant city is no exception. Thus, any municipality that is not permanently restricted by man-made walls or natural barriers will always extend its borders. It is not surprising then that within a few years of European settlement on the south side of Sydney Harbour, a number of adventurers crossed the river to settle on the other side.

These settlers, no doubt, were driven by their need for food, energized by exploration and also perhaps inspired to seek out some solace and privacy amid the chaos of the new colony. However, among all these positive goals, the end result was negative. Their independence had led to isolation. It was this very isolation that would eventually and inevitably compel them to build a bridge back to the original community. Their experience teaches us some crucial principles for the growth of our relationships.

Independence provokes rebellion

In our increasingly selfish and competitive world, independence has become a positive word. It is a concept that is promoted in our modern society. We are told that it is good to 'do your own thing', to 'go it alone' or to 'do whatever validates you' often without concern for the consequences either to ourselves or to others. However, this wilful independence, this drive to be set apart from others, this passion to rise to the top at all costs, can lead to two dangerous conclusions. Firstly, it deceives us into thinking that we don't need anyone else, including God, in order to be successful. We can do it ourselves. This is the basis for rebellion. Secondly, it forces us to conclude that we are slightly better than other people are. This is the height of arrogance.

The Bible describes God as a Shepherd and humankind as sheep. Modern-day shepherds tell us that goats are more independent than sheep. The Bible highlights this difference by equating rebellious people with goats (Matthew 25:31–33). Yet some sheep also have a tendency for independence and separate themselves from the protection of the shepherd and safety of the flock, thus endangering themselves. Occasionally one of my responsibilities as a child was to look for these independent sheep on our family farm, and we would drive around the perimeters of the fields. Sometimes we were able to rescue them but more often than not it was too late and all we found was their remains. The independence that took them from the rest of the flock had caused them to become the victim of a predator. This image is used in the Bible to describe the sinful condition of humanity:

> 'We all, like sheep, have gone astray,
>   each of us has **turned to his own way** ... '
>
> (Isaiah 53:6, emphasis mine)

What is made clear in the rest of the passage is that it was for this sin of wilful independence that Christ died: '... *and the* LORD *has laid on him the iniquity of us all'*.

The same theme is repeated during the rule of the Judges of Israel. The country was in a cycle of disobedience and restoration. In the seasons of disobedience, a God-sent leader such as Gideon or Deborah would arise and through repentance bring the nation back to God. Due to the compassion of God, restoration took place again and again (Nehemiah 9:28). As an explanation for the lawlessness and idolatry experienced in the nation during the periods of disobedience the Bible describes the prevailing attitude by saying,

> 'In those days Israel had no king; **everyone did as he saw fit.**'
>
> (Judges 17:6, emphasis mine)

The love for wilful independence that was prevalent in Israel at that time is equally common in today's society. Not only has it failed to bring us the success we desire, it has, in fact, set us up against God, divorced us from His favour and isolated us from the love that we crave from others. The truth is, we were created with the need to love and relate. We are dependent on God and interdependent with each other.

Segregation inhibits development

A study of nature gives the same evidence as the Bible. In an experiment conducted by Robert A. Butler, monkeys were kept alone in a dimly lit box. Even at three days old, they would crawl across the floor and press a lever hundreds of times in a few hours simply to see what was outside. If they saw another monkey, the normal and innate curiosity and subsequent lever-pressing was greatly increased. The desire for that same-species contact seems to be imbedded in our God-created universe. It is not only humans who have a passion for exploration.

Similarly, in 1959, after much research on affection in infant Rhesus monkeys, Harry F. Harlow described them as having an 'overwhelming compulsion to seek bodily contact'.[1] One of his experiments was to put infant monkeys in a cage with two surrogate mothers. The surrogates were wire models that very vaguely resembled another monkey. One model consisted of bare wire containing a bottle of milk. The other, also made of wire, was covered in towelling and therefore was more comforting for the infant monkey to hold. Yet this model had no supply of food. We know that hunger is a 'primary drive' in animals and so possibly would expect the baby monkeys to choose consistently to go to the model that provided sustenance. In fact the reverse was the case. The infant monkey seemed to prefer the comfort to the food. On top of that Harlow showed that lack of bodily contact hindered their development. He concluded that, 'The deprivation of physical contact during their first eight months had plainly affected the capacity of these infants to develop the full and normal pattern of affection'.[2] If this is the case in monkeys, how much more in human beings, who the Bible teaches are separately and specifically created in the image of the God of love and communication.

One of the names used in the Bible to describe the Church is the 'Body of Christ'. Like a living organism it grows and develops under the guidance of the Head, which is Christ. One of the purposes of ministers within the Church is to ensure that all its members develop and grow into maturity:

> *'It was he who gave some to be apostles, some to be prophets, some to be evangelists, and some to be pastors and teachers, to prepare God's people for works of service, so that the Body of Christ may be built up until we all reach unity in the faith and in the knowledge of the Son of God and become mature, attaining to the whole measure of the fullness of Christ.'* (Ephesians 4:11–13)

Any who decline to go to such a live church for whatever reason are immediately robbing themselves of the possibility of growth. They cannot develop in the way God intended.

The manner in which this process of maturation takes place is through building bridges with God and each other. We need to learn how to relate in a Christian community. As Paul continues,

> *'Instead, speaking the truth in love, we will in all things grow up into him who is the Head, that is, Christ. From him the whole body, joined and held together by every supporting ligament, grows and builds itself up in love, as each part does its work.'*   (Ephesians 4:15–16)

This concept seems to be ignored by many people I have met who will not attend a local church. They usually say that, 'Religion is a private matter'! (An idea that is blatantly untrue since it completely opposes the basis of Christianity!) Or they say, 'I choose to worship on my own in my own way'! This is akin to the aspiring soccer player who refuses to join a team because they won't play the way that he wants. (Someone needs to tell him that he will never be a soccer player. He is only a ball-kicker in the back yard!) The reality is that if we segregate ourselves from a God-inspired method of growth we stunt our development.

Solitary confinement invites insanity

Reading the Bible and observing nature give us ample evidence for the need of relationships, yet history testifies as well. Between 1830 and 1853 over 70,000 convicts were sent from Great Britain to the island prison of Tasmania, Australia (originally Van Diemen's Land) for 'punishment and reform'. From 1850 onwards, the more serious offenders who were incarcerated in the penal establishment of Port Arthur on the south coast of Tasmania were subjected to the 'Pentonville system of reform'.

This method of reform was based on a 'model prison' system developed in England in 1842. The idea was simple. Criminals needed to repent and also to be removed from any 'ungodly' influences. They, therefore, were submitted to a strict regime of religion and preaching and condemned to silence, anonymity and solitary confinement. The prisoners were allowed out of their cells for only one hour a day but were then compelled to wear a hood in order to conceal their identity and prevent communication. The 'success' of the neighbouring mental asylum built in 1867 is testimony to the failure of the prison. As a Port Arthur guide put it to me, 'After months of silent, repetitive incarceration, some men lost their sense of reality. Indeed, two out of every five were classified as insane'. The truth is that though we need God we also need each other. This misguided experiment with human souls should teach us all a vital lesson. We do not thrive in a disconnected environment.

In the twentieth century, numerous prisoners, including Nelson Mandela, have added weight to these observations and have spoken of the destructive power of isolation. The South African leader describes an incident while incarcerated in 'Pretoria Local' in November 1962. After refusing to eat the inadequate prison food or wear the required short trousers, he was placed in solitary confinement with better food and long trousers. He described the experience by saying, 'An hour was like a year. I was locked up in a bare cell, literally with nothing, nothing to read, nothing to write, nothing to do, and no one to talk or turn to ... I suffered the isolation for two months and finally concluded that nothing was more dehumanizing than isolation from human companionship'.[3] He subsequently exchanged his improved clothes and rations for human company. He had discovered painfully that we all have an innate desire for social contact that is fed by simple communication with others. When deprived of it, we feel as though a vital piece of our human puzzle is missing. God designed us with a spirit, soul and body and we need to keep each part healthy (cf. 1 Thessalonians 5:23).

Loneliness promotes torment

As a Bible-believing Christian I know that Satan is not only a real, though unseen, enemy but also a liar, in other words, a completely untrustworthy witness (John 8:44). Yet, it is his actions and not his words that are convincing in this discussion. Whereas God, who is committed to our welfare, leads us into relationship, Satan, who is committed to our destruction (John 10:10), drives us to isolation.

The story of the man from Gadara illustrates this well. He, according to the Bible, lived among the tombs, rejected by the community and sentenced to loneliness; that is, until he encountered Jesus Christ. Luke recounts the incident as follows:

> *'For Jesus had commanded the evil spirit to come out of the man. Many times it had seized him, and though he was chained hand and foot and kept under guard, he had broken his chains and had been **driven by the demon into solitary places.**'*
>
> (Luke 8:29, emphasis mine)

This tormented man was impelled by the demons within to a path of self-destruction, running naked through the tombs and cutting his flesh with stones.

This story may seem a little distanced from the often clinical world we tend to inhabit. Yet, on an overseas trip, the miracle of the Gadarene took on a new meaning for me. I was helping a friend who was working on a project of educating gypsies. These gypsies are alienated from the local population because of their different beliefs, lifestyle and culture. Many are condemned to a squalid existence on the rubbish dumps on the outskirts of the cities: desolate, lonely and rejected outcasts. On one particular day, as we approached one of these tented communities, a group of wild-looking children, aged between maybe four and eight, ran screaming to 'greet' us. They were filthy, half-naked and carried long knives. I thought for a moment that we were going to be attacked but then the children all stopped just in front of us. I have to say that I was somewhat shocked by what happened next. They all started cutting themselves with the knives, some sticking them into their flesh until the blood flowed. We, almost instinctively, commanded them to stop and despite not comprehending English, they immediately discontinued their self-mutilation. Nonetheless, I was left with an abiding image of the torment of rejection.

Seclusion ensures diminishment

The Gadarene, in his saner moments, although fully aware of the torture of his enforced loneliness, would probably have justified his seclusion as so many rejected people do. Nonetheless, when freedom was offered, he ran to meet it. His instincts told him that he was part of the human family and he needed the contact that had been denied him. Without it, he was less of a person than he should have been. He was incomplete.

The sixteenth-century English poet John Donne reached a similar conclusion, as he lay dying of typhus. He clearly understood that we are diminished by the loss of relationship when he wrote,

> 'No man is an island, entire of itself, every man is a piece of the continent, a part of the main. If a clod be washed away by the sea, Europe is the less, as well as if a promontory were, as well as if a manor of thy friend's or of thine own were; *any man's death diminishes me, because I am involved in mankind*; and therefore never send to know for whom the bell tolls; it tolls for thee.'[4]

In Donne's case, however, the loss was unavoidable. What if the seclusion is a personal choice? What if we choose to divorce ourselves from relationships?

In answer to this, the Bible not only establishes that wilful independence is wrong but also wilful isolation. In the creation story God says, *'It is not good for the man to be alone'* (Genesis 2:18). It must be noted that Adam was not completely alone when he was told this, since not only was God with him but he was also surrounded by animals. So it was the need for human contact to which God was referring. This may seem an irrelevant point until one meets people who, for instance, shun human contact, usually due to mistrust or disillusionment, and receive their necessary quota of affection solely from animals, or alternatively draw comfort from a hermitic lifestyle! At the best, this kind of behaviour is described as 'not good'. Why? Because God's plan for humankind is blessing, fruitfulness, increase and dominion (Genesis 1:28) and any rebellion against God's commission diminishes us as people, reduces our potential for blessing and decreases our effectiveness on earth. We, therefore, cannot and must not ignore the truth of God's statement to Adam if we are to discover the success that is destined for us.

Having now looked at the testimony of five 'spokespersons', the Bible, nature, history, Satan and instinct, we are left with the inescapable conclusion that isolation is highly destructive. However, in order to establish completely the case for our need for bridges we must fully grasp the positive argument for connection. Using the same 'spokespersons', I would like to discuss some principles that attest to the fact that God-given connection and dependence is a positive force both in civil and relational bridge-building.

Connection is constructive

In most towns or cities there is some sort of geographical or historical divide that separates one part of the city from another. This barrier may be a hill or a river such as the Thames in London, or the Seine in Paris. Or it might be an old city wall such as is found in Jerusalem, or a more mundane road or railway track. In Sydney, of course, it is the harbour. When growth of the city or some other circumstances demanded building the other side of this divide, the two communities often developed their own character. Names are coined to describe these distinct areas: names such as West Bank, East End, South Side, or in Sydney's case, North Shore. Expressions develop such as 'on the other side of the track' or 'outside the city'. In each case the names and expressions connote different things and engender strong feelings, often of dislike, contempt or prejudice which are directed to those living on 'the other side'. Yet, invariably, if some sort of connection is built to join the two halves, the fruit of the project is always constructive.

The Sea of Galilee, in the time of Jesus, was similarly divided. In this case, the division was political. He ministered among the Jews on the north-western shore in villages such as Capernaum and Magdala. The eastern and southern shores around to the town of Tiberias, established at the point where the Jordan River flows out of the lake towards Jerusalem, were inhabited by Gentiles. It was the region known as the Decapolis, which was greatly influenced by the Romans and therefore was 'out of bounds' to the religiously strict Jews. It was in this context that Jesus said to the disciples, *'Let's go over to **the other side** of the lake'* (Luke 8:22, emphasis mine). It was then that they set out to Gadara which was situated on the eastern shore. The disciples would have been very reticent. Not only were there stories about mad men in tombs, but it was 'the other side'! Jesus, of course, was unfazed. He crossed over, connected with the Gadarene and sent him back healed to build a bridge again with his community in the Decapolis. Jesus was trying to teach His disciples the power of connection. However, there is no record of Peter or the other disciples, the future 'bridge-makers', even leaving the boat!

Belonging inspires effectiveness

In its explanation of the correct function of the Church, the Bible, as we have observed, uses the imagery of the body. Using this image again, Paul the apostle, writing to the Corinthian church this time, draws two important conclusions: firstly, the body needs its parts and, secondly, the parts need the body! In the first case he teaches that the community needs every one of us if it is to operate successfully. There are no vestigial organs in God's economy! Each is a vital part of the whole. We belong to one another. The second conclusion that Paul comes to is that we all need the community if we are to function correctly. Each part needs to belong to the whole if it is to be effective.

'Now the body is not made up of one part but of many. If the foot should say, "Because I am not a hand, I do not belong to the body," it would

not for that reason cease to be part of the body. And if the ear should say, "Because I am not an eye, I do not belong to the body," it would not for that reason cease to be part of the body. If the whole body were an eye, where would the sense of hearing be? If the whole body were an ear, where would the sense of smell be? But in fact God has arranged the parts in the body, every one of them, just as he wanted them to be. If they were all one part, where would the body be? **As it is, there are many parts, but one body. The eye cannot say to the hand, I don't need you!** *And the head cannot say to the feet, "I don't need you!"'*   (1 Corinthians 12:14–21, emphasis mine)

Paul was teaching the Corinthian church and is teaching us that each one of us is significant. Each one of us possesses God-given gifts which are vital for the health and destiny of the community in which we live. Some of us are eyes, some ears and some noses! The body needs the eye in order to give sight to its action and the eye needs the body in order to put legs on its vision. It is great freedom for the leg to discover that it doesn't have to smell and the nose to discover that it doesn't have to run!

This concept of community was part of the foundation and fabric of the early Church. Thus Paul was reminding the Corinthians to remain true to the communion in which they were forged. Whether our community is a suburb, a church, an office or a family, teamwork is as essential for us today as it ever was for Paul's Greek audience.

Teamwork produces success

As a former biologist, I have often been intrigued by the 'wisdom' that God has invested in nature. In fact, since King Solomon advised us to *'go to the ant'* (Proverbs 6:6) and Jesus Christ told us to *'consider the ravens'* (Luke 12:24), it would be wise for us to do so! However, for the sake of my argument I would like to 'think about the bee'! (The word 'ant' in Proverbs 6:6 is translated 'bee' in the Septuagint!) I don't like bees, but they, along with other social animals, have taught me the significance of teamwork. On their own, they are at my mercy but in a hive they are terrifying! They are synergetic: the swarm is a far greater threat than the sum of the workers it contains. Not only that, but their complex social behaviour creates and maintains a constant temperature and healthy environment in the hive so that every individual can flourish. Every bee in this complex society has a task that is often individually pointless but corporately beneficial: where one gathers, another builds; where one guards another dances!

The power and wisdom of such teamwork can of course be observed within numerous animal species: whether musk ox or meerkat. However, occasionally two species will combine in a symbiotic relationship where both species rely on and benefit from each other. For instance, certain species of hermit crab have what could be described as an obligatory association with a type of sea anemone. Neither partner can do without the other. Their teamwork produces success. Parasitism, on the other hand, is a relationship where only one party benefits and the other is often destroyed. In 1845, millions of Irish men and women either starved to death or were dispossessed as a result of the parasitic fungus that causes potato blight! We don't need to be a genius to observe that the need for positive associations is fundamental to the world in which we live. We would all do well to learn from nature and choose symbiotic rather than parasitic relationships.

Communication releases power

Two of the key elements in the success of animal societies are the power created by unity and the language that promotes and maintains it. This is also true of humanity. The power and practice of communication will be discussed in some detail in the subsequent chapters, however it would benefit us at this stage simply to illustrate this point from history since it gives us ample evidence for the principle. Although many people may dispute the interpretation of the story of the 'Tower of Babel', the Bible tells us that the inhabitants of the plain of Shinar wanted to make a name for themselves by building a tower that reached the heavens. God objected to their arrogance and prevented their folly by confusing their language. However, prior to this event, the book of Genesis makes an amazing observation. It records that God said,

> *'If as one people speaking the same language they have begun to do this, then nothing they plan to do will be impossible for them.'*
>
> (Genesis 11:6)

As a completely united and interdependent community, the people could have built anything.

This capability is evident in the numerous nations that have arisen under one banner and with one language to conquer their known world. Edward Gibbon, when describing the rise of the Roman Empire, wrote, 'So sensible were the Romans of the influence of language over national manners that it was their most serious care to extend, with the progress of their arms, the use of the Latin tongue'.[5] They clearly understood the power of unity and communication. Although the concept can be misused, history leaves us in no doubt that connection and the subsequent interdependence are indescribably powerful.

Unity attracts blessing

Our fourth spokesperson, Satan, as I have mentioned, is an unreliable witness. Nonetheless, if we are to assume that he is not only real but also totally evil, then it follows that anything that he hates and seeks to destroy is fundamentally good. The Bible establishes that unity is not only powerful but also basically good. I say 'basically' because even good qualities can be abused. However, because 'God is one' and humankind is created in His image, humanity shares God's passion for unity. Thus the Bible promises that *'when brothers live together in unity'* God *'bestows his blessing'* (Psalm 133:1, 3). Since Satan hates God and His creation, it is in His interests to 'divide and destroy' and so rob humanity of a God-commanded blessing. This satanic policy of division and destruction can be readily observed in societies, relation-ships and even minds.

I encountered one such painful division on a trip to Spain in the 1980s. A friend of mine, a widow, took us to the museum in Toledo that exhibited some of the horror of the civil war that tore Spain apart between 1936 and 1939. She left us to enter on our own while she waited in the square. The scars of her divided family, brother against brother, were still so tormenting in her mind that she couldn't face another reminder. The influential Spanish artist, Pablo Picasso, lived through this war and wanted to portray something of what he saw. So in 1937, in horrified reaction to the bombing of the small Basque town of Guernica in the north of Spain on 26 April of that year, Picasso began to paint perhaps his most powerful painting. 'Guernica', as it is entitled, is a vast black and white canvas filled with startling evoca-tions of cruelty, destruction and ruin. At the time, Picasso said that he wanted these images to 'crawl up on the canvas, like roaches'. He was trying to capture what my widow friend was experiencing, the stark and terrible hand of division. This kind of division has all the malevolent fingerprints of Satan.

Whereas God occasionally divides 'like from unlike' as illustrated by the parable of the sheep and the goats (Matthew 25:32), He never divides 'like from like', that is, sheep from sheep. Satan, on the other hand, delights in separating and weakening those things that should be united. He undermines the covenant of marriage, severs children from their parents and disconnects people's minds. This negative argument is evidence enough for the blessed properties of God-given connection and warning enough to compel us to fight for interdependence and belonging.

Togetherness increases survival

We are the final spokespersons for connection and community. Our instincts and common sense tell us of its attributes and benefits. In his book *The Three Musketeers* Alexander Dumas coined an expression which captures the essence of unity. When his heroes, Athos, Porthos and Aramis, swore their allegiance to each other they proclaimed, 'All for one and one for all!' Although the phrase has subsequently become somewhat overworked it contains a truth that all of us need to hear. Their individual survival and their corporate destiny were dependent on their unity. They needed each other and so do we!

As we have seen, Solomon emphasizes this truth when he says,

> 'Two are better than one ...
> A cord of three strands is not quickly broken.'   (Ecclesiastes 4:9, 12)

The increase of the power of togetherness and subsequent survival rate is exponential. In other words, two together are more than twice as powerful as two are apart. Three together may be ten times more powerful than three are apart. This pattern is observed throughout nature. A pack of dogs or a pride of lions is considerably more dangerous than a single animal. Equally, a herd of oxen or a flock of sheep together statistically has a greater chance of survival than the lone straggler. Any predator will tell you that! They instinctively know the mathematics of unity. *'Five of you will chase a hundred, and a hundred of you will chase ten thousand ...'* (Leviticus 26:8).

It should be abundantly clear from my arguments so far in this chapter that civil and relational bridges are vital for the community. It is evident and therefore essential that we should all reach out to one another. I have given the various demerits and merits of isolation and connection and I have begun to lay the foundational stone of the first premise of bridge-building, the fact that we must know that the bridge is necessary. I have reiterated the point so we can be motivated by as many arguments as possible in order to overcome the numerous difficulties and challenges of bridge-building. It has been well said that, 'people who need people' are not the 'luckiest people in the world ... they are the only people!'[6]

Summary and advice

1. **The building of 'life bridges' is not an option, it is a necessity.** God requires us to build bridges both to Him and to others.

2. **Isolation is destructive.** If we divorce ourselves from relationships we must be prepared to pay the consequences.

3. **Independence provokes rebellion.** God-excluding seminars that teach self-development may not be a wise investment!

4. **Segregation inhibits development.** If we want to grow and develop we can only do so alongside others.

5. **Solitary confinement invites insanity.** Our mental health is determined by our relational health.

6. **Loneliness promotes torment.** Rejecting other people unnecessarily puts us in the same category as torturers.

7. **Seclusion ensures diminishment.** Avoiding intimacy will always make us smaller people and decrease our effectiveness and joy in living.

8. **Connection is constructive.** Building good relationships is an integral part of our health and wellbeing.

9. **Belonging inspires effectiveness.** Each part of the body works at optimum effectiveness only when it is joined to another.

10. **Teamwork produces success.** Symbiotic win-win relationships save life whereas parasitic win-lose relationships destroy it.

11. **Communication releases power.** Speaking with one voice helps build impossible dreams.

12. **Unity attracts blessing.** Prosperity in our homes starts with a decision to acknowledge disunity as the enemy that it is.

13. **Togetherness increases survival.** Stragglers get killed. Don't stick out from the crowd unless you are leading it.

Notes

1. Harry F. Harlow, 'Love in Infant Monkeys', *Scientific American Inc.* (1959), published in *Animal Behaviour, Readings from Scientific American,* ed. Eisner and Wilson (W.H. Freeman & Co.).
2. Harry F. Harlow, 'Love in Infant Monkeys', *Scientific American Inc.* (1959), published in *Animal Behaviour, Readings from Scientific American.*
3. Nelson Mandela. Quoted in Martin Meredith, *Nelson Mandela – A Biography* (Penguin Books, 1997).
4. Meditation XVII from Devotions Upon Emergent Occasions. Emphasis mine.
5. Edward Gibbon, *The Empire of Rome. AD 98–180* (Phoenix).
6. Ronald B. Adler and George Rodman, *Understanding Human Communication* (Holt, Rinehart & Winston, Inc., 1988).

THE SECOND
PREMISE

Bridges
Overcome Obstacles

Chapter 5

An Honest Analysis

The Decision to Build a Bridge

In common with many large civil engineering projects, the building of the Sydney Harbour Bridge was preceded by years of political wrangling and financial negotiation. Long before the tender of Dorman Long & Co. Ltd of Middlesborough, England was accepted in 1924, people had argued about the viability of such a massive undertaking. Between 1857, the year of the earliest recorded drawing of a harbour bridge by Peter Henderson, and 1924, numerous engineering proposals had been assessed and discarded, committees set up and abandoned, parliamentary bills presented and rejected. It could never be said that the building of Sydney Harbour Bridge was not thought through!

Every one of us has crosses to bear. These are the incidents in our lives that scar us for life. For some they are seemingly insurmountable: maybe the shocking tragedy of an earthquake that devastates and torments us with recurring fears; or the offensive sexual abuse of a relative that leaves us with violent bitterness that screams betrayal and refuses forgiveness; or the overwhelmingly negative circumstances of poverty that seem to create a cycle of failure. For others they are almost insignificant at the time, yet in the end can be equally destructive.

The latter are in fact common to all of us. They are like seeds planted in our souls, seeds of uncertainty, hopelessness and rejection. Given the right environment, they grow into life-dominating problems. These problems, if fostered, damage our self-image and subsequently ruin our relationships. For me, in common with many others, the seeds of doubt were sown at school.

On a recent perusal of my school reports that were all kept and filed away, I was reminded that the words 'poor', 'disappointing' and 'slow' occurred all too frequently! One teacher said, 'I cannot make out whether he is stupid or just lazy'! Another wrote, 'I find him a most unsatisfactory person to teach'. Yet another commented that my progress was hampered by an 'inability to express himself clearly'. In the summer term of 1968, the headmaster, who in our school was rather grandly referred to as 'the master', summed up the general feeling of the staff and school by writing, 'A nice boy but no great intellect'!

In addition to this, one of the schools that I attended had the habit of publishing amusing comments or mistakes made by pupils in the school magazine. In 1966 my geography essay was the target of a great deal of mirth and was duly published, thankfully without my name printed at the bottom. Some years later the school celebrated its centenary and consequently published a magazine. In it was printed my essay in full. Now my exam answer had become an example of the worst piece of writing in one hundred years of the school's history! Thousands laughed at my expense. On the outside, I laughed with them.

These remarks about my character and performance seem fairly harmless, yet when reinforced with other negative observations over a period of time, they had a profound effect on me. I developed a very poor self-image with a tendency to be retiring, shy, fearful and often lonely. I found it difficult to relate to others and did not believe that I could achieve very much at all with my life. Of course, I was told that 'Sticks and stones can break your bones but words can never harm you' but soon discovered that the proverb was completely erroneous!

The experiences that I have described, along with numerous others, were creating obstacles in my life, barriers that needed to be bridged if I were going to make any fulfilling connection in my life. Every time I pursued a relationship, I feared that I would be rejected. Every time I attempted to achieve something, I assumed that I would fail. It didn't seem to matter how many times I succeeded, I still tended to believe the nagging doubts in my mind that had been planted over the years. In order to deal with these problems in my life, it was necessary for me to grasp fully the second premise of bridge-building. I needed to really believe that a bridge has the power to overcome all the obstacles arrayed against it. I had to learn the various steps that a civil engineer takes in order to bridge a previously impassable ravine. It had to start with a decision.

Developing an appropriate mindset

A bridge-builder who wants to build a new structure has first to win a battle in his mind. He has to decide that it is technically possible to build the proposed bridge. If no one has ever built such a bridge, he must trust in his education that says it is feasible despite the previous evidence to the contrary. If a bridge has failed or collapsed in the past he must conquer the fear of failure and ridicule that tells him that he cannot succeed. He knows very well that, despite all the statistics and mathematics at his disposal, there is still an element of risk. His faith in the project must overcome the fear of the unknown in his thinking. He must make up his mind, with all that that entails, to build a bridge that nobody has built before. Similarly, I had to win the mental contest that told me that my personal obstacles could not be overcome.

Most of the more destructive conflicts of our lives take place in our minds. It is here that the insidious and poisonous seeds of doubt are sown and here that they can take root, flourish and bear their divisive fruit. When the apostles Paul and Barnabas went to Iconium in Asia Minor, the whole city was divided. On one side the crowd supported them and listened to the Good News that they brought, on the other the hostile mob threatened to execute them and drove them away. The source of the problem was a mindset change. The Bible says,

> *'But the Jews who refused to believe stirred up the Gentiles and poisoned their minds against the brothers.'*   (Acts 14:2)

A simple change of mind had robbed a whole city of the gospel.

Equally, when we are dealing with constantly recurring negative thought patterns we need to understand that the primary cause is doubt and the inevitable result, division. This was re-emphasized by James the brother of Jesus, when he wrote,

> *'he who doubts is like a wave of the sea, blown and tossed by the wind. That man should not think he will receive anything from the Lord; he is a double-minded man, unstable in all he does.'*   (James 1:6–8)

Our divided mind robs us of good news and hence our destiny. While I believed my negative school reports and doubted the good ones, I was unable to fulfil my potential.

On the other hand, if our minds are the sites of our greatest defeats they can also be the arenas for our greatest triumphs. If we can replace the negatives with positives, the bad news with good news, the doubts with faith, then the result will not be division, it will be unity, and unity, as we have seen, attracts blessing. So single-mindedness should become our goal. The reason that Joshua and Caleb, two of the Jewish leaders who were sent by Moses 'to spy out the land', succeeded while those around them failed was simply because, though fully aware of the problems, they chose to focus on the possibilities (Numbers 14). They believed the promises of God, rejected the doubt that would have caused division, and promoted a unity of thinking that attracted blessing.

Paul reiterated this truth when he encouraged the Philippian church to think positively:

> *'Finally, brethren, whatever things are true, whatever things are noble, whatever things are just, whatever things are pure, whatever things are lovely, whatever things are of good report, if there is any virtue and if there is anything praiseworthy – meditate on these things.'*
>
> (Philippians 4:8) [1]

If Paul were alive today, I think that he would say something like this to me, 'Don't listen to the negative reports that your teachers wrote about you or it will cause you to doubt and achieve nothing. Make a decision to be single-minded. Choose to believe the good things that God says about you in the Bible. Think and speak about those things and you will be successful in every area of your life.'

This line of reasoning will help us all to develop the necessary mindset that we need in order to build relational bridges in our lives. As well as this we need to act on three simple truths that will help us to overcome the seeds of doubt in our minds that attempt to rob us of any fruitful relationships. They are based on one of Paul's most famous statements. It reads,

> *'No temptation has seized you except what is common to man. And God is faithful; he will not let you be tempted beyond what you can bear. But when you are tempted, he will also provide a way out so that you can stand up under it.'*   (1 Corinthians 10:13)

We are not on our own

The language of inadequacy and self-pity proclaims proudly that 'No-one understands', 'My situation is worse than others', 'If anyone else had my problem he would behave as I do'! It is a language of self-justification and failure. While we think that we are on our own we will never overcome our difficulties which is why Jesus Christ con-stantly reminded His disciples that He would never leave them. However, this verse expressly states that our problems are *'common to man'*. We are all in exactly the same 'boat'.

The reason that this gives us hope is that if other people can extricate themselves from this mess then so can we! The obstacle looks insurmountable but if others have overcome it, so can we. The temptation of the civil engineer is to spend his time thinking that no one has built this bridge before rather than concentrating on the hundreds of people who have successfully built other bridges. On this same line of argument, I remember years ago hearing a story that greatly encouraged me. A man was driving his car up a twisty mountain road in the United States. Near the top the road narrowed to such a degree that it looked impossible for him to continue. As he attempted to turn his car around in order to return he noticed a small plaque attached to the rock wall. It simply said, 'You can do it, millions have done it before you'! On reading this, the man carefully and successfully negotiated the previously 'impassable' road and continued safely on his way.

If then, I was going to overcome the obstacles of my youth I needed to realize that others had succeeded in life after having encountered problems at school. For me, the inspiration came from Sir Winston Churchill. He stammered as a boy and still became one of the century's greatest orators. He continually failed at school causing his mother to remark, 'your work is an insult to your intelligence',[2] and yet won a Nobel Prize for literature! His father, Lord Randolph Churchill used to criticize his son constantly. He wrote to Winston on 9 August 1893 saying, 'I am certain that if you cannot prevent yourself from leading the idle useless unprofitable life you have had during your schooldays and later months, you will become a mere social wastrel one of the hundreds of the public school failures, and you will degenerate into a shabby unhappy and futile existence'.[3] Despite this parental disapproval, Winston Churchill went on to become one of the great leaders of the twenti-eth century.

God is bigger than our problem

The second truth that is contained in Paul's simple statement to the Corinthian Church is that *'God is faithful; he will not let you be tempted beyond what you can bear'*. In other words, whatever circumstances may come our way, God will never let us down but will always give us the strength and grace to succeed. He is always bigger than our problem. If I was to overcome the relational problems of my adolescence, I had to grasp that God as the ultimate 'designer of bridges' had the ability to build something in my life that was greater than my background, my failures or my discouragement.

My wife Amanda, though never a failure at school, had her own barriers to overcome. She had a middle-aged teacher who though tremendously kind was not noted for her beauty! On one occasion she was discussing growing old with Amanda and commented that, like herself, Amanda had no need to worry about ageing since 'she had no looks to lose'! I don't think she had any idea how devastating this remark was for her relatively shy and sensitive seventeen-year-old pupil. Despite this setback to her self-esteem, however, Amanda determined that she was not only going to get married but that she was going to marry a minister. On announcing this to a member of her family she was told that she was 'not pretty enough to be choosy'! Nonetheless, in 1976, in answer to her prayers, she was married, 'the first female member of her family on her father's side', she was told, 'to be married this century'! In common with Sir Winston Churchill, she took no notice of her school reports.

However, in order to be successful in her marriage, it was necessary for her to believe that not only was God bigger than her problem and was able to solve her insecurities but also the marriage itself was powerful enough to heal her. As I have stated, the second premise of bridge-building is that the bridge is able to overcome obstacles. As she committed herself in faith to a positive and loving marriage she soon discovered that it freed her from the negative reports of her schooldays.

There is always a way out

The statement made by Paul, from which we are drawing these conclusions, is written primarily about a temptation to sin. When we are tempted, he says, there is always 'a way out': there is always a choice, there is never an excuse for doing the wrong thing. Nonetheless, there is another interpretation. Paul is talking about Israel's failure in the past. He says that since they failed we can also fail. However, there is always a way out, there is always the possibility of success. We, therefore, can never excuse our failures.

Israel's history is rich with examples of people who found the way out, people who shook off the failures of the past and determined to succeed in life. They had a potential excuse but didn't succumb to it. Gideon the mighty warrior was the *'least in his family'* (cf. Judges 6:15), Peter the apostle was *'unschooled'* and *'ordinary'* (cf. Acts 4:13), and Jeremiah the prophet was *'only a child'* and did not know how to speak (cf. Jeremiah 1:6). David the king was an anonymous shepherd, and the powerful Joseph a prisoner. The list goes on and on. Jesus Christ Himself came from a poor family, was relatively uneducated, despised for His origins, constantly bore the stigma of illegitimacy, a political refugee, rejected by His family and friends, betrayed and tortured and yet never once complained or used His circumstances or suffering as an excuse for failure.

In each of these cases, a difficult past was not allowed to determine the effectiveness of the future. Negative circumstances were overcome and negative people ignored. They all believed that there was a way out. As I have already mentioned, Caleb, the Israelite leader and soldier, who lived among the failed generation about which Paul was writing to the church at Corinth, never used their constant idolatry, immorality and grumbling as a reason for depression or hopelessness. He didn't give in to their carping and never joined in with their criticism. When the opportunity came, though surrounded with unhelpful and dissenting voices he and Joshua brought a good report (Joshua 14:7). It was this attitude that enabled the two of them to survive and enter into the land that God had promised them (Numbers 14:38).

Every one of us may well have circumstances and reports in our past that suggest that we are going to continue to be disqualified in life and fail in our relationships but if we believe and correctly apply these three truths we are guaranteed success. In the light of the fact that others have been tempted, God does remain faithful, and there will always be a way of escape, we should always reject those negative reports of our life and replace them with positive ones.

Surveying the facts

While studying zoology at university I made a number of friends who were studying engineering. They had enthusiastically enrolled in various branches of the subject such as civil, electrical, electronic, mechanical, mining and so on. Each had different aspirations and reasons for doing the courses. Some were fascinated by computers, others by machines or even by coal! However, almost all of them complained to me about the first year of the course! The course was the same for all of them, an introduction to engineering, and it involved, among other things, a study of fluids and solids. The complaint was usually, 'What has this got to do with my future career?'

This scenario could of course be repeated in any form of instruction. The aspiring pilot cannot avoid the incessant disciplinary drill of the first few months of his training. The budding doctor has to spend months studying dead bodies before she can be trusted with a live one! Similarly the civil engineer, the potential bridge-builder, has to comprehend all aspects of fluid mechanics before one girder is joined to another. In all professions there are certain skills, fundamentals, that are essential for ongoing success in their chosen career. In both civil and relational bridge-building one of these fundamental skills is surveying.

The British contractors, Dorman Long & Co. Ltd, the builders of Sydney Harbour Bridge, and their various consulting engineers used a variety of detailed surveys in its construction. Cartographic and topographical surveys informed them of the surrounding geography. Geological surveys gave them the necessary information about the rocks and their ability to withstand the huge pressures that such a bridge exerts. They would have needed hydrographic surveys, which mapped the bottom of the harbour and possibly even a geodetic survey that takes the earth's curvature into account! The latter seems un-necessary until one realizes that the towers of the Humber Bridge in England, which at the time of its opening in 1981 was the world's longest single-span suspension bridge at 1,410 metres, are built 36mm out of parallel in order to compensate for it! The purpose for these surveys is simply to assess all the various obstacles before building a bridge to overcome them! It is a simple appraisal of the pros and cons. We would save ourselves a great deal of grief if we would do the same with our relationships.

Charles Darwin, the nineteenth-century biologist, wrote on a scrap of blue paper a 'for and against' list, some time prior to his marriage to Emma Wedgwood on 29 January 1839. In it he jotted down some 'positive' arguments about the idea of marriage which read as follows: 'Children – (if it Please God) – Constant companion (& friend in old age) who will feel interested in one, – object to be beloved and played with. better than a dog anyhow. – Home, & someone to take care of house – Charms of music & female chit-chat. – These things good for one's health. – but terrible loss of time'![4] Darwin cannot be commended for his appalling self-centredness and patronizing manner yet may be praised for his careful planning. Too many people today, compelled by, often unreliable, feelings, launch into all manner of personal and business relationships without ever 'facing the facts'.

This type of honest analysis is not only imperative for the success of our future relationships but also for our lives in general. It is a truth that is observed in the life of one of the great patriarchs of the nation of Israel. Abraham had been promised children by God. He had been told that his children would be as innumerable as the stars in the sky or sand on the seashore. However, there were a few small obstacles! It had been many years since the promise was given, his wife Sarah was unable to have children and they were now both in their nineties!

Nevertheless we are told that Abraham *'faced the fact that his body was as good as dead ... Yet he did not waver through unbelief regarding the promise of God'* (Romans 4:19–20). In other words, he correctly assessed that the positives were greater than the negatives, the opportunities more compelling than the obstacles, and therefore retained his confidence. However, in order to come to this conclusion, he had to survey the circumstances honestly. As we have already observed, Winston Churchill was able to overcome the failures of his past because he was prepared to face the facts fairly and squarely and challenge them correctly.

One of the major reasons for failure in people's lives is therefore a form of dishonesty, an inability to assess the situation accurately. Such people fall into two broad categories, the over-confident and the under-confident. The over-confident ones, in their determination to succeed and fulfil their vision, tend to ignore the very real obstacles and subsequently get caught out by them. The under-confident, on the other hand, tend to concentrate on the problems, fail to face up to the huge opportunities and therefore never take hold of them.

This inability in the lives of people, especially leaders, is often best observed in times of war because the consequences of their failures are so stark. Napoleon Bonaparte, for instance, the despotic eighteenth-century French general, was renowned for his dishonesty, regularly lying to his supervisors, the Directory, about the success of his campaigns. He falls into the category of the over-confident! He was so convinced of his attributes that he was almost completely unaware of his faults. This blind dishonesty and ambition drove him to invade Egypt in 1798. The expedition was described by his own secretary, Bourrienne, as 'disastrous',[5] a debacle from beginning to end, ill conceived and poorly executed, resulting in a cruel and unnecessary loss of life.

Napoleon had failed to plan appropriately or precisely determine the climate, terrain, opposition or food and water supplies. Many of his own troops died of thirst, hunger and disease. It was an appalling episode in his life. Subsequently, Napoleon returned to France, abandoning his army in Egypt to their fate. Simply stated, Napoleon's failure to face facts, his refusal to assess the obstacles to his 'dream', had inexcusably resulted in the death of thousands of people.

To be aware of a problem then, or to analyse an impediment carefully is not a sign of weakness. Rather, it is evidence of wisdom. Military commanders and politicians planning a campaign, and scientists and civil engineers building a project must all survey the facts and plan accordingly. And you and I must not be afraid to face the challenges of a relationship honestly before we pursue it with confidence, knowing full well that the bridge we are building has the power to overcome all obstacles. However, when we have honestly surveyed all the facts, we have to make a decision whether to proceed or not and therein lies a dilemma. To build or not to build: that is the question!

Making the right choice

Every day we each make countless choices that involve both the mundane and the profound. We make decisions about where we go, what we eat, what we say, and so on. Life is the sum total of these decisions. The ramifications of our daily choices are so complex and the consequences so dramatic that many of us are terrified of making them. We are frightened that we will make a mistake or take the wrong path in life. When faced with such a huge array of options we either hesitate and consequently miss opportunities, stagnate and fail, or we hurry our deliberations and rush into mistake after mistake.

In order to overcome our weaknesses in this area we first simply need to reduce the possible choices in order to make the decisions simpler. For instance, the commander may ignore the plan that would have resulted in too many casualties or the surveyor may reject a proposal that would have incurred too great an expense. Charles Darwin, as we have noted, attempted this procedure, in a typically unemotional and scientific manner, when choosing a wife. It seems that he discarded certain possible companions because they would be injurious to his health and eventually married Emma Wedgwood. She must have been a remarkable woman! Nonetheless, for most of us, in the case of relationships, the issue of decision making is not so black and white. We need some guidelines.

The Bible, as usual, makes this considerably easier for us although this may not be clear to everyone initially. In the books of Leviticus and Deuteronomy the nation of Israel was given what seems at first glance to be a very involved system of rules and regulations. To attempt to fulfil every one of these laws must have seemed to be an impossible task at first. However, at the end of the book of Deuteronomy, in order to communicate clearly to the people, Moses, under the inspiration of God, reduced the options. He simply said,

> *'See, I set before you today life and prosperity, death and destruction . . .*
> *This day I call heaven and earth as witnesses against you that I have set*
> *before you life and death, blessings and curses.* **Now choose life**, *so that*
> *you and your children may live . . . '*
>
> (Deuteronomy 30:15, 20, emphasis mine)

In all our decision-making, therefore, we need to weigh up the various options, reduce them to those that produce God's blessing and those that don't, and then always choose life. In the event that two possibilities will both invite God's favour, we choose the path that will, in our opinion, produce the greatest fruit, since fruitfulness is a sign of life, blessing and prosperity.

William Shakespeare identified the dilemma of indecisiveness in his play about Hamlet, the Prince of Denmark. The first lines of his famous soliloquy find the troubled hero grappling with thoughts of suicide, 'To be, or not to be: that is the question'.[6] What follows is a poetic summary of the various merits of life and death, or, as he puts it, 'sleep'. Eventually, after considering the various options, he rejects the unknown, 'the dread of something after death, the undiscovered country from whose bourn no traveler returns' and chooses to stay awake!

Hamlet's choice, however, was relatively simple. It is obvious that he should have chosen life – although, with the current increase in suicides, murders and abortions in most countries of the world, it is evidently and tragically not always as clear to some people. The problem is that sometimes we simply do not know which of our decisions will produce fruit. We need more clarity.

Again the passage in Deuteronomy provides us with an answer. It says,

> *'This day I call heaven and earth as witnesses against you that I have set before you life and death, blessings and curses. Now choose life, so that you and your children may live **and that you may love** the LORD your God, listen to his voice, and hold fast to him. For the LORD is your life, and he will give you many years in the land he swore to give to your fathers, Abraham, Isaac and Jacob.'*
>
> (Deuteronomy 30:19–20, emphasis mine)

In other words, a choice for life will always result in love. And, as I have already pointed out, love is the foundation of all relational bridge-building. Life, then, is not simply a choice to live and bear fruit, it is a choice to love. In fact it is a choice between two loves.

The French Catholic priest Michel Quoist succinctly describes this principle of decision making in his book *Prayers of Life*. In one of his poems entitled 'There are two loves only', he writes: 'There are two loves only, Lord, love of myself and love of you and of others, and each time that I love myself, it's a little less love for you and for others, it's a draining away of love, it's a loss of love, for love is made to leave self and fly towards others. Each time it's diverted to myself, it withers, rots and dies'.[7] He explains the poem by saying, 'To live is to choose between these two loves'. In our loveless and egocentric world this kind of reasoning often falls on deaf ears. Nonetheless it is true, as we shall see, and it is the basis of all successful decision making.

Whether our decisions involve the building of businesses or the building of relationships, the principles that were taught by Moses to Israel about three thousand four hundred years ago in the book of Deuteronomy are as applicable today as they were then. A summary of his teaching could read as follows:

- We must make decisions or our indecision will rule our lives.

- We must make right decisions because it is necessary for God's favour and therefore success in life.

- We are capable of making right decisions in life only because the Spirit of God promises to help us and we have the guidance of the Bible.

- We must make decisions that result in life, blessing and prosperity and avoid decisions that draw us away from God.

- We must always make decisions that result in love for God and others and avoid decisions that only benefit ourselves.

- We must make right decisions in faith, believing that they will lead to a hopeful future, and avoid decisions made in doubt.

- We must make decisions with courage and avoid those made in anxiety or fear.

Here then are some clear guidelines for decision making in all aspects of our life. However, as a relational engineer, how do we put these principles into practice? For instance, how do we know whom to marry? How do we know with whom to build a bridge or develop a friendship? Can we choose or is it just a matter of chance? Many believe that their mistakes are a product of misfortune. They say, 'I ended up with the wrong man' or, 'I am afraid he got in with the wrong crowd', as though it was some bad luck that was beyond their control, whereas actually they chose incorrectly. It is therefore imperative that we learn to apply this Mosaic blueprint for life. Take, for example, a Christian making a decision about their life partner. What are the questions they should ask themselves before they choose? If the answer to any of these questions is no, they need to think seriously about their choice!

- Am I free to make this decision?

- Does my proposed partner share my faith, my commitment to live biblically and my convictions about serving God?

- Am I making my decision according to both the 'witness of the Spirit' and the tenets of God's Word?

- Does my relationship with my proposed partner enhance my relationship with God?

- Will I love and am I 'in love' with my proposed partner?

- Do I believe that any personal discords, relational barriers or cultural differences that separate us can be successfully bridged?

- Am I entering this relationship without any irresolvable fear or anxiety?

These are the kind of frank questions that all relational engineers should be able to ask themselves before they begin to build a relationship. As we learn to think positively and are courageous enough to face the facts honestly, we will be increasingly free to build loving and fruitful relationships at all levels.

Summary and advice

1. **We need to overcome our mental barriers in order to build bridges successfully.** Every one of us has had negative experiences that can hinder our pursuit of fruitful relationships. Honestly admitting our problems is the first step to conquering them.

2. **We must develop an appropriate mindset.** Positive single-mindedness rids us of doubt and attracts the blessing that comes with unity.

3. **We are not on our own.** Realizing that we are not the only one with challenges inspires us to change.

4. **God is bigger than our problem.** There is no wound that God cannot heal or dream that He cannot realize.

5. **There is always a way out.** There is always an opportunity for success if we choose to grasp it.

6. **We must all accurately and truthfully survey the facts.** Careful planning is evidence of wisdom. In order to build good relationships we need to conclude that the positives presented by the relationship outweigh the negatives that challenge it.

7. **We need to learn to make the right choices.** Our decisions must always result in life, fruitfulness and love. We should make right, possible, living, loving, faith-filled and courageous decisions!

Notes

1. The Holy Bible, New King James Version (Thomas Nelson Inc., 1982).
2. Charles Darwin. Quoted in Adrian Desmond and James Moore, *Darwin* (Michael Joseph Ltd, 1991).
3. Alan Schom, *Napoleon Bonaparte* (Harper Perennial, 1998).
4. Martin Gilbert, *Churchill. A Photographic Portrait* (Wings Books, 1993).
5. Ibid.
6. William Shakespeare, *Hamlet*, Act III, Scene I.
7. Michel Quoist, *Prayers of Life* (Logos Books, 1966).

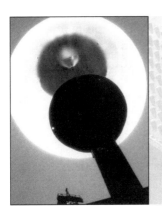

Chapter 6

Unintentional Arrogance

Recognizing the Power of Obstacles

When the explorer Captain Cook sailed passed Sydney Heads in 1770 and gave the harbour the official name of Port Jackson, he recognized it as a place of opportunity. When the navigator Captain Arthur Phillip established the colony on 26 January 1788, he described the port as a place of safety, writing that it was 'the finest harbour in the world',[1] in which a thousand ships could sail in perfect security. However, when various engineers proposed plans for the construction of a bridge from as early as 1815, all they saw was difficulty: a shark-infested body of water that was twenty-one metres deep and stretched nearly five hundred metres between Dawes' Point in the south to Milson's Point in the north. For the bridge-builder, the harbour was an obstacle that had to be overcome.

There is something irresistibly potent about the elegance and majesty of large bridges. They seem indestructible, almost eternal. Some have, in fact, spanned two millennia. In his Pulitzer-prize-winning novel *The Bridge of San Luis Rey*, Thornton Wilder wrote, 'The bridge seemed to be among the things that last forever; it was unthinkable that it should break'.[2] It is this kind of blind respect for bridges that has led to numerous tragedies.

Two of the most famous 'bridge disasters' of the twentieth century involve the Quebec Bridge and the Tacoma Narrows Bridge. The former, built over the River Lawrence in Canada, collapsed on 29 August 1907 killing seventy-five workmen as a result, among other things, of a type of unintentional arrogance. One of the consultant designers who, despite his respectable track record and teaching on the importance of careful preparation, increased the length of the main span without the proper recalculation of the resultant stresses. According to Judith Dupré, his mistake was that he believed that, 'a bridge's stability was more reliant on the engineer's instincts than "merely upon a theory of stresses".'[3] In other words, scores of men lost their lives as a result of a 'gut feeling'.

The Tacoma Bridge disaster involved similar short-sightedness. The Narrows, the body of water in Washington, USA over which the bridge passed, was not only swift running but had an unsuitable riverbed for piers, the intermediate supports of a bridge. The consultant engineer, therefore, designed a long and very narrow suspension bridge. Only one of the several engineers participating in the project foresaw the danger of aerodynamic forces on the bridge. Yet on 7 November 1940, just four months after its opening, the bridge, nicknamed 'Galloping Gertie', twisted, buckled and collapsed in winds of only forty-two miles an hour. In this case, the only casualty, apart from the bridge itself, was a dog, called Tubby!

Of course, disasters such as these result in much soul-searching. After the Tacoma Narrows Bridge collapse, the design of suspension bridges around the world reflected the lessons learned in Washington. Nevertheless, the reason that both bridges collapsed is still the reason why every bridge has ever collapsed in the long history of bridge-building. Despite the engineers' experience, research and planning, they failed to build a bridge that overcame the various obstacles that 'opposed' it. The power of the obstacles was not accurately assessed or clearly identified.

In common with all my observations of bridges, the lessons learned by these myopic engineers can help us avoid such unnecessary and inglorious collapses in our far more precious relationships. A number of years ago I had the opportunity to counsel a couple who, like the engineers, were only wise after the event! They came to me with a *fait accompli*. They had been living together and had decided to get married, so had come to me, as a minister, to marry them. They assumed that since they were doing the 'right thing' I would be immediately supportive of their decision.

I obviously took time to assess the situation before I committed myself. In the course of the conversation, which incidentally revealed numerous problems that they had failed to identify, I simply said that in order to be successful in their relationship they would have to learn to say sorry. It seemed like a simple and obvious piece of advice. However, the response took me completely by surprise. The future husband looked at me with a mixture of anger and determination and said defiantly, 'I have never said sorry in my life and I have no intention of starting now'!

It seemed that he thought that a commitment to the bridge of marriage would automatically resolve this fundamental flaw in their relationship. Both of them had failed to judge the enormity of the obstacle that they were facing. After my evidently shocked response, I decided to highlight the inevitable outcome of such a destructive philosophy. I ended my conversation with three simple statements. 'Firstly,' I said, 'if you have never said sorry, then you are not a Christian which you profess to be. Secondly, if you cannot say sorry, then your future relationship cannot prosper and, thirdly,' I concluded, 'if you will not say sorry, then I will not marry you!' My conclusions may seem harsh in retrospect, however, at the time, I felt that they were completely justified. As Kathryn Kuhlman said, 'Be careful of the person, whether they're a member of your family, whether you work with them, whether they are an employee; be careful of the person who can't say, "I am sorry". You will find that person very self-centred ... Such a self-centred person usually draws disease to themselves like a magnet.'[4]

The couple were, perhaps understandably, somewhat offended at my comments. However, I foresaw a tragedy and didn't want to stand silently by, carelessly watching them injure each other so unnecessarily. I felt like the lone engineer who warned against the building of the Tacoma Narrows Bridge. Nonetheless, they rejected my advice, angrily left my office and were married soon afterwards in a registry office. I thought that they would never contact me again, but three months later the husband phoned to ask for some counsel. He and his wife had separated because of irreconcilable differences. The marriage had collapsed as predicted. They had entered it with blind and unreasonable expectations and both failed to take into account the power of the obstacle of unforgiveness that opposed it.

In all of these cases of failure, the people concerned seemed unable to see the problems arising. Maybe their blindness was a result of being too close to the issue. The engineers were caught up in the enormity of their vision, while the courting couple were involved with the passion and intensity of the relationship. In both situations good advice went unheeded. In order to avoid the tragic outcome of these mistakes, we need not only to realize the power of the obstacles in our path but also clearly recognize them long before we have to encounter them. I have therefore chosen four common obstacles that must be overcome by the relational engineer. Since love is the goal of all relationships, each of these obstacles is antagonistic to love.

Selfishness – the opposite of love

In order to comprehend fully the power and poison of selfishness I need to define what I mean by real love. When most of us think of love we think of romance, sex, friendships and family affection. All of these expressions are essential in our lives but they remain incomplete without the foundation of true love. True love is not the unreliable and sentimental love portrayed in so many movies that avoids commitment and follows feelings. It is only fully exemplified by God. It is a wilful giving action that seeks another's good at one's own cost. Although it demands a response it doesn't require it. It puts others first without desiring recognition. It is a selfless choice to give sacrificially.

The Bible, in fact, gives its own definition of love. It says,

> *'This is how we know what love is: Jesus Christ laid down his life for us. And we ought to lay down our lives for our brothers. If anyone has material possessions and sees his brother in need but has no pity on him, how can the love of God be in him? Dear children, let us not love with words or tongue but with actions and in truth.'*   (1 John 3:16–18)

In other words, it is not good enough just to feel in love, or to sing love songs or say, 'I love you' to a friend. Our expressions of love must include an act of giving. Though possible to give without loving, it is impossible to really love without giving. This kind of love should be the basis of all of our relationships.

How then do we ensure that true love is exemplified in our lives? What exactly will this look like in practice? True love will give time to an acquaintance in a busy workplace. True love will complete a task at home without being asked. True love will seek to please a partner within the sexual intimacy of marriage. True love will visit a lonely person without a sense of obligation. True love will go out of its way to find a gift for a friend. True love will give courtesy to a stranger. True love will make a commitment to love and keep it. No one is fully convinced by words alone we all need action! As a frustrated Eliza Doolittle expresses to her useless 'admirer' in the musical *My Fair Lady*, 'Don't talk of stars burning above. If you're in love show me'![5]

The love of self, on the other hand, has no understanding of giving. It revolves around taking. It is a commitment to put ourselves first at the expense of others and is so ingrained in our competitive society that we fail to recognize its dangers. The Bible warns of its destructiveness,

> *'There will be terrible times in the last days. People will be **lovers of themselves**, lovers of money, boastful, proud, abusive, disobedient to their parents, ungrateful, unholy, without love, unforgiving, slanderous, without self-control, brutal, not lovers of the good . . . '*
>
> (2 Timothy 3:1–3, emphasis mine)

This kind of self-love destroys relationships. It is not just an obstacle to love: it is the opposite of it.

St Augustine evidently believed this when he stated that, 'Two cities have been formed by two loves; the earthly by the love of self, even to the contempt of God, the heavenly by the love of God even to the contempt of self'.[6] Michel Quoist continues the thought, writing in his prayer 'There are two loves only' that the 'love of self indulges my senses and supplies them from the table of others'. He goes on to say, 'What is more serious, Lord, is that love of self is a stolen love. It was destined for others, they needed it to live, to thrive, and I have diverted it. So the love of self creates human suffering, so the love of men for themselves creates human misery'.[7] Now we can begin to understand the power of selfishness. It has the ability not only to repel love but also to advance hatred.

Let us consider what exactly our selfish choices can create. Our pride and arrogance causes inferiority in others. Our self-consciousness leads to loss by robbing others of what we should be giving them. Our extramarital affairs generate rejection and loneliness, our immoral relationships produce shame and disease and our selfish addictions promote poverty and domestic violence. We may say that we are not personally responsible, however our failure to act, or worse still our indifference, allows these miseries in our society. Not only that, but our corporate selfishness creates wars and our prejudice, apartheid. No wonder Nelson Mandela, the former President of South Africa, in his inaugural address on 10 May 1994, said, 'The time for the healing of the wounds has come. The moment to *bridge the chasms* that divide us has come. The time to build is upon us' (emphasis mine).[8] Like Mandela, we all need to believe that a commitment to love has the power to destroy the selfishness that opposes us all.

Fear – the enemy of love

The Bible is full of giants: spiritual and even natural giants who were at enmity with the people of God. These included the Nephilim, the *'men of renown'* (Genesis 6:4) who lived in the time of Noah, the Anakites who fought against Joshua in the land of Canaan (Numbers 13:28, 33), and, of course, Goliath of Gath (1 Samuel 17:4) who was defeated by David in the valley of Elah. The goal of the Nephilim was to pollute the earth in order to prevent its redemption. The purpose of the Anakites was to rob the children of Israel of their promised inheritance. Goliath's desire was to enslave the Israelites and so limit their prosperity and influence.

The principal weapon of giants, in fact or fairy tale, is not the club that they traditionally brandish, but fear. Their size is their strength and the fear that it spawns is immensely powerful. Og, King of Bashan, for instance, one of the Rephaites who confronted Moses, had a bed that was about four metres long and almost two metres wide (Deuteronomy 3:11)! (In other words, he was either very restless or extraordinarily large!) These giants evidently terrified their onlookers.

The power of fear is illustrated by the story of the spies who accompanied Joshua and Caleb in the exploration of Canaan:

> *'But the men who had gone up with him said, "We can't attack those people; they are stronger than we are." And they spread among the Israelites a bad report about the land they had explored. They said, "The land we explored devours those living in it. All the people we saw there are of great size. We saw the Nephilim there (the descendants of Anak come from the Nephilim). We seemed like grasshoppers in our own eyes, and we looked the same to them."* (Numbers 13:31–33)

Thankfully none of us have had to face such fearsome opposition. However, for us Satan is the giant and fear his primary weapon. His operation and purpose is exactly the same as the biblical giants and the solution the same as that discovered by Moses, Joshua and David.

Fear operates in two main ways in the minds of those of us who struggle with it. Firstly, it enlarges the size of the opposition. Fear always exaggerates the problems (*'The land we explored devours those living in it'*) and so causes us to run from them, telling others of their massive dimensions (*'All the people we saw there are of great size'*). Secondly, it diminishes the size of the onlookers. Fear always makes us feel inferior and powerless (*'We seemed like grasshoppers in our own eyes, and we looked the same to them'*) and consequently lies to us about the effectiveness of the solution. Fear, therefore, works like a pair of binoculars. If we look at a man through binoculars, he seems like a giant to us whereas if the man looks back through the same binoculars we seem like a dwarf to him. It changes our perspective. We are unable to assess our surroundings accurately. That is why people are warned never to use binoculars near a cliff since they are likely to misjudge the danger and fall down the precipice!

Satan, therefore, always encourages fear since it makes him look more powerful and us less so. It also fulfils his purpose, as I have already intimated, of polluting us and thus preventing our redemption, robbing us of our God-given inheritance and enslaving us in order to limit our influence and prosperity. In fact, apart from selfishness, it is possibly the most destructive and powerful of the barriers to love and relationships. It is the 'enemy' of love.

Some time ago in Manchester, England I sat down next to a woman at the end of a meeting that we had both attended. She looked extraordinarily troubled and I inquired whether I could help her. During the course of the brief conversation, a group of three men walked past us, and the woman, evidently terrified, immediately fainted and fell onto my shoulder. After I had managed to bring her round I asked her the reason for her fear. She nervously and somewhat reluctantly told me her story. A number of months previously she had been raped by four men, her scarred wrists a testimony to her subsequent torment. Whenever a group of men came near her, she was so distraught with fear that she often passed out. I offered her counsel and encouragement but she turned it down. I told her that she was not guilty, and that God could release her and give her life back, as I had seen Him do many times before. However, her fear would not allow her to accept it. She simply promised me that she wouldn't kill herself and left me sitting alone, holding an old tobacco tin which she had given me: it was filled with rusty razorblades.

The story of this woman graphically illustrates how fear works in our lives. When we are offered a life-changing relationship, whether with God or people, fear opposes it. Love says that we are beautiful but fear denies it. Love presents us with a gift but fear pushes it away. Love desires success for our lives but fear prevents us receiving it. Love buys us freedom but fear stops us enjoying it. Love tells us that we have a destiny but fear will not believe it.

However, as Moses, Joshua and David discovered when they faced the giants of fear, not only is fear the enemy of love, love is also the solution to fear. It was because these men understood that God loved them that they were able to conquer all that opposed them. John, the 'apostle of love', gave us an insight to this in the first of his letters when he wrote,

> *'And so we know and rely on the love God has for us. God is love. Whoever lives in love lives in God, and God in him. In this way, love is made complete among us so that we will have confidence on the day of judgment, because in this world we are like him. There is no fear in love. But perfect love drives out fear, because fear has to do with punishment. The one who fears is not made perfect in love.'*   (1 John 4:16–18)

John is saying that because of the love of God the Christian should understand that he or she is forgiven, no longer under judgment and therefore has no reason to be tormented by fear. Satan, on the other hand, cannot be forgiven, is under God's judgment and therefore is terrified. Thus love has turned the binoculars around! The lens now magnifies us and condenses the obstacle of fear. This is the key to success in our relationships, not that we love ourselves in order to love others, but that we realize that God loves us. For as John goes on to say, *'We love because he first loved us'* (1 John 4:19). If the lady from Manchester had genuinely received this love much of her torment would have been over.

Rejection – the absence of love

When I was growing up on a farm in England, I became fascinated with the wildlife living around me. It wasn't long before I transferred some of it from the garden to my bedroom. My mother became used to discovering my latest project in a makeshift cage on my windowsill. My interest lay primarily in rescuing wounded or abandoned animals, looking after and observing them and then releasing them back into the garden. Over the course of a few years I had looked after all manner of birds, reptiles, amphibians and small mammals. I was never fond of fish! Too wet! A common feature of this exercise was that I ended up with numerous wounds. The animals on which I lavished my attention never seemed to appreciate it! The reason for this was, of course, a natural self-protective mechanism, a response that I would have expected from any wounded animal. I was soon to discover that such a caged and violent response was not confined to animals.

Years later in Spain, I was working in a drug rehabilitation centre and, seeing a young man in need, I simply put my hand on his shoulder. The reaction was immediate. I will never forget the pain and consternation in the man's face and the venom in his voice as he viciously removed my hand. It was as though I had maliciously tortured him with a red-hot iron. His eyes were wide with fear and filled with tears as he walked away. He desperately wanted and needed the love that had been offered but the numerous disappointments of the past compelled him to reject it. The American singer songwriter Don Francisco wrote the song, 'Bird with broken wing locked up in tiny cage' about such a person. Its chorus graphically describes the dilemma of those who are broken by pain: 'Soaring far above the storm on wings spread strong and wide is the vision that you've buried in despair, you dash yourself against the stones and flutter terrified when my love would heal your wounds and lift you there'.[9]

The young Spanish man felt rejected because there had been some absence of love in his life. Maybe he had suffered genuine loss through death or tragedy, however such feelings of rejection are often birthed in betrayal. Possibly, he had an absentee father, a mother who had abandoned him, a relation who had abused him or a friend who had broken a promise. I don't know. Sadly he never let me find out. However, I do know that he responded to my outstretched hand in the predictably unpredictable way of a typically rejected person. The expected response has two sides. Firstly, a rejected person, like a fearful one, pushes love away because he or she feels unable or unworthy to receive it. For instance, a girl who has been molested by a poisonous touch will initially mistrust a healing one. This creates a barrier through which friendship has difficulty passing. Secondly, a rejected person protects himself or herself through anger, hatred, violence or rebellion. Behind the hand that holds others at a distance is a clenched fist. If the new friend gets past the first line of defence they will soon receive the scars of committed affection!

One day, while I was living in England, these two sides of rejection were memorably illustrated in our living room. My wife Amanda was sitting on our settee, next to a friend whom we were endeavouring to help. She had been mistreated and abandoned as a young girl. Amanda showed her a verse in the Bible that promised her freedom if she would simply accept God's love for her. In the course of the conversation the offer of kindness and concern reminded her so painfully of the lack in her childhood that she literally threw herself on the floor and curled up into a foetal position. She gradually came to her senses and with apologies took her place again on the chair. A few minutes later, without warning, she lashed out at Amanda, narrowly missing her face but instead tearing the Bible that was lying opened on the settee. After she left we discovered that the woman's fingernails had torn out the very verse that my wife had been reading to her. The feeling of rejection was so powerful in her life that both God's love and our friendship were repulsed.

Rejection with its associated feelings is so real that it deceives people into thinking that they cannot build relationships. It denies the truth and believes a lie. It rejects acceptance and exaggerates its power of separation. The reality is that, though rejection is a huge obstacle that needs to be overcome, it cannot compete with the power of love. The Bible asks the question,

> *'Who shall separate us from the love of Christ? Shall trouble or hardship or persecution or famine or nakedness or danger or sword?'*
>
> (Romans 8:35)

To which we can add 'or rejection'! It goes on to give the answer,

> *'No, in all these things we are more than conquerors through him who loved us. For I am convinced that neither death nor life, neither angels nor demons, neither the present nor the future, nor any powers, neither height nor depth, nor anything else in all creation, will be able to separate us from the love of God that is in Christ Jesus our Lord.'*
>
> (Romans 8:37–39)

Lust – the counterfeit of love

On a brief trip to Argentina some years ago, I decided to take the opportunity of purchasing an inexpensive leather jacket for which, I was told, the country was well known. I was taken into a shop where I examined the huge array of coats with considerable care. I did not want to be deceived into buying a cheap imitation! The owner, on observing me checking the seams of a particular jacket, approached me with anger. 'All of these coats are made of leather,' he shouted. 'They are all good quality! They are not synthetic.' He snatched the coat out of my hand and in a swift movement lit his cigarette lighter and held it under the sleeve. 'Look, it's not melting. It's not plastic.' It passed the test and I duly bought the jacket and quickly left the shop before I incurred any more of the owner's wrath!

In this case, my suspicions were evidently unjustified. However, sadly we do live in a world where increasingly we are duped into buying fakes, inferior products or even using counterfeit money. These imitations invariably fail the tests imposed on them. 'They are not the same as they used to be! They just don't last', is the catch cry of the consumer society! Of course, ultimately, it doesn't really matter if sometimes we mistakenly end up with some piece of bogus merchandise. What is much more tragic is when we purposely exchange the genuinely and eternally valuable for something temporary and cheap. Swapping love for lust is one such pitiful exchange.

Paul the apostle described and challenged the godless people in Rome, a city of statues, when he wrote,

'For although they knew God, they neither glorified him as God nor gave thanks to him, but their thinking became futile and their foolish hearts were darkened. Although they claimed to be wise, they became fools and exchanged the glory of the immortal God for images made to look like mortal man and birds and animals and reptiles.' (Romans 1:21–23)

Their idols were man-made counterfeits. They wilfully bartered lies for truth and chose to worship stone instead of Spirit. God, saddened by the glibness of their actions, withdrew and left them to reap the consequences of their choices. As the Bible puts it, *'God gave them over to shameful lusts'* (Romans 1:26). The city of idolatry became a city of immorality. One imitation became another. Of course, the same principles apply to us. If we choose to make the same fateful exchanges we will suffer for it. If we choose to love money, sport, the environment or ourselves for instance, more than we love God, we will reap a harvest of cheap 'forgeries'. The counterfeit of lust that we all suffer in our cities and relationships is a direct result of the choices that we have made.

In our day-to-day relationships lust is totally destructive. Whereas love is self-giving, lust is self-absorbing. Lust is hedonistic, seeking personal pleasure at someone else's expense. Lust takes without asking permission. Lust doesn't take no for an answer. It always demands more and is never satisfied. It heartlessly robs people of their money, their innocence and their life. It despises God's laws and promotes the freedom of choice above all else. It lies about its authenticity. It says that it is love but it is only a cheap imitation that will never pass a genuine test and will never last. Any relationship based on lust will eventually break down and fail.

Edwin Louis Cole describes the glory of virginity in his book, *Communication, Sex and Power,* and how we must preserve it for marriage. In the book he writes, 'Don't let some cheap, tawdry relationship in the back of a van, or at a cheap motel, or on a sandy beach blanket, or in hushed whispers in the living room, rob you of the greatest moment of your life'![10] When presented with genuine love, the most powerful and wonderful gift of all, how can we possibly exchange it for a fake lifestyle of lust? This is one obstacle we must overcome.

Summary and advice

1. **We cannot be arrogant about the obstacles that face the bridge-builder.** Blind faith can be as disastrous as perceptive doubt. We have to be realistic about the power of those things that oppose our relationships.

2. **The power of the obstacles should be accurately assessed and clearly identified.** When encountered, the obstacles must be overcome. If we need to say sorry we must do so!

3. **Selfishness is the opposite of love.** The love of self not only 'over-feeds' me, it starves others. True love, on the other hand, is a wilful giving action that seeks another's good at one's own cost. This kind of selfless giving is a vital ingredient of all fruitful relationships.

4. **Fear is the enemy of love.** Fear robs us of a correct perspective in life, enlarging our problems and diminishing us, whereas the love of God frees us from this thief and restores our vision. Failure to deal with fear will always limit the growth of our relationships.

5. **Rejection is the absence of love**. Rejected people protect themselves from further pain by refusing the love they know they need and fighting those who offer it. Of all the antagonists to love, rejection is the most deceptive because it makes people believe that they cannot be loved. God's love, however, is a truth that will not yield.

6. **Lust is the counterfeit of love**. Lust is the tragic but inevitable outcome of our idolatry. It is the lifestyle that a godless society chooses for itself. It seeks pleasure at another's expense. Love is the genuine article!

Notes

1. Capt. Arthur Phillip. Quoted in Manning Clark, *A Short History of Australia* (Penguin, 1987).
2. Thornton Wilder, *The Bridge of San Luis Rey* (1927). Quoted in Judith Dupré, *Bridges* (Könemann, 1998).
3. Dupré, *Bridges*.
4. Kathryn Kuhlman, in a sermon entitled 'Not doing what we like, but liking what we have to do'. Quoted in Roberts Liardon, *God's Generals* (Albury Publishing, 1996).
5. Frederick Loewe and Alan Jay Lerner, *My Fair Lady*, 1956.
6. Augustine, *Civitas Dei* XIV 28. Quoted in Paul Brownback, *The Danger of Self Love* (Moody Press, 1982).
7. Michel Quoist, *Prayers of Life* (Logos Books, 1966).
8. Nelson Mandela. Quoted in Martin Meredith, *Nelson Mandela. A Biography* (Penguin Books, 1997).
9. Don Francisco, 'Bird with Broken Wing'. Recorded on *Power* Album, Ariose Music (ASCAP), administered by Gaither Music, 1987.
10. Edwin Louis Cole, *Communication, Sex and Money* (Honor Books, 1987).

Chapter 7

The Mechanic and the Mystic

Understanding the Strength of Bridges

It has been suggested that Sydney Harbour Bridge was first foreseen by the poet Erasmus Darwin. A few short months after Governor Phillip had landed in 1788, he wrote a poem about Sydney Cove, in which he penned the remarkable lines, 'There the proud arch, Colossus-like, bestride Yon glittering stream and bound the chafing tide'![1] His grandson Charles Darwin, who sailed into the same cove on *HMS Beagle* in 1836, described the new colony as a 'paradise to the worshippers of mammon'![2] Each viewpoint was equally valid yet wholly different. The first was the buoyant vision of an artist, the second the more practical description of a scientist. Ever since then, the poets and pragmatists have voiced their opinions of the Harbour and its bridge, and all of them have added something to its mystique. There is no doubt that there is more power in a bridge than in the strength of its steel.

When people cross a noteworthy bridge for the first time, they are often struck by its enormous power: the power to inspire; the power to withstand the elements; the power to transport goods; the power to unite a city. As Judith Dupré said, 'Since the first log fell across water, people have been fascinated with bridges and their power to bring together what has been separate. Bridges can evoke exhilaration, triumph, and fear, sometimes simultaneously'.[3] The power of bridges creates faith in us: the faith that we need every time we cross them. In fact, a truly great bridge allures us like a siren in the mist. It invites us to approach its span and put our trust in its piers and trusses. However, the faith that this power inspires is not blind. It is based on a mutual respect for our common obstacles yet a fundamental understanding that the bridge is stronger than those obstacles. We believe that the bridge has the power to guide us safely across the divide.

There is therefore science and poetry in our appreciation of bridges. The engineer and the artist are equally awestruck by a great bridge. It becomes the subject of study in both metallurgy and photography classes! The scientist is more concerned with the properties of the materials used whereas the poet values their lines and feel. Both viewpoints are not only valid but also essential in our understanding, recognition and building of bridges. Poetry based on science is the foundation on which our faith in bridges is built.

Until the latter half of the eighteenth century, timber and masonry (stone or brick) were basically the only structural materials used in the building of bridges. These materials then gave way to iron, steel and concrete, or a combination of these, and, more recently, aluminium and even plastic. However, in all of these cases, the workers of these materials, whether carpenters, stonemasons or blacksmiths, have combined technical expertise with aesthetic enjoyment. For example, Francis Whitaker, a well-known American blacksmith, who died in 1999 with, as requested, a hammer in his hand, said, 'Iron has a strength no other material has and yet it has the capacity for being light, graceful and beautiful. It has this capacity – but no desire. It will do nothing by itself except resist you. All the desire, and all the knowledge of how to impart this desire to the iron, must come from the smith'.[4] This tough artisan evidently incorporated mystery into his lifetime of moulding metal.

The ironworker Abraham Darby was also persuaded to combine the two powers of poetry and science into the design of his bridge at Coalbrookdale in England. The Iron Bridge, which was erected over the River Severn in 1779, comprises 363 tonnes of cast iron forming a graceful thirty-metre arch over the valley. The strength of this relatively new building material was tested and proven in 1795 when the Severn flooded and the Iron Bridge was the only one that survived. The power of its beauty still attracts thousands of visiting tourists and artists.

These complementary powers are equally essential in the building of relationships. A successful friendship or marriage contains both a quantifiable set of necessary ingredients and an indefinable mystical element. The mechanics, or science, of companionship may be applied but for a relationship to flourish it must have an additional and non-empirical 'chemistry'! The danger is that people will concentrate on one and thus be robbed of the benefit and balance of the other.

In countries where arranged marriages are the expectation, couples have to choose to love each other if their marriage is going to have any hope of success. This is an essential foundation, but often the partnership lacks the 'sparkle' that God desires for them. However, this is also true in the Western world. I have had people come into my office and announce grandly, 'God has shown me whom I have to marry'! When questioned they informed me that they didn't particularly like the person concerned but in obedience to God they would choose to love them! When I suggested to them that maybe this was not enough I was criticized for being unspiritual! On the other hand, I have also had people come into my office and tell me that they are no longer 'in love' with their partner and therefore they are going to divorce them. When I suggested to them that they should choose to love on the basis of the vows that they made, they told me that that would be hypocrisy! The fact is that for a marriage to thrive we need both to love and be 'in love' with our marriage partner! The mechanic and the mystic in our soul must be satisfied.

Much of our problem in understanding this principle stems from the English language. The word 'love' means different things to different people. We love God, our friends and apples with the same word! The Greeks simplified this by using four separate words for 'love'. The word *agapao*, on the one extreme, is the giving love which God exemplifies and with which He enables us to choose to love. *Phileo* is mutual friendship love, *stergo* is best described as family affection and, of course, *eros* involves the romantic chemistry on the other end of the spectrum. A marriage needs the selflessness of *agapao*, the warmth of *phileo*, the comfort of *stergo*, and the intoxication of *eros*. These are the powerful materials used by the relational engineer in the construction of bridges and the ones in which he or she has to believe. They are all facets of love and they have the power to overcome every obstacle of selfishness, fear, rejection and lust that combine against them.

I have mentioned all of the various facets of love because I don't want you to think one will work effectively without the other. I have taken time to explain the necessity of both science and poetry, the complementary sides to a bridge's power, because I don't want you to apply religiously or clinically just one principle contained in this book,

thinking that by doing so you will automatically succeed! Relationships rarely work like that! I have discovered that it is usually a
combination of factors that produces results. In our marriage, for
instance, which, despite its faults, is remarkably blessed, we have
sought to apply the characteristics of each of the 'four loves'. However,
rather than go through all of these in detail, which has already been
done by better authors than myself, including C.S. Lewis, I have
chosen four qualities that have proven powerful in our lives and
relationships in the hope that you can apply them to your own.

Willpower – a commitment to vows

As a marriage celebrant I have the privilege of leading scores of couples
in their marriage vows. The exact words used vary from service to
service. However, many have looked lovingly into each other's eyes
and promised 'I will' after committing themselves 'for better for worse,
for richer for poorer, in sickness and in health, to love and to cherish,
till death us do part, according to God's holy ordinance'.[5] These are
not idle words but are made before each other, family and friends,
society and, of course, God. The Bible describes this as a marriage
covenant (Malachi 2:14). In fact, every biblical covenant, of which
there are many examples, consists of three elements: the giving of a
promise, the recognition of a sign and the shedding of blood. In the
case of the marriage covenant, the promise is seen in the vows, the sign
in the rings and the blood in the loss of virginity. Thus the marriage
is not finalized or consummated until each of these elements is
complete.

The reason that we perform such a ceremony is not simply because
of tradition but because God has made the same loving covenant with
us. As the Bible says,

> *'Know therefore that the LORD your God is God; he is the faithful God,
> keeping his covenant of love to a thousand generations of those who love
> him and keep his commands.'*   (Deuteronomy 7:9)

We are, therefore, simply following the example that He has set. The
Bible says that the Lord Jesus Christ is the bridegroom of His bride, the
Church. He has made a promise to love 'her', given her the sign of
the Holy Spirit in order to guarantee an inheritance and shed His own
blood for her (Ephesians 1:7, 13–14; 5:22–33). In other words, the

Church has a promise of love, a guarantee of blessing and a commitment to sacrifice. God cannot and will not break His promise, has sworn on oath that He will bless us and has already demonstrated His love by dying for us. This is the basis of marriage.

Speaking for myself, if I am going to be successful in my marriage I must abide by these three principles of covenant. My wife must know that I will keep the promise I made to her on our wedding day. She must be secure in the knowledge that I will love her in all circumstances. It was not a conditional promise nor is it conditional love. I made a decision and a confession that I would love her in good and bad times and I will not break my word! She must be totally convinced that all that I have is hers and that I am completely committed to her honour, welfare and prosperity. I have told her that I will put my life on the line in order to assist her to enter into her inheritance and to protect her from anything that attempts to rob her of it. Let me assure you, this kind of unconditional commitment will always elicit a powerful response! We all tend to respond positively to true love. As the Bible says, *'We love because he first loved us'* (1 John 4:19).

Why is it then that so many couples, especially in the Western world, end up in the divorce courts? One of the reasons is that many are unfamiliar with the concept of covenants and the requirements involved. They enter into a covenant without the first idea of what it means, without the least intention of keeping it and without God, the only One who could help them maintain it. Some even put a signature to their misunderstanding by drawing up a pre-nuptial agreement in order to safeguard their own property in case of a possible divorce.

I am fully aware of the trauma experienced in many marriages, and I am also fully aware of the biblical teaching on divorce and the fact that on occasion it is justified. Jesus Christ Himself said that 'marital unfaithfulness', the wilful breaking of a covenant, was a possible reason for divorce (Matthew 5:32). This is known to theologians as the 'exception clause'. However, I am also totally convinced that we would all avoid a great deal of pain in our relationships if we would only think before we act. If we don't want to keep our vows we shouldn't make them! The uncommon 'exception clause' should not be turned into a common 'escape route'! Putting a ring on someone's finger and saying, 'All that I am I give to you' is not just a moment of romance, it is a lifelong responsibility.

Nonetheless, I wouldn't dare to make such a commitment without the help of God. Thankfully I have discovered that the love that He promises me enables me to keep my marriage covenant and is more powerful than any natural or supernatural antagonist. The love of God bridges all divides and overcomes all obstacles. As Paul says,

> *'For I am convinced that neither death nor life, neither angels nor demons, neither the present nor the future, nor any powers, neither height nor depth, nor anything else in all creation, will be able to separate us from the love of God that is in Christ Jesus our Lord.'*
>
> (Romans 8:38–39)

Forgiveness – a decision to forgive daily

In March 1984, I visited the remains of the Second World War concentration camp in Majdanek, near Lublin in the east of Poland. It was bitterly cold as I slowly walked past the sentry towers, barbed wire and endless line of wooden huts. I talked freely with my companions on entering the prison but soon the cold and my imagination silenced me. There are no words to describe the horror of what took place there. A display case of the poisonous gas 'Zyklon B' outside the rusted door of the gas chamber gave harsh and needless information about its use. The eight hundred thousand pairs of shoes collected from various camps and now discarded in these huts were more eloquent. Today it remains a grisly monument to inhumanity. Yet even with such graphic scenes the visitor can scarcely begin to comprehend the unimaginable cruelty of the captors. It would be easy to conclude that these crimes must not be forgotten and cannot be forgiven. Should we forgive such monstrous savagery and indeed can we forgive when we are not the victims ourselves? In a world that is filled with tyranny and atrocity, this is our universal dilemma. Can we forgive the soldier who burns a village and rapes the captives? Should we forgive the terrorist who plants a bomb in a shopping centre or a schoolboy who shoots his classmates? Must we forgive the relatives who come into our room at night and rob us of our innocence?

Many people come to me and tell me of horrendous abuses in their lives. They tell me stories of how their mother would come home drunk, strip and beat them, or how their father would molest them and then slip money under their door or give them presents in order to 'prove his love for them'. Many of these people explain away their angry and negative responses: 'My revenge is completely justified', 'It's only fair that he pays for it. I have suffered and so should he', 'She has ruined my life, I am a helpless victim'. When I suggest forgiveness, they are incredulous. 'How can I forgive that animal for what he has done?' These reactions and arguments are totally understandable but completely unhelpful. They are still trapped by the crime perpetrated against them years before; they still have nightmares and still feel unclean and guilty as though somehow it was their fault. Their resentment and bitterness prevents healing. Unforgiveness is not just a powerful 'river' that separates two people, it is a polluted one. Yet it is the knowledge of this pollution that should drive us to find a solution. Philip Yancey argues for the power of forgiveness by writing, 'The strongest argument in favour of grace is the alternative, a world of ungrace. The strongest argument for forgiveness is the alternative, a permanent state of unforgiveness'.[6] The question is: can forgiveness bridge such a treacherous and corrupted stream? The answer, of course, is an unequivocal 'Yes'!

In her celebrated book *The Hiding Place*, Corrie Ten Boom, a wonderful Christian Dutch woman, describes how God enables us to love the unlovable and to forgive the unpardonable. Her family, who were respected Haarlem watchmakers, harboured fugitive Jews in the Second World War. As a result Corrie and her sister Betsie were arrested and imprisoned in Ravensbruck concentration camp where Betsie died in appalling conditions. After her release near the end of the war Corrie travelled extensively and spoke of her experiences and the lessons that she had learned about the love of God. After one church service in Munich one of her former jailers approached her and testified how he had recently been forgiven by God and had become a Christian. Initially she felt unable to shake his hand, let alone forgive him, until she desperately cried out for God's help. This kind of forgiveness was beyond her comprehension or capacity, yet in answer to prayer, she writes that, 'Into my heart sprang a love for this stranger that almost overwhelmed me. And so I discovered that it is not on our forgiveness any more than on our goodness that the world's healing hinges, but on His. When He tells us to love our enemies, He gives, along with the command, the love itself.'[7]

In 1948, during the communist uprising in Korea, Pastor Son, a Christian minister, heard that his two sons, who themselves were training to be ministers, had been murdered. In an extraordinary act of love and forgiveness, Pastor Son sent a message to another pastor saying, 'Tell him that those who killed my sons, if they are found, must not be beaten or put to death. I will seek to convert them and adopt them as my own sons'! The murderer Chai-sun was subsequently found, forgiven and embraced by the Son family. Some time later the newly converted Chai-sun wrote to Pastor Son from the Bible Institute of Korea where he, like his victims, was training for the ministry. In the letter he wrote, 'Father, forgive me for everything. Because of your love to me given you by God, I shall try to fulfil your desire for me and follow in the footsteps of St Paul. I shall do all in my power to follow after my two brothers.'[8] Such forgiveness is powerfully redemptive.

In a slightly less dramatic scenario, John, a friend of mine, told me how a commitment to forgiveness had released him from the emotional scarring of an alcoholic father. When he was ten years old, his father returned home in a drunken state. He picked up his terrified son, who had seen him angry and violent many times before, and placed him firmly on the dining-room table. Looking him straight in the eye he said, 'I am not your father. You are adopted. I don't want you anymore so I am going to get rid of you. I am going to send you away to boarding school. You're useless, now get out here and go to your room.' John was totally devastated and understandably terrified of his unpredictable father until he discovered the power of forgiveness. Interestingly, all the offenders in these stories responded to the grace shown them by becoming Christians themselves!

In each of these cases, the 'victims' were able to release themselves from resentment because they had discovered the truths contained in a story that Jesus told. In the parable of the unmerciful servant (Matthew 18:21–35), Jesus related how a servant would not forgive a colleague the debt of a few pounds despite having been forgiven by the king himself a debt of the equivalent of millions of pounds. As a result the servant was imprisoned and tortured until he repaid everything that he owed. In the economy of the day, this was an impossible task. The simple interpretation of the story is that if Jesus Christ has forgiven us of every sin with which we have hurt Him, how much more must we forgive others of each sin with which they hurt us; if we don't, our torment and captivity is guaranteed. As George Herbert puts it, 'He who cannot forgive another, breaks the bridge over which he must pass himself'.[9]

Corrie Ten Boom, Pastor Son and John were all Christians and as a result had the cross of Christ both as an example and an empowerment. They had all experienced God's forgiveness, all understood His command to forgive, and all realized the consequences of unforgiveness. As a result they were enabled to love and forgive in a way that they previously thought impossible. Jesus taught this same principle when he questioned a religious leader,

> *'Two men owed money to a certain money-lender. One owed him five hundred denarii, and the other fifty. Neither of them had the money to pay him back, so he cancelled the debts of both. Now which of them will love him more?'* (Luke 7:41–42)

Simon the Pharisee reluctantly replied correctly, *'I suppose the one who had the bigger debt cancelled.'* So the ability to love and forgive others is founded in our realization of being forgiven. To paraphrase Jesus Christ's teaching to Simon, the more we realize how much we have been forgiven the more we want to forgive. Grace gives birth to grace. This grace not only frees us from our own sin but it also allows us to free ourselves from those who sin against us. In the case of the three examples I have given, it enabled them to free themselves from the frightful results of torture, murder and abuse.

Coming closer to home, forgiveness is not only applicable in cases of major offence but also in the day-to-day running of our households. We must learn the grace of forgiveness if we are to relate successfully. When we face the innumerable irritations and sinful habits of those around us we must never keep a 'record of wrongs' (1 Corinthians 13:5) or we have failed to keep one of the vital components of love. Once again Christ is our example. The Bible says that each of us had a certificate of debt that we were unable to pay. It represented a criminal charge. But Jesus Christ 'nailed it to His cross' as a testimony to the whole world that He had paid it (Colossians 2:14). How then can we keep a mental list of sins against others? For instance, if we ever say to someone, 'That's the third time you have done that today', it is evidence that we failed to really forgive them for the first two offences! Real forgiveness treats each re-occurring transgression with the same grace as if it were the first! It will not fall into the 'trap of offence' nor will it grow a 'root of bitterness'. It will not hold onto a past hurt nor will it carry a grievance over into another day. Real pardon can overcome any hurdle and bridge any obstacle. As Pat Conroy writes in his novel *The Prince of Tides*, about a wounded family in South Carolina, 'In families there are no crimes beyond forgiveness'.[10]

Why is forgiveness so important to relationships, the essential tool of the relational engineer? Why is it the secret to success in marriages, why so vital in homes? It is because it deals with the ultimate barrier.

When Jesus Christ was questioned about divorce, He started His reply with the words, *'Haven't you read ... that at the beginning ... ?'* (Matthew 19:4). In other words, if we refer back to the creation account in the book of Genesis, we will find some answers. The world started with the harmony that we all crave. Yet, the one factor that destroyed the perfect relationships was sin. This was the sole gulf that drove God and human beings apart and stands between them now. It is the only chasm that divides humanity. We can attribute the breakdown in our relationships to communication failure, irreconcilable differences, personality clashes or just incompatibility but the reality is far simpler. The problem is sin. Any 'bridge' that fails to deal with the obstacle of sin is bound to fail eventually. We cannot avoid it. There is no way around it. Time may heal but it doesn't build bridges. Ignoring the problem tends to add to the gap rather than span it. The only solution is forgiveness. It is the one and only bridge that can connect a holy God with sinful humankind. It is the one and only bridge that can heal every rift in a relationship. As the Bible says,

> *'Above all, love each other deeply, because love covers over a multitude of sins.'*   (1 Peter 4:8)

Transparency – an ability to be honest

Conjoined or 'Siamese' twins are joined to each other at birth. They sometimes share an organ and in such cases one cannot live without the other. The original 'Siamese' twins, Chang and Eng Bunker, were born in 1811 and died in 1874. Despite both marrying and fathering twenty-two children between them, they were never separated because at the time it was believed that to do so would endanger their lives! In theological terms, love and truth are 'Siamese twins'. They are different but they cannot survive apart from one another. Jesus Christ embodies both. He must not be divided. Paul tells us to speak *'the truth in love'* (Ephesians 4:15) because he understood that to tell someone the 'truth' without compassion, robs it of an essential quality. Jesus challenged the lawyers and teachers of His day because they attempted to teach rules without grace. The 'vital organ' that truth and love share is reconciliation.

This 'Siamese quality' of love and truth is highlighted for us in the writings of John. Perhaps of all Christ's disciples, John had a true understanding of God's love. It was he who understood that God did not just give love, He is love (1 John 4:16). He knew God loved him. This was the basis of his identity and security. He didn't describe himself as 'a professional fisherman', 'a Galilean', 'one of the sons of Zebedee', or even 'a leader in the Church' as many in his position would have done. He identified himself simply as *'the one Jesus loved'* (John 20:2). He also understood, as we have seen, that God's love challenged and empowered him to love others. He expresses it in the first of his letters when he writes,

> *'Dear friends, since God so loved us, we also ought to love one another ... We love because he first loved us.'*   (1 John 4:11, 19)

This was the pattern and foundation of his ministry. The story is told of John that at the very end of his life, as he was regularly carried to church in Ephesus by the disciples, all he was able to say was, 'Little children, love one another.' When questioned about his constant repetition of this message, he replied, 'Because it is the Lord's command, and if this only is done, it is enough.'[11]

However, John did not just establish that God is love, he also embraced the twin concept that God is light (1 John 1:5). It was John who recorded Christ's immortal statements, *'I am the light of the world'* and *'I am the truth'* (John 8:12; 14:6). In John's teaching, light and truth were almost synonymous:

> *'This is the message we have heard from him and declare to you: God is light; in him there is no darkness at all. If we claim to have fellowship with him yet walk in the darkness, we lie and do not live by the truth.'*
>   (1 John 1:5–6)

Truth, for John, was not an abstract concept or a philosophical principle. Truth was a person. Truth was a friend of his, whom he dare not offend. Honesty was not the *best* policy, it was the *only* policy. He knew that fellowship with God should be everyone's goal and telling the truth or 'walking in the light' is the only way to achieve it. Yet this truth is not solely applicable in our friendship with God, it can be applied in any relationship. He went on to say,

> *'But if we walk in the light, as he is in the light, we have fellowship with one another, and the blood of Jesus, his Son, purifies us from all sin.'*
>   (1 John 1:7)

In other words illumination leads to reconciliation. If we want real fellowship with anyone we have to tell the truth. It has been this revelation and our commitment to transparency that has been one of the four foundation stones to our successful marriage. However, it is not necessarily easy to do! Once again, John has some sound advice!

In perhaps the most famous chapter in the Bible, John gives some conclusions about light that we would do well to consider:

> 'This is the verdict: Light has come into the world, but men loved darkness instead of light because their deeds were evil. Everyone who does evil hates the light, and will not come into the light for fear that his deeds will be exposed. But whoever lives by the truth comes into the light, so that it may be seen plainly that what he has done has been done through God.'   (John 3:19–21)

I would like to draw three vital observations from this passage that we need to apply to our relationships. Firstly, everyone loves darkness. Despite what some sociologists tell us, humankind is not inherently good. Until we face this we are simply deceiving ourselves. Our selfish and deceptive behaviour ruins our relationships. That is why most of the world has rejected Christ and why most of us choose not to be completely honest with each other. Secondly, everyone tends to run from the light. From the time of Adam and Eve human beings have been hiding. We don't want to admit our faults because we don't want to change. We don't want to be found out because we fear that others will reject us if they know what we are really like! Finally, everyone benefits from the light. When we do finally overcome what Grant Howard calls the 'trauma of transparency'[12] and confess our failings we discover that truth always sets us free.

The Bible not only teaches us these principles but also illustrates them in the lives of ordinary people so that we can see how to apply them today. Judas Iscariot is one person who can train us in the power of dishonesty! We know little of Judas' background. The name Iscariot either means 'an assassin' or 'man of Karioth'. If the latter is the case, then it is possible that Judas was the only disciple from Judea. Maybe this was the reason he felt divorced from the other disciples from Galilee. Maybe this feeling of disconnection drove him to bitterness. We simply don't know. However, what we do know is that he betrayed truth with a kiss.

One of Judas' weaknesses was that he loved money. It spread through his life like a cancer until finally he exchanged the Saviour of the World for four months' wages (today's equivalent of thirty pieces of silver). His weakness inexorably drew him into a world of lies. He deceived himself into thinking that he was significant because he was Jesus' treasurer. He deceived the disciples into thinking that he cared for the poor when in fact he was simply helping himself to the widows' offering. Perhaps worst of all, he attempted to deceive Truth Himself by pretending to be a follower. He listened to the stories, followed the sign-hungry crowd and sat down to eat with the disciples, but for Judas, it was sometimes 'Rabbi' but never 'Lord'. He was falling into the hands of his true master, Satan, the father of lies. As far as we know Judas never practised sorcery or divination but he was certainly a lover of the occult. The word 'occult' literally means 'hidden' and as such perfectly describes the dark, secret and dishonest world in which Judas was living. At the Last Supper, Jesus seemed to offer Judas one final opportunity to repent when He gave him a morsel of bread. Judas took the bread but rejected the offer. Satan entered him and he scuttled for cover like a cockroach. One awful verse records,

> *'As soon as Judas had taken the bread, he went out. And it was night.'*
> (John 13:30)

Toward the south-west of Jerusalem lies one of its three valleys, the Hinnom Valley. Historically it was a valley of slaughter, the site where repulsive idolaters had sacrificed children: an unclean place of burning, a rubbish dump, the valley that Christ compared to the everlasting fire of hell which He called 'Gehenna' (a Greek word that is derived from the Hebrew for 'Valley of Hinnom') (Matthew 10:28). It was here that they found Judas' disembowelled body. His deception and dishonesty had pushed away his companions and banished him to the outskirts of the old city where he hung himself in remorse. Eventually, he was replaced by Matthias, as Luke graphically and starkly comments, *'to occupy this ministry and apostleship from which Judas turned aside to go **to his own place**'* (Acts 1:25, emphasis mine).[13]

Extreme though the story of Judas may seem, it accurately portrays the ultimate price of dishonesty. If we commit ourselves, for whatever reason, to a path of deception, half-truth, innuendo, exaggeration or 'white lies', we are bound to end up in isolation or worse. Whether we realize it or not we are choosing a lifestyle of the occult with its obvious ramifications.

Whereas the power of dishonesty to separate is evident in the life of Judas, in contrast the power of honesty to connect is even more apparent in the life of David. Like Judas, David was chosen by God and yet had potentially destructive flaws. He was not so much tempted by the love of money as the lust of the flesh. However, unlike Judas, although initially deceptive, he chose the painful but positive pathway of confession. In order to illustrate my point, I want to consider his life story at a time when he was already king of Israel. For one reason or another, when he should have been leading his men in battle, David found himself one evening, frustrated and alone on the flat roof of his palace. Clearly he was in the wrong place at the wrong time. From this vantage-point he was able to look down on the city and he saw a beautiful woman bathing. It turned out to be the compliant wife of one of his friends and, when sent for, Bathsheba, perhaps unable to resist the power of the king, came and slept with him. She left quietly in the morning and nothing more was said until Bathsheba became aware that she was pregnant. It was evidently David's child since Bathsheba's husband Uriah was away and she had only just finished her monthly period when David slept with her. Prior to this news, it seems that David was just going to pretend that this betrayal had never occurred. Uriah need never know. However, now he had to act in order to cover up his wrongdoing. He therefore arranged to have Uriah killed, took his pregnant widow and hurriedly married her. The cover-up was complete but Scripture records, *'the thing that David had done was evil in the sight of the Lord'* (2 Samuel 11:27).[14]

Although, as king of Israel, David was expected to uphold God's law, he had already broken at least three of the Ten Commandments, the sixth (murder), seventh (adultery) and tenth (covetousness). Now, however, he added a fourth transgression by breaking the ninth commandment, *'You shall not give false testimony against your neighbour'* (Exodus 20:16). In common with anyone who has committed adultery in secret, David embarked on a life of lies, constantly justifying himself and blaming others. Hardly anyone knew of his sin and that was the way it was going to stay. He had gotten away with it, or so he thought. His life was in fact now similar to that of Judas and it was beginning to take its toll. His guilt was eating him up and his deceit was affecting his health. Thankfully, God stepped in and through a prophet challenged David to own up to his sin. Unlike Judas, David chose to be honest and face the consequences of his actions. His truthfulness, confession, and genuine repentance brought him freedom. When his wrongdoing was brought into the light he received forgiveness. Once again illumination had led to reconciliation. David recalls his experience in a song,

> *'Then I acknowledged my sin to you*
> *and did not cover up my iniquity.*
> *I said, "I will confess*
> *my transgressions to the LORD" –*
> *and you forgave*
> *the guilt of my sin.'* (Psalm 32:5)

If we are to build any connecting bridge to another, whether to God, our partner or our family and friends, we must shun the valley of deception that Judas so readily embraced. Although it is occasionally traumatic to own up to our sin that has ruled us or face the past experience that has haunted us, it is imperative that we fight to nurture truth or we will also lose love, the twin with which it is interconnected.

Optimism – a confident expectation that life improves

One of the goals of building bridges, as we shall see, is humankind's in-built desire to explore new territory. Every one of us wants to discover. This is one of the attractions of making a new acquaintance or starting a friendship. Sir Ernest Shackleton, the Edwardian hero, poet and adventurer, who attempted to reach the South Pole in the early part of the twentieth century, named optimism as one of the necessary qualities of an explorer. He said that, 'Optimism nullifies disappointment and makes one more ready than ever to go on'.[15] Optimism is not blind to reality, as many pessimists would have us believe! It faces the facts and overcomes them. It surveys the valley of disappointment and then spans it! It is a quality that all bridge-builders must possess.

The doctrine of optimism is perhaps best described as a combination of faith and hope. Faith enables the 'born again' Christian to overcome obstacles or, in the context of our subject, to build bridges:

> *'For whatever is born of God overcomes the world. And this is the victory*
> *that has overcome the world – our faith.'* (1 John 5:4)[16]

Alongside this overcoming faith is hope. Christian hope is not an uncertain, 'hope so' mentality but a positive outlook to life that comes from a true understanding of God's nature of goodness, His unbreakable promises and His determination to bless us. Hope is a confident expectation of good things to come. Jeremiah, despite his tag as 'the weeping prophet', was remarkably optimistic. In the middle of devastating circumstances, with his nation on the brink of defeat, he was able to speak positively about the future:

> ' "For I know the plans I have for you," declares the LORD, "plans to prosper you and not to harm you, plans to give you hope and a future." '
>
> (Jeremiah 29:11)

This positive approach to life does not ignore its harsh realities nor does it guarantee a trouble-free existence. It simply helps us to overcome difficulties, bridge obstacles or, as Shackleton put it, 'to go on'. And unlike the uncertain longing of the prospector or the temporary fortune of the gambler, the hope of God cannot disappoint us because the God of hope cannot fail us:

> 'And hope does not disappoint us, because God has poured out his love into our hearts by the Holy Spirit, whom he has given us.'
>
> (Romans 5:5)

In fact a lifestyle of optimism and hope opens up other avenues. It gives us a better understanding of God's character, makes us more attractive to others and empowers us for life. As Paul wrote,

> 'May the God of hope fill you with all joy and peace as you trust in him, so that you may overflow with hope by the power of the Holy Spirit.'
>
> (Romans 15:13)

It is a blessing that is available to us today.

Both hope and faith are not only part of the character of God but also are inextricably involved with love (1 Corinthians 13:13). If we are to build loving relationships successfully we must adhere to a theology of optimism. A number of years ago I was teaching on relationships. One of my students was an unmarried woman in her late thirties. In common with many of us, she came from a somewhat dysfunctional background. As a result she had an inaccurate and rather jaundiced view of marriage. Some time later, after I had conducted her wedding, she revealed to me that a comment I had made in class changed her thinking completely and freed her not only to pursue a relationship but enjoy it. The comment was simply that our wedding, despite what numerous people believe, should not be the happiest day of our life!

The comment was made on the basis of a simple biblical principle. King Solomon gave his sons wise advice when he wrote,

> *'The path of the righteous is like the first gleam of dawn,*
> *shining ever brighter till the full light of day.'* (Proverbs 4:18)

In other words, the lives of the righteous should steadily improve every day until they reach their zenith. This verse doesn't allow for any waning at the end. This principle and promise is not just for the remarkably wise or the scrupulously pious, it is for all Christians. As born-again Christians, we, though undeserving, have been made righteous in Christ (2 Corinthians 5:21). Therefore, for me, today is the best day of my life and tomorrow will be even better! This is a biblical fact and not a wishful assumption and I have claimed it for my marriage. Of course, it doesn't mean that nothing will ever go wrong. While on this earth we will all experience pain. Nonetheless, I always anticipate blessing. Like David the psalmist I count on green fields to precede me, comfort to accompany me and goodness to follow me. I confidently expect my life and relationships to improve in every area. If events turn against me, though somewhat surprised, my God-given optimism sees me through. The Bible promises that the one who fears God and delights in His commands *'will have no fear of bad news; his heart is steadfast, trusting in the* LORD. *His heart is secure, he will have no fear;* **in the end** *he will look in triumph on his foes'* (Psalm 112:7–8, emphasis mine). Optimism is a product of the faith that comes from these promises. It is an attitude of heart and mind and is essential for all bridge-building.

When faced with the numerous and often seemingly impenetrable obstacles that stand in the path of our friendships or seek to destroy our marriages, it is essential that we believe in the capacity of bridges to overcome them. The relational engineer must appreciate the poetic power of covenant, forgiveness, transparency and optimism and fully understand the scientific energy of these loving building materials. If we do access this wisdom, then no evil is beyond forgiveness and no relationship impossible. The valleys of self-sufficiency and destructive desire can be levelled. While on this earth, no 'gulf' is un-bridgeable and no 'bridge' is un-constructible!

Summary and advice

1. **Every relationship must contain both poetry and science.** The mechanic and the mystic in our soul must be satisfied. We need to maintain balance in our relationships.

2. **A balanced marriage should reflect every facet of love.** We need the selflessness of God's love, the warmth of friendship, the comfort of affection and the intoxication of romance. Time must be given to developing each of them.

3. **The strength of willpower: a commitment to our vows.** The Lord Jesus Christ established a covenant with His bride, the Church, and gave her a promise of love, a guarantee of blessing and a commitment to sacrifice. It is only this kind of wilful resolution that will establish a platform for our marriages and friendships.

4. **The strength of forgiveness.** If we choose not to forgive others, we will continually suffer the torment of bitterness and guilt. A decision to forgive, however, has the power to overcome even the most horrific crimes. Christ's example of forgiveness not only demands that we make this decision, it empowers us to do so. His forgiveness covers sin and keeps no record of wrongs. This daily practice has to be like breathing in all of our homes.

5. **The strength of transparency and honesty.** Love and truth are like 'Siamese twins'. In the Bible truth is synonymous with light. Illumination leads to reconciliation. We all tend to run from such transparency because we are afraid that we shall be seen for what we are. In our relationships, however, we can either be like Judas Iscariot who hid from his crimes and died alone in disgrace or be like King David who faced his failings, repented of his sins and lived in companionship and honour.

6. **The strength of optimism.** Optimism is a combination of faith and hope that does not guarantee a trouble free existence but nonetheless always expects a good outcome. It gives us a better understanding of God, enables us to be filled with good things, increases our trust, makes us more attractive to others and empowers us for life. Relationships that always 'fear the worst', usually experience it!

Notes

1. Dr Erasmus Darwin. Quoted in 'The Men Who Talked the Bridge', *The Bulletin*, 23 March 1932.
2. Charles Darwin. Quoted in Adrian Desmond and James Moore, *Darwin* (Michael Joseph Ltd, 1991).
3. Judith Dupré, *Bridges* (Könemann, 1998).
4. Francis Whitaker. Quoted by Douglas Martin in obituary, *Sydney Morning Herald*, 6 November 1999.
5. *The Book of Common Prayer*, Solemnization of Matrimony (1662).
6. Philip Yancey, *What's so Amazing about Grace?* (Zondervan, 1997).
7. Corrie Ten Boom, *The Hiding Place* (Hodder & Stoughton, 1971).
8. Pastor Son. Quoted in Yong Choon Ahn, *The Seed Must Die* (Inter-Varsity Press, 1965).
9. George Herbert. Quoted in Yancey, *What's so Amazing about Grace?*
10. Pat Conroy, *The Prince of Tides* (Bantam Books, 1986).
11. Jerome's Bible Commentary. Quoted in John Stott, *The Epistles of John* (Tyndale Press, 1971).
12. J. Grant Howard, *The Trauma of Transparency* (Multnomah Press, 1979).
13. The New American Standard Bible (The Lockman Foundation, 1977).
14. Ibid.
15. E.H. Shackleton, 'The Making of an Explorer', *Pearson's Magazine* (August 1914). Quoted in Roland Huntford, *Shackleton* (Hodder & Stoughton, 1985).
16. The Holy Bible, New King James Version (Thomas Nelson, Inc., 1982).

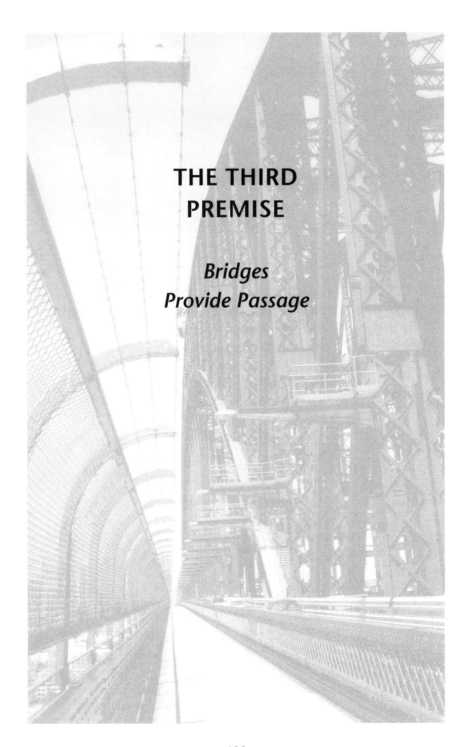

THE THIRD PREMISE

*Bridges
Provide Passage*

Chapter 8

Mr Milson and
Lt Dawes

A Theology of Communication

Sydney Harbour Bridge connects Milson's Point on the north side of the harbour to Dawes' Point on the south side. James Milson arrived in Sydney in about 1804 and lived in the west of the city until 1822 when he leased some property on the north shore of Port Jackson in order to become a dairy farmer. He delivered milk to the numerous ships that plied the harbour and provided a 'milk house' in order to refresh the day visitors from the other side. The point at which they landed was appropriately named after him. Lt Dawes, on the other hand, was an explorer, scientist, linguist, and above all an astronomer. It was he who, under instructions from England, established the observatory on the south shore of the harbour, after arriving with the 'First Fleet' in 1788, and the area eventually carried his name. Who could possibly have predicted that time would turn a dairy farmer and an astronomer into bridge ends?! Yet the two are inextricably linked and are the richer for it!

There has always been a certain antipathy between France and England. They are natural sporting antagonists! They share different languages, customs and passions. Despite fighting together in the two world wars, the English have always resented the fact that the French were the last nation to invade their shores successfully. The fact that it is nearly one thousand years since William, Duke of Normandy, crossed the Channel doesn't seem to enter into it! A traditional and island mentality has a long memory! From the French perspective, the emperor Napoleon summed it up when he said, 'With God's help, I will put an end to the destiny and very existence of England'.[1] Nonetheless, despite this cultural antagonism, the Channel Tunnel was officially opened on 6 May 1994 connecting the two countries for the first time since the last ice age! What was it that overcame hundreds of years of hostility and a body of water that numerous invaders had failed to cross?

The Channel Tunnel, along with numerous other similar engineering projects the world over, aids communication, facilitates trade, fulfils a desire for exploration and achievement, and secures a better connection between the two countries. Despite humankind's incessant ability to divide communities, the Channel Tunnel represents our drive for attachment, our passion to establish passage between two severed societies. What the kings and politicians had failed to achieve in centuries, the tunnellers and bridge-builders had accomplished in a few short years. The unassuming civil engineer, perhaps unconsciously, contributes immeasurably to humanity.

On the other side of the world, Sydney Harbour Bridge bears testimony to the same passion. The great steel arch effortlessly spans the harbour from Milson's Point in the north to Dawes' Point in the south. When it was built the engineers had not only provided passage between two settlements but they had permanently united two very different people, Mr Milson, a farmer, and Lieutenant Dawes, an astronomer! C.H. Bertie described Dawes as 'much engrossed with the stars' and Milson as 'much engrossed with the earth'.[2] Thus the bridge has not only actually joined the north with the south but symbolically connected nature and science, the earth with the stars.

This may seem to be a far-fetched illustration of the gulf between two people and the power of a bridge to provide 'passage' between them, but it bears remarkable similarities to the day-to-day communication of a normal couple, as I know from personal experience. Amanda and I may never have contemplated marriage had we completed a 'compatibility test' prior to our relationship! We were total opposites and, despite the theory that opposites attract, it wasn't bearing fruit in practice! I was an unemotional scientist, Amanda an emotional musician; I was a nature-loving countryman and she was a book-loving city woman; I loved watching sport, she remained disinterested! At the time, my mother considered that our faith was the only thing that we had in common and since that wouldn't last, in her opinion, she gave us two years maximum! That was over twenty-five years ago. In the same way as the communities on the north and south sides of Sydney Harbour are now seen as one city because of the connecting power of the bridge, my wife and I had to build a bridge that enabled us to become one. We had to find common ground, develop mutual interests and learn to communicate.

Conversely, if my wife and I had not learned to communicate we would have remained separated and probably ended up in the divorce courts. It could also be argued that if Sydney had not built a bridge, the divided city would not be as influential and successful as it is today. Jesus said,

> *'Every kingdom divided against itself will be ruined, and every city or household divided against itself will not stand.'*   (Matthew 12:25)

Since miscommunication can cause nations to war, cities to decay and households to falter, it is imperative that we all embrace a theology of communication.

The idea of communication incorporates the concepts of exchange and commonality. A definition might read:

▶ *The process of exchanging information, ideas or feelings via a common pathway, passage or system of signals.*

Therefore a bridge is a form of communication since it enables the exchange of goods via a common or shared passage. In relationships communication involves the sharing of lives: it is sharing in common with another.

This sharing is a fundamental ingredient of Christianity and indeed any committed relationship. As he draws his letter to a close, the writer to the Hebrews gives a final exhortation on sharing,

> *'Through Jesus, therefore, let us continually offer to God a sacrifice of praise – the fruit of lips that confess his name. And do not forget to do good and to **share** with others, for with such sacrifices God is pleased.'*
> (Hebrews 13:15–16, emphasis mine)

The original Greek word used here for 'share' is *koinonia*. In the King James Version of the Bible the same word is translated 'communicate'. It is evident from this passage that communication requires discipline, sacrifice and Jesus' help! However, what exactly does *koinonia* mean to us in our everyday lives and how are we going to live it? In the rest of the New Testament *koinonia* is used in a variety of contexts and is translated in a number of different ways. Sometimes it is interpreted as 'fellowship' and at other times 'contribution'. Evidently, *koinonia*, like the English word 'communication', is a rich and evocative word that has many shades of meaning. Before we look at the science of communication in the next chapter, we need to understand the concept from a biblical perspective.

Partnership – a common cause

> '... *In all my prayers for all of you, I always pray with joy because of your partnership* [Gk. koinonia] *in the gospel from the first day until now.'* (Philippians 1:4–5)

The father of Alexander the Great, Philip II of Macedonia, gave his name to the town of Philippi in Northern Greece in the fourth century BC. It was here, in about 50 AD, that Paul the apostle was summoned by a vision to establish the first European church. He was beaten and imprisoned for his efforts, something to which he became accustomed!

Some years later, Paul was in prison again: this time in Rome. The Philippian church heard of his predicament and sent Epaphroditus to encourage him and take care of his needs. Paul responded to this generosity with a thank-you letter, the epistle to the Philippians, in which he rejoices in their *'partnership* [Gk. koinonia] *in the gospel'* (Philippians 1:5). He goes on to thank them for 'sharing' in his troubles (4:14), challenges them to 'share' in the sufferings of Christ (3:10) and encourages them that they also will 'share' in God's grace with him (1:7). There is no doubt that the Philippian church was concerned for Paul's plight but it is evident that they also were suffering. In fact, Paul writes,

> *'For it has been granted to you on behalf of Christ not only to believe on him, but also to suffer for him, since you are going through the same struggle you saw I had, and now hear that I still have.'* (Philippians 1:29–30)

Paul's Philippian partners were prepared to suffer for the same gospel and die for the same Saviour. They shared a common cause.

The concept of partnership, which Paul was espousing, contains both the warmth of companionship and also the power of covenant, and is fundamental to successful communication. It suggests a unity of purpose, working together toward the same goal. In fact, Paul describes his friend Epaphroditus as a 'fellow worker' and 'fellow-soldier' (2:25) and another is called Syzygus which means 'yoke fellow' (4:3): in other words, they all shared their work, battles and burdens. Nonetheless, two of the congregation in Philippi had fallen out with each other over some anonymous and no doubt petty matter. Euodia and Syntyche, whose names apparently mean 'prosperous journey' and 'pleasant acquaintance' respectively, were not living up to their names. Their communication was neither prosperous nor pleasant! Paul begs for reconciliation by reminding them of the cause of the gospel:

> *'I plead with Euodia and I plead with Syntyche to agree with each other in the Lord. Yes, and I ask you, loyal yokefellow, help these women who have contended at my side in the cause of the gospel, along with Clement and the rest of my fellow-workers, whose names are in the book of life.'*
> (Philippians 4:2–3)

Had they remembered the cause, they would have continued to contend for it and not with each other.

Milson and Dawes, on the other hand, the historical representatives of the north and south shore of Port Jackson, were united around the common goals of a shared project. The prejudice, competition and selfish programmes of the two communities were put aside as Sydney Harbour Bridge took shape. They committed to a cause that was beyond themselves. It is this same vision and passion that will cement even the most vulnerable of relationships. As my senior minister, Brian Houston writes, 'The power of any relationship is the cause or reason that binds it together'.[3] A couple who genuinely build their relationship around a shared cause or common purpose are very difficult to part. They work with each other, not against each other. Their hands are committed to creating a dream rather than holding a position. There is no time for destructive and idle remarks. There is no place for blame shifting. They no longer face each other from distant and opposing shores but stand together against a common threat, the challenges that oppose them. The yoke they bear is shouldered equally. Both sides feel the losses and both sides enjoy the triumphs.

This is not just a fanciful picture. It is a real and necessary part of our relationships. Our communication requires a partnership in a common cause. So many couples today live independent lives under the same roof. They have their own jobs, friends, interests and agendas. It is no wonder that they divorce. Others do share a common purpose in working on their relationship, bringing up their children and may occasionally unite over a building project or a shared holiday but so often the dream is temporary and they drift apart when the enthusiasm wanes. What we need is an eternal cause: a purpose that is beyond our ability; a message that leaves no room for self-interest. It was for such a message that Paul and the church at Philippi gave their lives and such a cause that gave them their rich and lasting partnership.

Fellowship – speaking the same language

> *'They devoted themselves to the apostles' teaching and to the fellowship* [Gk. koinonia], *to the breaking of bread and to prayer.'*   (Acts 2:42)

The early Church was birthed and empowered on the Day of Pentecost. This was the second of the three major Jewish festivals. The expectation was that God-fearing Jews would travel to the place of worship in order to celebrate and bring offerings. So Jerusalem was crowded with international visitors on the day that Peter and the other disciples met in the upper room. According to Luke's account in the book of the Acts of the Apostles there were numerous nationalities represented:

> *'Parthians, Medes and Elamites; residents of Mesopotamia, Judea and Cappadocia, Pontus and Asia, Phrygia and Pamphylia, Egypt and the parts of Libya near Cyrene; visitors from Rome (both Jews and converts to Judaism); Cretans and Arabs ... '*   (Acts 2:9–11)

In other words, people, literally, from all the points of the compass descended on Jerusalem.

A riot of nations gathered for the feast. They had the one purpose, yet they also came with their own national perspectives and above all their own native languages. Jerusalem was filled with commotion and confusion, an ever-increasing babble of tongues. Imagine the frustration and miscommunication! Among the travellers were some Parthian Jews, modern inhabitants of ancient Babylon. They of all people would have known the story of the building of the Tower of

Babel (Babylon) where the languages of the world were confused. Until then humankind had '... *one language and a common speech'* (Genesis 11:1). As they pushed through the clamour the returning Parthians would have rued the day that the ancient Babylonians had tried to make a name for themselves. Yet unbeknown to them they had walked into Jerusalem on one of the most significant days in its history.

It was in this context that God poured out His Spirit as promised. The one hundred and twenty Christians who had been waiting in Jerusalem since Jesus' resurrection were miraculously filled with power and began to speak in the numerous different languages represented in the visiting crowd. The multicultural and multilingual crowd listened in astonishment to Peter who explained the phenomenon and three thousand subsequently became disciples on that first day. The Bible then makes what, in my view, is a remarkable statement, quoted at the beginning of this section. Once again *koinonia* is used in the sense of fellowship. In other words, the crowd once separated by human tongues was now united by a divine one. Where once rebellion had confused their communication devotion had now fused them. They not only shared a common cause, they now shared a common language. Of course they maintained their distinctives but there was a commonality in what was being said. They all spoke the language of the Spirit. Whereas before they misunderstood one another, now they understood.

When the Channel Tunnel was built between France and England, the signs had to be in both French and English. There is no new tongue. France still speaks French and England speaks English! However, for the project to succeed there has to be a greater degree of unity in their communication with one another. Equally when the Sydney Harbour Bridge was built, the two shores with their own perspectives and choices had to begin to 'speak the same language'. This could be said about any community that is attempting to build a bridge to another. When England and the United States allied in the Second World War, two countries, which George Bernard Shaw said were 'separated by a common language',[4] had to share the same spirit if they were to survive together.

Much has been written recently about the differences between the genders. It has been argued that they almost speak different languages! In the book *Men Are from Mars, Women Are from Venus* John Gray asks the readers to imagine that men and women are from different planets since this explains the consistent confusion in their communication!

He argues that, 'The Martian and Venusian languages had the same words, but the way they were used gave different meanings'.[5] Any of us who have attempted any sort of bridge-building between the genders knows this to be true! A word may denote one thing in a dictionary and yet connote a completely different thing in the heart. The answer to this dilemma is fellowship, *koinonia*, a true commitment in spirit. It is this kind of spiritual connection that will unite the most divergent of couples with the most diverse of backgrounds. If we are one in spirit, the actual words that we use are secondary.

I remember travelling in Spain some years ago with a Spanish pastor. On one occasion we had a long journey together that gave us opportunity to talk. We conversed in Spanish until he realized that my Spanish was limited to say the least. We changed to English only for me to discover the same problem with his English. Amid much laughter we tried French. Again, as soon as the conversation became 'deep and meaningful' my vocabulary let me down. We both became immensely frustrated. We wanted to communicate but seemingly were unable to do so. In the end, in desperation, we prayed! Suddenly all the barriers were removed. The words that we used were irrelevant. We were speaking the same language. It was true what Paul wrote to the Corinthian church, *'For who among men knows the thoughts of a man except the man's spirit within him?'* (1 Corinthians 2:11). I knew instinctively what he was saying and vice versa. We both got out of the car saying, 'We had great fellowship!'

This fellowship is essential for all bridge-builders. It is inspired by the divine empowerment that brought Jew and Arab together in Jerusalem two thousand years ago. It is the kind of communion that we take for granted in my home church in Sydney where over seventy different nationalities gather each Sunday morning to worship one God, commit to the same cause and speak a common language. It is this kind of true communication that is essential in all relationships.

Commonality – joint ownership

> *'All the believers were together and had everything in common* [Gk. koinos] ... '   (Acts 2:44)

The first church meetings in Jerusalem not only had a common language they *'had everything in common'*. They shared their food, goods, possessions and homes. There was evidently a sense of community and wellbeing. This was not an enforced policy that demanded equality; it was simply a voluntary response to the needs of their new family. Barnabas is cited as one example of a landowner who sold a field and freely gave the money to the newly formed church (Acts 4:36–37). The tragic deaths of Ananias and Sapphira recorded in the fifth chapter of the Acts of the Apostles were not as a result of their refusal to share their inheritance, it was because they colluded in lying to God (Acts 5:4–9). They both were totally free to keep or sell their property and then free to dispose of the proceeds as they both saw fit, as Peter, a house and business owner himself, reminded Ananias.

It is difficult in retrospect to determine why the early Church felt so compelled to share with one another even by the selling of property. I suspect that it was a combination of factors. Many believed that the Lord Jesus Christ would return very soon in order to establish His kingdom. This would give reason enough to sell fields and houses. Others, perhaps, were caught up with the euphoria of the moment or even partially motivated by the fear of what happened to Ananias and Sapphira! If these three reasons are correct it would explain why, with the passing of time, the practice declined in the Church. However, I believe there were two further reasons why such sacrifice was common: genuine love for others and a correct understanding of eternity. The believers instinctively knew that real fellowship involved sacrificial care. They now shared a faith that was bigger than themselves and their temporal assets seemed less significant. They possessed goods but held them lightly. They understood the often misunderstood balance between personal responsibility and joint ownership. This is the balance for which we must strive.

When the Sydney Harbour Bridge was built it was started from both sides at the same time. Each side took personal responsibility to build its section. There may have been some friendly rivalry between the teams of each section. Some of the workmen may have claimed that their side was the best. Yet when the bridge was complete both North and South boasted to their colleagues, 'Look at our bridge that we have built!' It could be genuinely said that both shores had 'everything in common'. Their once separate individual needs were subordinated to the needs of the new larger community. They jointly shared the load but also jointly owned the bridge.

A prosperous newly engaged couple may have two homes and two bank accounts. As they approach the covenant of marriage, where 'two will become one', they usually pool their goods and possessions. They are about to vow that, 'All that I have I share with you'. One may have had more to bring than the other but they end up with a single home and a joint account. They are committing to a relationship that is larger than the sum of either of their individual lives. They know that successful communication within it is based on the balance between two people carrying their respective loads and yet both sharing the one load. Couples who refuse joint accounts on the grounds of a need for independence are often admitting to a deeper problem. Their actions are usually indicative of selfishness or a lack of trust, commitment or hope. Sadly their happiness is often doomed from the start since all of these problems oppose healthy relationships.

Of course, this principle is often not as easy in practice. I have the privilege of travelling a good deal in my work. As a result my car is not being used during the time that I am away. In keeping with my commitment to the church I have often lent my car to a needy person within the community. A number of years ago I lent my car to a friend with the strict instructions to care for it as if it were his own! Just after my return someone else whom I didn't know well approached me and said, 'Your car goes really well'! 'How do you know?' I protested. 'Your friend lent it to me while you were away!' My immediate reaction was one of anger. How could my friend have been so irresponsible? My car could have been damaged. However, I soon realized that in fact my reaction was inappropriate. My friend had simply acted within his brief. In retrospect, he should not have lent it without permission but I should not have been so possessive. In common with marriage, true fellowship, as exemplified by the early Church, demands it is my car, but it is also ours!

Communion – a faith agreement

> *'Do not be yoked together with unbelievers. For what do righteousness and wickedness have in common? Or what fellowship* [Gk. koinonia] *can light have with darkness?'* (2 Corinthians 6:14)

In chemical terms milk could be called an emulsion, a mixture of two distinct liquids. It consists of tiny droplets of fat or oil suspended in water. When fresh and mixed it looks and tastes good, but since 'oil and water don't mix', as we all know, it will inevitably separate! When stale and separate, it is both repellent and noxious. This is an observation that might have proved helpful for some groups in the early Church. In their desire for peace and unity they were attempting to mix two totally opposite viewpoints. In theological terms this is called syncretism: trying to combine the characteristics of differing belief systems or religious philosophies. Paul was trying to explain to the Corinthian church that there could be no communication or fellowship between Christianity and idolatry (2 Corinthians 6:14–16). Initially, it may look good to some, but ultimately it will prove poisonous. A similar argument could be applied to certain aspects of ecumenism. There are groups in the Church for whom the goal of unity, it seems, must be reached at all costs – the means of achieving it irrelevant. Although we should all promote Christian unity, there are some beliefs that are so divergent that an attempt at symphony can only result in a temporary mixture – ultimately rather than the desired concord discord will inevitably erupt.

Genuine unity, according to Paul's theology, involves a true communion of faith, a harmony of philosophy, an agreement of belief. It was only when Paul had become a believer that the Christian leaders in Jerusalem were able to give him what he calls the *'right hand of fellowship'* (Gk. *koinonia*) (Galatians 2:9). This is the basis for good communication. Bridge-builders must shake hands over the contract and agree to the terms of the covenant between them. If they cannot agree, the project cannot advance successfully. In the same way, a couple not only needs to share a cause if they are going to communicate effectively, they need to share a system of beliefs. Where they do the power of agreement is released in their relationship.

This is reiterated in the teaching of the Lord Jesus Christ. He said,

> *'Again, I tell you that if two of you on earth agree about anything you ask for, it will be done for you by my Father in heaven. For where two or three come together in my name, there am I with them.'*
>
> (Matthew 18:19–20)

In my view, this is a verse that is regularly misquoted in churches around the world. I have heard it argued in small lifeless meetings that God is definitely present because of the size and purpose of the gathering: two or three have gathered in the name of Christ. Yet, surely it is not just the size and purpose alone but the spiritual condition of the group to which Jesus was referring. If two of us agree (Gk. *sumphoneo*), then and only then, is the presence of the God of unity assured. The issue here is communion. If one hundred Christians gather in the name of Christ, yet in dissension and disharmony, God cannot bless the gathering.

This explains Paul's teaching on the sacrament of 'the breaking of bread'. He writes,

> *'The cup of blessing which we bless, is it not the communion* [Gk. koinonia] *of the blood of Christ? The bread which we break, is it not the communion* [Gk. koinonia] *of the body of Christ?'*
>
> (1 Corinthians 10:16)[6]

The basis of the ceremony is fellowship with God and each other. If we are out of fellowship with God or one another we should not share in the sacrament. That is why he goes on to condemn fellowship with demons (1 Corinthians 10:20–21) and discourages those who are not in good fellowship from participating.

> *'Therefore, whoever eats the bread or drinks the cup of the Lord in an unworthy manner will be guilty of sinning against the body and blood of the Lord.'*
>
> (1 Corinthians 11:27)

This is the foundation of a theology of communication. We may share interests, passions and even a language but if we don't believe the same thing the future of our relationships is in jeopardy. We will constantly disagree and therefore consistently drive a wedge between us. Our faith is the most intimate aspect of our lives; it is the foundation on which we build. That is why the Old Testament teaches that the Jews were not to marry those outside their faith. The leader Nehemiah condemned the interfaith syncretistic marriages of his time because by mixing their faiths they had destroyed their fellowship and communication both with God and each other.

No wonder Paul reiterates the sentiment to Christians in the New Testament. As we have seen, he says, *'Do not be yoked together with unbelievers'* (2 Corinthians 6:14). The image of a yoke that he uses is very descriptive and would have been readily understood by his audience. Both the Law of Moses (Deuteronomy 22:10) and common sense forbade ploughing a field by yoking an ox and a donkey together. The different statures, strengths and behaviour of the animals would have made ploughing painful for all concerned, if not impossible. Being unequally yoked doesn't plough fields, build bridges or win races! Looking around it seems that many people have ignored this warning and have attempted to harness a cheetah with a tortoise in order to run their race!

Companionship – sharing the journey

'We proclaim to you what we have seen and heard, so that you also may have fellowship [Gk. koinonia] *with us. And our fellowship* [Gk. koinonia] *is with the Father and with his Son, Jesus Christ. We write this to make our joy complete.'*   (1 John 1:3–4)

The opening of a bridge is always a festive occasion. It is accompanied quite rightly by joy and celebration. In fact, in my view, a bridge should exude and symbolize joy throughout its life. This is certainly true of the Sydney Harbour Bridge. It is the centrepiece for extraordinary celebrations. Hundreds of thousands of people gather around it every New Year and its image, festooned with fireworks, is beamed around the world. The Australians know how to party and the bridge provides a focus. Other nations seem a little less exuberant! A lady from the West Indies once said to an English minister friend of mine that the greatest sin of the English was 'hidden joy'! Of course it is a generalization. However, occasionally our stolid, often dour personality doesn't help us; nor does the example of the traditional Church. Joy does sometimes seem to be in short supply!

This was not the case for John the apostle, who of all the disciples must have caught something of the infectious joy of the Christ. In his first letter to the Church he makes some startling observations. He writes that the reason that he was proclaiming the message of Jesus Christ was so that we might have fellowship (communication) with God and each other, and the reason for the fellowship was the completion of joy (1 John 1:4). John Stott, the noted English writer and preacher, comments on this passage by writing, 'What is the secret of fullness of joy ... ? It is in the fellowship which the proclamation creates; for if the immediate purpose of the proclamation is the establishment of fellowship, the ultimate purpose is the completion of joy. This is the divine order – angelia, koinonia, chara'.[7] (These last three Greek words mean: message, fellowship, joy.) We could also express their sense in the words 'incarnation, communication, celebration'. So we could conclude that if we are not full of joy we have not yet learned to communicate and if we cannot communicate properly we haven't yet fully grasped that the 'Word became flesh' and lived among us.

Once we have recognized, received and believed in the incarnated Christ (cf. John 1:10–13) how can we learn to communicate so that we can experience the completion of joy to which he refers? John uses the image of walking to describe the process of fellowship and communication and it may be helpful to maintain the image. In his first epistle, John tells us to walk in the light and not in the darkness and in his second he instructs us to walk in truth, obedience to Jesus' commands and love for one another (2 John 4–6). So honesty, integrity and compassion would all be essential ingredients of successful communication. However, perhaps the most challenging of John's statements is,

> *'Whoever claims to live in him must walk as Jesus did.'*   (1 John 2:6)

If we are to walk with one another we must first learn to walk with Him.

Walking together is about companionship, sharing a journey. It starts with agreement. Amos the prophet asks a rhetorical question,

> *'Do two walk together unless they have agreed to do so?'*   (Amos 3:3)

An alternate translation reads, *'Can two walk together, except they be agreed?'*[8] First we have to decide to be companions and then we have to share enough in common to make the journey together beneficial. In practical terms, if we are to accompany someone on a journey we have to start at the same place and time and agree on a mode of transport, route and direction. We must travel at the same speed and have the same destination. However, this is not enough. The success of a journey is also determined by the enjoyment that accompanies it. For a conversation to be enjoyable it has to be agreeable! This is not a shallow agreement. We should not only walk on the same path we should walk in the same shoes!

I have travelled on numerous plane trips which I would not rate as a success, since, though my fellow passenger and I visited the same airports together, we might as well have been living on different planets for all that we had in common! On one occasion, a large man sat next to me and immediately offered me some drugs. After I declined his offer I tried to make conversation only to be met with a torrent of abuse and cynicism. He swore loudly and fluently through-out the flight, made suggestive remarks to all the female flight attendants and was promptly arrested by the police as soon as we arrived at our destination. In retrospect, though we travelled together, we did not share the journey. Though we attempted to talk, we had nothing in common. There was no companionship. There was no agreement of spirit and therefore no joy!

Good fellowship or communication with another is therefore dependent on an agreement of purpose and destination. This at least puts us on the same map. However, it must also include an agreement of spirit. If we cannot be honest with one another, if our relationship is not founded on the tenets of God's word or we simply do not love one another, our communication and bridge-building will be robbed of the joy for which it was destined. Our life bridges are built to be celebrated.

Contribution – mutual grace

> *'For Macedonia and Achaia were pleased to make a contribution* [Gk. koinonia] *for the poor among the saints in Jerusalem.'*
>
> (Romans 15:26)

While in Corinth, nearing the end of his third missionary journey, Paul wrote to the Christians in Rome to outline the gospel that he was preaching and to inform them of a possible future visit. In the letter, he tells them that he is going to Jerusalem with a gift for the poor from the churches in Macedonia. He writes that the Macedonians were not only pleased to give, but they owed it to the Jews in Jerusalem. It was their duty, their responsibility. His argument was that since the Jews had spiritual blessings, which they shared with the Gentiles, the Gentiles in turn should share their material blessings with the Jews. The word he uses for this gift is 'contribution' (Gk. *koinonia*, Romans 15:26). Communication and fellowship involve committed and responsible giving.

On another occasion Paul writes to the Corinthian Church. He also encourages them with a report about the Macedonian giving. Despite their 'extreme poverty' the Macedonian Christians were extraordin-arily generous. In fact, Paul writes,

> *'they urgently pleaded with us for the privilege of sharing* [Gk. koinonia] *in this service to the saints.'*   (2 Corinthians 8:4)

He describes their giving as an *'act of grace'* (v. 6) since they were giving beyond their own ability. They therefore had to be empowered by God to do it. He challenges the Christians at Corinth to also *'excel in this grace of giving'* (v. 7). He goes further by saying that the 'liberal distribution' (Gk. *koinonia*, 2 Corinthians 9:13)[9] of the Corinthians was not only meeting the needs of God's people but was also resulting in prayer, thanksgiving and praise to God. Now we see that Paul's teaching on communication, fellowship and giving not only involved sharing responsibility but also included what I term mutual grace.

When the Sydney Harbour Bridge was built the community surrounding Dawes' Point on the south side was considerably larger than that around Milson's Point on the opposite shore. The Dawes' side, being the site of the original colony, was the more established and wealthier area. Nonetheless, despite these obvious differences, it would have been ridiculous for the North Shore community to expect the richer suburbs of Sydney to cover all the expenses. It was a shared project with shared benefits and therefore demanded equal responsibility. Not necessarily equal giving but definitely equal sacrifice. As the North Shore suburbs have grown more prosperous they have had to increase their giving for the upkeep of the bridge but still cannot be expected to pay everything. The building of bridges requires equal responsibility from both sides.

There is no doubt that a selfish attitude toward money can destroy relationships. Although gambling and debt are the most obvious causes of conflict, it is often the hidden agendas that are the most cancerous. A number of years ago I was preaching in a mining community. I was told that the tradition of financial management in the home consisted of many of the wives demanding the paycheque at the end of the week. The miner duly placed his hard-earned wages on the kitchen table and had a small amount of 'drinking money' returned to him! There was no agreed amount, no joint accounts, no discussion and definitely no trust! In another situation, when a family I know gathered together to read their mother's last will and testament, the distribution of the inheritance caused such acrimony and hurt to surface that they had to call in some counsellors for a day to resolve the problem.

It has been well said that the two major problems in a marriage are the 'bank and the bed'! It is argued that either money or sex – or both – is at the centre of marriage break-ups. However, it is not so much the money or the sex itself that causes the conflict but our incorrect and usually sinful response to it. Therefore, the bank and the bed themselves are not the problem: we are! This is not a hopeless comment, rather the reverse! The author, Jay Adams, in his book, *Christian Living in the Home*, writes that, 'The first and most important fact to remember about a truly Christian home is that sinners live there'.[10] An understanding of this truth gives us hope for transformation since with the help of God we can change our sinful behaviour.

Communication demands an honest appraisal of the challenges that confront our relationships. If we want to relate successfully, when we have first crucified the 'love of money', we are dared to live lives of mutual grace and radical liberality.

Sociability – like-mindedness

> *'Command them to do good, to be rich in good deeds, and to be generous and willing to share* [Gk. koinonikos].' (1 Timothy 6:18)

The tendency of the rich is to hold onto their riches. Thus Paul the apostle, in his letter to Timothy, didn't just suggest to the wealthy but commanded them to lay up treasure in heaven by being generous on earth. In this way they would *'take hold of the life that is truly life'* (1 Timothy 6:19). However, he didn't want the wealthy to give reluctantly. After all, there are numerous selfish philanthropists! He wanted them to be inclined to give, willing to share (Gk. *koinonikos*, 1 Timothy 6:18). He was not looking solely for an action in his disciples but also for an attitude. Peter the apostle challenged his readers with the same thought when he wrote,

> *'Offer hospitality* [lit: friendship to strangers] *to one another without grumbling.'* (1 Peter 4:9)

In other words, if you are going to be nice, do it nicely! Both Paul and Peter were requiring a selfless attitude toward others.

A like-minded attitude of selflessness is essential for communication. When a couple first get together they usually look for common ground. If they share a hobby, a passion for sport, an interest at work they find it easier to maintain a conversation. There is no doubt that this is an important part of relationship but it is not an integral one. As I have said, my wife Amanda and I shared few common interests when we first met. In common with Milson and Dawes, I was more interested in farming and soil and she was more interested in music and the stars!

Yet we didn't build on our differing selfish interests but on our shared interest in others. We were like-minded in our desire to help others. As a result, over the years, we have created common ground on which we can build.

If a couple don't have this common attitude they will constantly be at loggerheads. A personality clash is not as destructive as an attitude clash. For instance, the man may be the quieter of the two, relaxing by reading a book. The woman, on the other hand, may be a partygoer, relaxing by going out with a crowd of people. This clash of personalities may be frustrating, but it is not devastating to the relationship and simply requires understanding and compromise. However, if one is given to hospitality and the other is not, a more serious attitude clash occurs: selfish versus selfless. The couple becomes double minded and division ensues. Real fellowship and communication demand likemindedness.

Participation – shared pain

> 'Is not the cup of thanksgiving for which we give thanks a participation [Gk . koinonia] in the blood of Christ? And is not the bread that we break a participation [Gk. koinonia] in the body of Christ?'
>
> (1 Corinthians 10:16)

The greatest example of communication that the world has ever experienced is that demonstrated by the birth, life, death and resurrection of the Lord Jesus Christ. It was also the most costly. Remarkably, every time we participate in the sacrament of communion in a church we are invited to remember and identify with His suffering. We must never forget the price of communion. With our limited understanding we cannot possibly grasp what it really cost the Christ to die. Yet even if we are allowed the privilege to glimpse even a whisper of the enormity of His sacrifice it would fill us with wonder. Then to be allowed to identify with Him in His suffering is an act of profound grace. We don't know how Paul the apostle reacted to Jesus' challenge, 'I will show him how much he must suffer for my name' (Acts 9:16), but we do know that he came to understand that sharing in Christ's suffering was a high calling. He told the Philippians,

> 'I want to know Christ and the power of his resurrection and the fellowship [Gk. koinonia] of sharing in his sufferings, becoming like

*him in his death, and so, somehow, to attain to the resurrection from the
dead.'* (Philippians 3:10–11)

Many Christians suggest that we are not called to any form of
suffering. Although Jesus died in order to relieve us of a great deal of
pain, to suggest that we should never suffer is not only ridiculous but it
robs us of the joy of fellowship and identification. Peter was well aware
of the price of associating with Jesus Christ. He wrote,

*'Dear friends, do not be surprised at the painful trial you are suffering,
as though something strange were happening to you. But rejoice that you
participate [Gk. koinoneo] in the sufferings of Christ, so that you may
be overjoyed when his glory is revealed. If you are insulted because of the
name of Christ, you are blessed, for the Spirit of glory and of God rests
on you.'* (1 Peter 4:12–14)

James, too, taught Christians how to respond in the face of inevitable
difficulties,

*'Consider it pure joy, my brothers, whenever you face trials of many kinds,
because you know that the testing of your faith develops perseverance.'*
(James 1:2–3)

This identification with Christ's sacrifice is an integral part of our
relationship and participation with Him.

Real communication, then, is not just an idle chat in the corridor
with a colleague, a conversation over coffee with a friend or passing
the time of day with a neighbour over the garden fence. It is much
deeper than that. It involves building a bridge, and every exercise
of bridge-building, whether historical or relational, involves loss,
shared pain and even death! Some of my most precious relationships
have been birthed in shared tragedy. As a pastor I have been invited
into situations of immense grief, marriage break-up, the death of a
child, or bereavement as a result of suicide. In almost every case, our
shared tears have fused our hearts. Although pain can drive people
apart it can also bring them together in a way that few other things
can.

In my own relationships, I have discovered that the price of
intimacy is discovery and the price of discovery is vulnerability. In
other words, although it is true to say that the one who knows me best

loves me most, it is also true that the one who knows me best can hurt me most! Yet, those with whom I have been the most vulnerably honest have often proved the best of friends. It is not just joy that cements relationships, the celebration of companionship; it is also the obstacles that we have to overcome together that make bridge-building so fulfilling.

Summary and advice

1. **Communication incorporates the concepts of exchange and commonality.** The Greek word *koinonia*, which can be translated 'fellowship', 'participation', 'communion' or 'communication', is a good starting point to look at how we can share together in relationships.

2. **Communication is a partnership with a common cause.** A relationship built around a shared purpose is immensely strong. It stands together against common threats.

3. **Communication is fellowship: speaking the same language.** A true unity of spirit will unite the most divergent of people.

4. **Communication includes commonality or joint ownership.** Successful communication is based on the balance between taking personal responsibility and sharing each other's load.

5. **Communication is a communion, a faith agreement.** The Bible describes interfaith syncretistic relationships as 'unequally yoked'. They rarely prosper.

6. **Communication is companionship, sharing the journey together.** For a conversation to be enjoyable it has to be agreeable. We should walk on the same path and in the same shoes.

7. **Communication involves contribution or mutual grace.** In order for genuine sharing to take place with each other we need a common outward focus.

8. **Communication thrives on sociability and like-mindedness.** A relationship benefits from common interests but there must be a like-minded attitude.

9. **Communication is about participation which includes shared pain.** It is not only joy that cements a relationship but suffering: facing loss and common threats.

Notes

1. Napoleon. Quoted in Alan Schom, *Napoleon Bonaparte* (Harper Perennial, 1998).
2. C.H. Bertie, 'Dawes and Milson. The Men Who Gave their Names to Bridge Ends', Supplement to the *Sydney Morning Herald*, 19 March 1932.
3. Brian Houston, *For This Cause* (Maximized Leadership. Inc. 2001).
4. George Bernard Shaw, *Reader's Digest*, November 1942.
5. John Gray, *Men Are from Mars, Women Are from Venus* (Thorsons, 1993).
6. The Holy Bible, The King James Version (Cambridge, 1769).
7. John Stott, *The Epistles of John. An Introduction and Commentary* (Tyndale Press, 1964).
8. The Holy Bible, The King James Version.
9. Ibid.
10. Jay Adams, *Christian Living in the Home* (Baker Book House, 1972).

Chapter 9

A Plank Across a Stream

The Essential Ingredients of Communication

> Although the Sydney Harbour Bridge gives the impression of being a massively complex piece of engineering comprising 52,800 tonnes of steel including 6,000,000 rivets, 95,000 cubic metres of concrete, 17,000 cubic metres of granite facing and 272,000 litres of paint, it is actually remarkably simple. If you remove the virtually entirely ornamental pillars, the hanging roadway and the steel approaches, it is just one 39,000-tonne steel arch that spans what is arguably the most picturesque harbour in the world! Strong, simple and beautiful!

Diana had lots of breasts! They flowed down her chest like a cluster of ripe grapes! Statues discovered by archaeologists in Ephesus reveal her prolific mammarian collection! Artemis of the Ephesians, as the Greeks called her, was their mother-goddess, the mistress of the great temple in Ephesus, one of the seven wonders of the ancient world. The breasts signified her fertility.

I was attempting to use this image once while preaching in Poland. At the mention of the word 'breasts', my female interpreter went bright red with embarrassment and immediately stopped interpreting. She informed me, in the middle of the sermon, that although she knew the Polish word, she couldn't possibly use it in church. After some quick thinking, I changed the words in order to continue the message! Apparently, Winston Churchill encountered the same communication problem in the United States during the First World War. When offered chicken at a reception in Richmond, Virginia, he innocently asked for 'breast'. To which the shocked hostess replied that polite people use the word 'white meat' to describe that part of the chicken's anatomy! The next day, the ever-resourceful Churchill sent some flowers to the hostess with a note attached saying, 'I would be most obliged if you would pin this corsage on your white meat'![1]

The reason that I am telling you this story is not only to illustrate the innumerable communication problems that each one of us encounter every day, but also to illicit in some of you the same response as the hostess in Richmond. If the word 'breast' is a taboo word in your vocabulary, you may have been somewhat surprised that I used it at the start of the chapter and may have already prejudged my attitudes and motives. If that is the case, the message that I am trying to convey in the rest of the chapter will be tainted by your prejudice. Please forgive me! I don't want to offend you, but I do want to show you how easy it is to have a breakdown in communication. In fact, it is often significantly easier to destroy a bridge than it is to build one!

The way we get round these problems is to study the whole topic of communication: hence this book. As the Australian social commentator Hugh Mackay puts it, 'Communication is probably one of your favourite subjects – and so it should be. After all, we humans are "herd animals". We belong to communities. We thrive on relationships. We need to communicate.'[2] However, we also need to know how communication works. This is especially true if we are preachers attempting to bridge the hermeneutical gap between what the Bible meant to its writers and what it means to its readers: or as Fee and Stuart put it, 'moving from the "then and there" of the original text to the "here and now" of our own life settings'.[3] This can prove to be a seemingly insurmountable problem. After all, how can I, as an Englishman, accurately communicate a modern paraphrase of a new edition of an old translation of a Latin version of a Hebrew text to a Russian speaker in Australia?! It is these very complexities of the science of communication that demand that we break the whole process down into some simple but fundamentally necessary parts. Let me illustrate why this is important.

My aunt was a great cook! I particularly remember a groundnut stew that she had perfected when living in Africa. After her dinner parties, her guests would often ask for the recipes. Apparently, she would always oblige but, unbeknown to them, would leave out an essential ingredient! Their attempts at emulating her skills were therefore unsuccessful! The truth is, although the whole is greater than the sum of the parts, we need to know the parts in order to recreate the whole! Similarly, bridge-builders need the eyes of an architect and the fingers of a surveyor. We need to be able to see the whole and yet also count the parts! Although a bridge works as a complete unit, it consists of numerous components. It is only as we identify and understand the functions and qualities of these individual ingredients and learn how they fit together that we can create a masterpiece.

All of us want to build these great bridges: we long for successful relationships and strive to communicate effectively. Yet so often we get bogged down in details. When we tour a natural bridge we tend to be more fascinated in the number of rivets that it contains than the pillars on which it stands. We approach couples who have been together for fifty years and ask them their secret. One advises, 'Say "thank you" regularly.' Another reflects mistily, 'We hold hands every day' and yet another says, 'Never go to bed angry.' Yet, although this is all good advice, they are details and not the foundations on which their bridge is built. What we need to discover are the indispensable factors that make a bridge a bridge.

In her book on bridges, Judith Dupré begins with what she calls 'Bridge Basics'. In it she states, 'The distance between the main supports of a bridge is its *span* ... the plank across a stream is a *simple span*. A *continuous span* is supported along its length by *piers*; the outermost supports are *abutments*' (italics hers).[4] In other words, although she goes onto explain numerous fascinating details of bridge design she starts with the simplest of examples, a 'plank across a stream'. In communication terms, the 'basics' consist of seven ingredients. Each of these seven ingredients introduces a principle and contains a number of problems. Knowledge of these seven factors and how they work together can help us immeasurably in our bridge-building with one another.

The first abutment – the sender

The construction of the immense steel arch which forms the basis of the Sydney Harbour Bridge began on 26 October 1928. It was built by two half-arches being cantilevered from either side of the harbour. Of the two sides of the arch, the southern end, at Dawes' Point, was the initiator. By November 1929 it was well ahead of the northern arm, although the latter caught up and overtook its counterpart near the end of the project. These giant arms, supported by steel tendons, stretched toward each other until their ends, like hands longing to clasp, touched each other for the first time at 4.15 p.m. on 19 August 1930. They were finally joined later that day, amid much celebration. It was a successful courtship! After the half-arches of the bridge were riveted together, the cables that held each of them in place and had kept them apart were slackened and removed. They were no longer needed as the two halves were now drawing strength from each other. As Leonardo da Vinci described it, 'An arch consists of two weaknesses which leaning one against the other make a strength'.[5]

In every relationship, of which this is a good image, there are two parties seeking to be connected. At first, the two are totally self-supporting. Although they can live successfully on their own, they seek the added strength of partnership. Inevitably, however, one of these parties will take the initiative. In communication terms, the instigator of a message is called the 'sender'. Although both the 'sender' and the 'receiver' are equally responsible for the eventual success of the connection, the 'sender' must start the process. Jesus, for instance, taught that if someone is bearing a grudge against us because of our sinful behaviour, we need to take the initiative for the reunion (Matthew 5:23–24). If, on the other hand, someone sins against us, we are still required to take the first step toward reconciliation (Matthew 18:15). In both cases, we are required to be 'senders'.

Sooner or later, somebody has to take responsibility. Of course, the receiver also has a responsibility to listen carefully and hear the message, but if we are going to be successful communicators we must see it as our role as senders to ensure that our message gets through to others. As a former biology teacher, I would have loved to blame the students for their poor performances and their inability to learn in my class, but that would not have been good teaching. As Bruce Wilkinson says, 'Teachers are responsible to cause students to learn.'[6] Equally, this responsibility falls squarely on the shoulders of the parents in a home or the leaders in a community. It is not the congregation's fault if they get bored during a sermon: it is the preacher's!

I believe, however, that most of us are reticent to be 'senders'. In the area of courtship, there is often a marked reservation 'to make the first move' and ask someone out. In the public arena, many of us are trapped by a 'fear of public speaking'. We simply don't want to carry the responsibility. We are worried we will have nothing to say or are concerned about the possible reaction of the audience. 'What if they reject me?' 'What if they don't like what I say?' 'Let someone else do it.'

When reconciliation is involved, even the extroverts among us are not really inclined to take initiative. 'Why should I bother to speak to him; if he wants to get offended that's his problem', is a common retort. Or conversely, 'Why should I have to go to her; she is the one who messed up.' Either way, it is always someone else's fault! These excuses are the enemies of loving communication and must be eradicated. They include blame-shifting, diminishment, misrepresentation and pride. Each of them has a recognizable language. In a marriage breakdown, the adulterous husband's defence to a counsellor may sound something like, 'It's not my fault. If she ever had sex with me I wouldn't have looked elsewhere [*blame-shifting*]. She always was a lousy lover [*diminishment*]. I tried to tell her that I wasn't satisfied, but she never listens [*misrepresentation*]. What do you expect me to do? Beg for forgiveness? You have to be kidding [*pride*]! As I said, it's all her fault anyway!' Had this husband followed the biblical counsel and taken responsibility for being a 'sender' by first loving his wife *'as Christ loved the church'* (Ephesians 5:25), he may well have not ended up in the counsellor's office with a broken marriage.

The first pylon – encoding

The weight of the Sydney Harbour Bridge is carried by the steel arch that abuts into either side of the harbour. The main bridge deck is hung from this arch. The four stone pylons at each end of the Sydney Harbour Bridge are primarily ornamental. Although they support some of the roadway, part of which goes through them, they are really there to provide what Dupré describes as 'visual reassurance'. Nonetheless they provide a filtering point for the approaches to the bridge and an image for us. The transport that travels daily across the bridge goes between and through these pylons. They are a necessary part of the smooth routine of the bridge. If you want to cross the bridge in a car or by foot, there are numerous routes that you can take. People jostle for position on the approaches to the bridge. Some of the lane dividers are mobile in order to direct the traffic appropriately. A traffic jam or accident on such a vital artery through the city can prove disastrous and so the options are carefully monitored and reduced until finally the pylons are reached and the laneways fixed. They remain fixed until the other end of the bridge where the options once again are many and varied.

In our communication model, this process of filtering is called 'encoding'. If we choose to communicate with someone, there are many ways by which we can do so. Our goal is to use a method that will effectively convey our message to the other party. Our 'transport' must arrive safely and unchanged at the other end of the bridge. What we are trying to avoid is an 'accident' that will inevitably result in miscommunication. As we approach the conversation we automatically choose the appropriate words to use and filter out the possibly confusing options. The principle that we use is to select a route that aligns with the receiver, the other end of the bridge. The problem that most of us have in this process of encoding is simply selfishness. Instead of thinking of the other person and the way they may interpret our message, we tend to think of ourselves and how we want to convey it.

When I was training as a biology teacher I attempted to teach the subject of osmosis to a class of teenagers. It was chaos! Although I knew a great deal about the subject, I struggled to simplify the concept for my students. It was as though I had six lanes of information at my end of the bridge and they only had one lane at theirs. Eventually, my exasperated supervisor took over. She knew much more than I and yet quickly and simply explained the principle. I was embarrassed and the students were impressed! She had encoded her knowledge into their language. It was a lesson I will never forget. I realized that until I could convert uncommon ideas into common language I would never be a good teacher.

Jesus Christ, for instance, was passionate about His message being heard and so despite containing *'all the treasures of wisdom and knowledge'* (Colossians 2:3) told profound truths in uncomplicated stories and the *'common people heard him gladly'* (Mark 12:37).[7] Winston Churchill's word power was prodigious. He had a phenomenal grasp of the English language as is evidenced in his books. Yet, when he spoke to a nation he would only use the simplest and best of words. He once said, 'I like short words'.[8] One of his five rules of public speaking was 'simple language'.[9] Why did he choose to communicate in this way? Because he was thinking of his audience and not himself. When it comes to my communication to my wife, family or friends, I must unselfishly learn their languages and encode my love accordingly. As the Bible says,

> *'An unreliable messenger can cause a lot of trouble. Reliable communication permits progress.'* (Proverbs 13:17)[10]

The simple span – the message

A constant stream of all sorts of traffic flows across the Sydney Harbour Bridge. Apart from the eight lanes of road, there are two rail tracks, a cycle track and a pedestrian walkway. There are many ways to cross a bridge! That is a lesson we all need to learn when it comes to communicating with others. We tend not only to think that there is only one way to converse but also that the way we have always done so is the right way. Many of us are very stubborn when our message is not getting through. Instead of changing our methodology, we become frustrated and so jeopardize the relationship. I remember once encountering a particularly unpleasant Englishman on a train in Yugoslavia who couldn't make the guard understand his request. Instead of politely asking for help from someone who could speak the language, he started swearing at the guard, his voice becoming louder and louder the more the innocent official failed to understand. Eventually, amid a torrent of abuse, I was called in as a fellow English tourist to pacify the irate man. I very nearly lost my place on the train despite only being a bystander! However, the reality is that, though the 'tourist abroad' is famous for his ignorance, the majority of miscommunication takes place within the privacy of our homes.

What we need to grasp is that communication is more than words. We communicate with everything that we are, think, speak and do! We communicate by our mouths, our manner and our mannerisms. We communicate with the clothes we wear and places we live. We even communicate with our spirit. For example, our words in other mouths may carry a different meaning. In a well-documented study on personal communication Professor Mehrabian of UCLA suggested that there are three elements to our language: verbal (words) (7 per cent), vocal (e.g. intonation) (38 per cent) and visual (e.g. facial expression) (55 per cent)![11] In a study on the believability of these various aspects of our communication, Mehrabian discovered that when an inconsistent message is given we will tend to believe the visual element before the vocal or verbal elements. We can, therefore, easily detect insincerity ('"It's OK," he said, smiling through his teeth'), become offended at someone's manner ('It was not what he said but the way he said it that upset me') and judge people's appearance ('I didn't like the look of him').

When we first got married, my wife blamed me one day for being selfish! I was shocked, especially when she told me the reason. Every time she kindly decided to iron one of my shirts for me, she had to undo all the buttons first which frustrated her immensely! I had the habit of removing my shirts by pulling them over my head without undoing the buttons and then putting them for washing. It was what I had always done! Of course I expressed my gratefulness but my unconscious actions were communicating thoughtlessness not thankfulness. It was a proof that 'actions speak louder than words' and a lesson to me that love is communicated in a host of different ways and the quicker I learned them the better! Years later, she never has to undo a single button!

The second pylon – decoding

On 13 July 1966 the restriction for lane-changing on the Sydney Harbour Bridge was abolished. Motorists can now change lanes in between the pylons. In other words, although the laneways are fixed and the lanes and traffic passing through the second pylon are exactly the same as the first, the configuration of the traffic can now change. What the second pylon 'receives' is slightly different from what the first pylon 'sends'. A complex system of traffic monitors and indicators assess and control these changes, especially at times of peak traffic, in order to avoid or compensate for an accident. This is a powerful image of the problems of communication between two parties.

When I preach I am often shocked at the disconnection that occurs between the words that I speak and the words that are heard! I have often had a discussion with a member of a congregation after a church service who is convinced that I said something that I didn't say. When the video, tape or other people are consulted and it becomes clear what was actually said, the individual sometimes becomes intransigent: 'Well, I know what I heard, and it's not what you say that you said!' What we are seeing here is a problem of decoding! The traffic is crossing over between pylons! The same communication problem operates in the field of genetics. Information is passed from one generation to another via a genetic code. Sometimes, however, in the process of information exchange some sort of mutation or change takes place that causes the process to go awry. The information received is not the same as that passed down. The traffic is crossing over between generations!

The principle that we must be aware of if we are to receive the exact messages that are sent is that we all 'read' messages through our past hurt, our present circumstances and our prejudged expectations. In other words, we screen or decode messages through a filter, and occasionally that filter is not always clean! For instance, when I teach on the subject of relationships, occasionally I have read out a list of common words and asked the audience to write down their immediate feelings when I mentioned them. I then compare their answers. If I use the word 'father', for example, the feelings swing from 'love' and 'security' to 'hatred' and 'pain'. Their recorded emotions reflect their past. What I am attempting to illustrate to them is the difference between denotation and connotation. If we look up the word 'father' in the dictionary, it has a literal meaning or denotation, yet it may, as we have seen, have a completely different specific meaning or connotation to each of us. So if I use the phrase 'God is our Father' without explanation from the pulpit I am in danger of being mis-interpreted since everyone will decode the phrase differently. On top of the problem of connotation, people tend to add their feelings of rejection, their poisoned perceptions and their ill-informed expecta-tions. As 'senders' we are at pains to express clearly what is in our heart and yet we hear comments from the 'receivers' to indicate that our message is not getting through: 'When you mention forgiveness I feel ...' (connotation); 'When you say, "God loves you", I know that you couldn't mean me because ...' (rejection); 'I could have sworn that you said ...' (perception); 'I really thought that you were going to say ...' (expectation). Once again, a simple knowledge of these 'road conditions' can help prevent people getting hurt.

The second abutment – the receiver

The fact that the 'sender' of a message must take the initiative in communication, does not mean the 'receiver' is passive: quite the contrary. Many people, for instance, think of petition as 'one-way' communication. God is the 'Source' or 'Sender' and we are simply recipients. After all, the Bible says, *'For everyone who asks receives'* (Matthew 7:8) and the receiving suggests passivity. Yet the word for 'receive' here (Gk. *lambano*) is active and can be translated 'take' or 'lay hold of'. There is an action involved in receiving a gift. This is a lesson that some people who are passively waiting for the gift of the Holy Spirit need to hear. We need gratefully and actively to take the gift that was given to the Church on the Day of Pentecost.

On a similar note, a preacher will often encourage congregational participation, because they need to be active listeners. Almost as much energy needs to be exerted by the audience as by the speaker. There is an art to listening and it is the responsibility of the receiver to learn the necessary skills, and through feedback and reflection ensure that the true message has been heard. This was the commended and expected response of the Bereans when Paul the apostle visited them.

> *'Now the Bereans were of more noble character than the Thessalonians, for they received the message with great eagerness and examined the Scriptures every day to see if what Paul said was true.'*   (Acts 17:11)

Listening, however, is more than an art: it is a science, and one that we would do well to study. Apparently the Chinese character meaning 'to listen' incorporates the characters for undivided attention, ear, eyes and heart, which give us some indication of the expertise required. Larry Barker, in his book *Listening Behavior*,[12] also suggests that listening contains four separate components: hearing, attending, understanding and remembering. There is obviously a great deal of difference between listening and just hearing. Many husbands hear their wives but don't listen to them! As Mackay explains, 'The difference between hearing and listening is crucial in communication. When I hear, I simply receive a message which I may or may not think about. When I listen, I am involved in the transaction: I am not just hearing what you say, but I am attending, understanding and interpreting'.[13] The true 'receiver' of a message must therefore do more than hear it, they must listen to it. In order to do this effectively we need to take active steps to remove the barriers to listening, such as an inappropriate mindset ('I don't need to hear this'), internal distraction ('Sorry, I was miles away') and downright selfishness which includes interrupting a conversation because we think we have something better to say! As the Bible says,

> *'He who answers before listening –*
> *that is his folly and his shame.'*   (Proverbs 18:13)

When I was at school, I had the opportunity to fly as a passenger in a two-seater plane for which I was required to wear a parachute. Prior to my flight, the pilot instructed me what to do in an emergency. He started with a harrowing account of how a previous student had died by refusing to obey orders. Years later, I still remember exactly what he said because my life depended on it! I made the necessary effort to focus on his message, removed all distractions and said to myself, 'I need to hear this.' I didn't interrupt him once! If only we would put the same value on the sermons we hear or our conversations with our children, friends or partners.

Traffic hazards – noise

When the idea of climbing the Sydney Harbour Bridge as a tourist attraction was proposed not only was it met with an array of regulations but with objections highlighting the possible dangers, such as: 'The climbers would be a distraction to the motorists'; 'It could cause accidents'; 'What if a climber dropped something onto the road?' Years later, having overcome all these obstacles, the climbers ascend the long stairs safely attached to cables, camouflaged in 'bridge metal grey' and with even their handkerchiefs attached to their wrists! Of course the authorities were right: every potential traffic hazard must be avoided, if at all possible, in order to maintain traffic flow and safety standards. This is especially true at 'rush hour'. In communication jargon, the distractions that inhibit the traffic flow of words from sender to receiver are called 'noise'. (The word 'noise' describes all distractions, not just auditory ones.) In order for a message to be received by an 'audience' this 'noise' must be recognized, removed or, at the very least, reduced.

As a teacher, I have discovered that 'noise' in a classroom can range from the tiredness of the students to the uncomfortable seats or the temperature of the room. I must therefore do everything in my power to create an environment that is conducive to listening and learning. As a married couple, what we have discovered is that the timing of communication is crucial. Although my wife has a prodigious ability, in common with many women, to do numerous things at once, if I attempt to discuss something with her when she is cooking, I will be in trouble! She in turn has found out that if she tries to tell me some important news just as I come back from work or just as I return from a trip abroad, she is met with a completely blank look! Later, I will be blamed for being disinterested in her news and I will protest that she never told me. If, on the other hand, we communicate at the evening meal, the 'rush hour' is over, all the 'noise' has gone and conversation flows smoothly! As a consequence of these simple discoveries, watching television has always been banned in our family at mealtimes because that is when we talk. Whatever 'house rules' are imposed, I would recommend that every married couple avoids the 'rush hour' and thereby travels more safely!

Two-way traffic – feedback

In order to simplify the process of communication, I have illustrated how words flow from sender to receiver. In effect, I have described a bridge with 'one-way traffic', the transport moving across the span, through the pylons, from one abutment to the other. In reality, of course, communication is far more complicated than this. Like conversations, most bridges are 'two way'. Each end of the bridge is both 'sender' and 'receiver', often at the same time. In the case of Sydney Harbour Bridge, vehicles are constantly crossing in both directions. In a communication model, part of this two-way traffic is called feedback and is essential for conveying something accurately.

Good teaching, for instance, requires constant feedback. A teacher must know that his or her message is getting through and therefore will ask for an audience response in order to establish this. As a teacher, I am always teased for saying, 'Are you getting this?' 'Do you see?' or 'Does this make sense?' in the middle of my message. However, even Jesus did this. In the middle of teaching His disciples, He asked, *'Have you understood all these things?'* (Matthew 13:51). He was looking for some feedback!

True preaching, on the other hand, is more persuasive and therefore is more of a monologue and less of a dialogue. However, although this may be commendable in the pulpit it is inexcusable in the home! As a preacher, I have to learn to stop pontificating to my children and preaching to my wife and learn to shut up and listen! The Bible makes this clear:

> *'My dear brothers, take note of this: Everyone should be quick to listen, slow to speak and slow to become angry.'*   (James 1:19)

> *'When words are many, sin is not absent,*
>   *but he who holds his tongue is wise.'*   (Proverbs 10:19)

Nonetheless, as a leader in my home I do need to have a vision for my family, but I have to communicate this vision effectively. If, through lack of interaction and feedback, my family do not see what I see, then I have failed in my role as husband and father.

Summary and advice

1. **A simple model of communication can be represented by the components of a bridge.** If we fail to understand the seven ingredients of communication our 'relational bridges' are likely to collapse.

2. **The first abutment represents the sender.** The sender needs to initiate the process of communication and take responsibility for the message 'getting through'.

3. **The first pylon represents encoding.** The sender of a message must code it simply and selflessly so that it is clear and loving.

4. **The simple span represents the message.** Communication is more than words. We communicate with everything we are, speak, think and do.

5. **The second pylon represents decoding.** When we hear a message we automatically interpret and filter it. If our filter is polluted the process will be flawed.

6. **The second abutment represents the receiver.** The recipient of a message is not passive but actively involved in the communication process. A huge barrier to effective listening is an inappropriate mindset.

7. **Traffic hazards represent 'noise'.** In communication, 'noise' describes those distractions that prevent the passage of the message. These 'accidents' need to be avoided!

8. **Two-way traffic represents feedback.** Communication is a two-way process. As teachers we all need feedback and therefore have to learn when to be quiet and listen!

Notes

1. Winston Churchill. Quoted in James Humes, *The Language of Leadership* (The Business Library, 1991).
2. Hugh Mackay, *Why Don't People Listen?* (Pan Macmillan Publishers Australia, 1994).
3. Gordon D. Fee and Douglas Stuart, *How to Read the Bible for all Its Worth* (Zondervan, 1993).
4. Judith Dupré, *Bridges* (Könemann, 1998).
5. Leonardo da Vinci. Quoted in Mario Salvadori, *Why Buildings Stand Up* (W.W. Norton & Co., 1980).
6. Bruce Wilkinson, *The Seven Laws of the Learner* (Multnomah Press, 1992).

7. The Holy Bible, The King James Version (Cambridge, 1769).

8. Winston Churchill, Margate, 10 October 1953. Quoted in J.A. Sutcliffe (ed.), *The Sayings of Winston Churchill* (Duckworth & Co. Ltd, 1992).

9. Winston Churchill. Quoted in James C. Humes, *The Language of Leadership* (The Business Library, 1991).

10. Living Bible (Tyndale House, 1971).

11. Professor A. Mehrabian. Quoted in B. Decker, *The Art of Communicating* (Crisp Publications, Inc., 1988).

12. Larry L. Barker, *Listening Behavior* (Prentice Hall, 1971).

13. Hugh Mackay, *Why Don't People Listen?* (Pan Macmillan Australia, 1994).

Chapter 10

Traffic Lights

The Power and Control of Our Words

Every day tens of thousands of vehicles queue at the Sydney Harbour Bridge toll gates in order to go south into the city of Sydney. For many drivers the resultant traffic jams are a constant cause of complaint! They would like the Harbour Bridge simply to be a powerful icon, a magnificent stage for the New Year's fireworks and above all a free access to work! However, a bridge without traffic is a contradiction in terms. The toll, the congestion and the potential accidents are all part of the cost of communication. The answer is effective traffic management and not toll avoidance.

Bridges are designed for traffic. Their purpose centres around their ability to promote communication. Abraham Darby's Iron Bridge in Coalbrookdale in England was closed to vehicular traffic in 1934. It was one hundred and fifty-five years old at the time and was officially termed an 'ancient monument'.[1] As I have already described in a previous chapter, it remains an extraordinarily elegant piece of engineering and is still visited by numerous tourists. Yet its design prevented its ability to change along with the traffic conditions. It therefore became obsolete. It may now be the highlight of a museum visit but it no longer maintains the significant place in the town for which it was lovingly conceived. It is no longer an essential artery, and a bridge without traffic is like a vessel without blood.

Although there is merit in visiting the Iron Bridge out of historical interest there is no joy in visiting a life bridge that is similarly positioned. A relationship without communication is moribund. It is either dead or bleeding to death. I have had the sad task of going to many homes where the communication has broken down, in order to attempt to bring reconciliation. In many cases the husband has been profane and abusive, the wife brooding and silent and the children rejected and confused. In other situations it has been the teenagers who have been the culprits. In every instance, I have come away with a heightened understanding of the power of words to corrupt and destroy. However, I have also had the privilege of staying in many homes where the language has been positive and uplifting. The difference between the two is staggering.

A functional bridge, like a relationship, must facilitate a smooth traffic flow that brings credit to its designer, suits its capability and serves the world in which it is placed. Traffic congestion is avoided by effective direction of both the individual vehicles and the overall flow of traffic. Traffic lights, for example, serve this purpose. They are vital to a town because there is nothing like a traffic jam to enrage individuals or stall communities! It is therefore in everybody's best interest if we learn how traffic behaves both positively and negatively and how we can control and direct it. In each of our lives traffic consists of the words we use and the way we use them. If our life bridges are to bring benefit they must include working traffic lights!

Traffic is an indicator

In June 1976, the one billionth vehicle crossed the Sydney Harbour Bridge! This incredible statistic is an indication of the popularity and the necessity of the bridge. After it was opened in 1932 the average daily traffic volume in both directions was just fewer than eleven thousand vehicles whereas at its seventieth anniversary in 2002 the figure was nearer one hundred and sixty thousand vehicles. As the city has grown, the traffic flow across the bridge has increased steadily with a few notable exceptions. In 1943, for instance, the crossings were down to less than nine thousand vehicles a day due to wartime vehicle shortage and petrol rationing. There was also a sudden dip in the daily traffic when the Harbour Tunnel opened in 1992. All of these figures are clear indicators of the growth and prosperity of the city, the usefulness and limitations of the bridge and also the alternatives that are available. If traffic is a good analogy for communication in our relationships, then we would also expect communication to be an indicator. Our character, for instance, determines whether we are loquacious or taciturn. We are also told that women speak at least twice as many words in a day than men. Although with my ability to talk at length I rather think that this would be untrue in our family! We also know that words tell us a great deal about the moods and morals of those around us. There is no doubt that verbal traffic is an indicator of our personalities, our gender and our attitudes.

When challenging the Pharisees, Jesus Christ made it abundantly clear that the evil words they spoke were the fruit of their hearts and that fruit does not lie.

> *'Make a tree good and its fruit will be good, or make a tree bad and its fruit will be bad, for a tree is recognised by its fruit. You brood of vipers, how can you who are evil say anything good? For out of the overflow of the heart the mouth speaks. The good man brings good things out of the good stored up in him, and the evil man brings evil things out of the evil stored up in him.'* (Matthew 12:33–35)

If we think that we are neither Pharisees nor vipers we are sadly mistaken! The Bible teaches that all of us are sinners and that wrong-doing finds its expression in what we say. Speaking of Jew and Gentile alike it says,

> *'Their throats are open graves;*
> *their tongues practice deceit.*
> *The poison of vipers is on their lips.*
> *Their mouths are full of cursing and bitterness.'*
> (Romans 3:13–14)

Despite the sociologists telling us that we are all inherently good, the Bible categorically states that without God in our lives our hearts are wicked (Jeremiah 17:9) and our words betray our condition. There is no better way of discovering what is in people's lives than listening to them when they are under duress or when they drop a brick on their foot! Our words definitely describe the condition of our heart!

Martin Luther King had a dream for the state of Alabama that he voiced in his famous speech given in Washington in 1963. In it he describes the opposition of the current governor whose 'lips' were 'dripping with the words of interposition and nullification'.[2] He judged that the governor's opposing words revealed a prejudiced heart.

Whether we like it or not our words, however disguised, will eventually expose our heart motives. Our idiolect, the words that we regularly use and the way we use them, is an accurate gauge. It measures what is in a person. In this case, the governor's lips were a gauge of his prejudice, but lips can also be a gauge of other passions or poisons in our life, our intimacy or our impurity. When Moses, for instance, was making excuses about his commission he said to God,

> *'If the Israelites will not listen to me, why would Pharaoh listen to me, since I speak with faltering lips?'*   (Exodus 6:12)

It was a dangerous comment since it manifested an attitude that had previously incurred God's wrath (Exodus 4:1–14). The word 'faltering' is translated 'uncircumcised'[3] in some versions of the Bible. Apparently, his uncommitted heart had found expression on uncertain lips.

However, at least Moses was honest about his faults. There are many who attempt to disguise their failings with flattery and dishonesty or, in the case of the Pharisees, hypocrisy. As Jesus said,

> *'Isaiah was right when he prophesied about you hypocrites; as it is written: "These people honour me with their lips, but their hearts are far from me."'*   (Mark 7:6)

All of us have the capacity to do this. We say one thing but think another. It may take the fairly innocent form of, 'Just what I always wanted', when receiving a useless gift from a distant aunt or it may be the more serious 'I love you' when our heart and actions clearly deny it! Either way our insincerity will be discovered. As the book of Proverbs says,

> *'A malicious man disguises himself with his lips,*
> *   but in his heart he harbours deceit.*
> *Though his speech is charming, do not believe him,*
> *   for seven abominations fill his heart.*
> *His malice may be concealed by deception,*
> *   but his wickedness will be exposed in the assembly.'*
>   (Proverbs 26:24–26)

Since our verbal traffic will always give us away, it would be wise to change our heart and not just our words.

Traffic has power

I have described how traffic flow is an indicator of the usefulness of a bridge and the affection with which it is held in the community. But now I want to look at the power that it has either to damage or serve the bridge. Bridges are regularly destroyed by the vehicles that they are meant to carry or the vessels which are intended to pass through their span. I have already mentioned the destruction of the Hobart Bridge in 1975 that was caused by the sudden impact of a ship. However, normally the process is more gradual. The failure of the Mianus River Bridge on 27 June 1983 in Connecticut is a case in point. The story reveals a pattern common to many disasters. Unnoticed weaknesses and corrosion develops in a poorly designed bridge over a number of years and the 'Repeated pounding of the traffic causes a fatigue crack to develop ... initiating the collapse'.[4] Despite carrying over one hundred thousand vehicles every day, the three of them that ended in the river were the final load that broke the bridge's back.

The Mianus tragedy is a sobering parable for every one of our relationships. Our communication, the verbal traffic that we carry daily, is normally beneficial for us. So it should be. We are designed for it. It serves us and brings connection, prosperity and even credibility to our lives. Nonetheless, this traffic does add pressure and if the traffic is uncontrolled, the load too great or our relational bridge flawed, it can injure us irreparably. What is meant for blessing becomes a curse. When describing blessings and curses, Derek Prince writes that, 'They are vehicles of supernatural, spiritual power. Blessings produce good and beneficial results; curses produce bad and harmful results'.[5] It is because of this power that we have to be very circumspect about our language. However, it is not so much the few damaging words that pass between us in one day that usually cause the problems; it is the years of 'repeated pounding', the recurring negativity! Most of us can put up with a few harsh words, but it is the continual complaining or nagging that is really hard to take! The Bible gives the example of a contentious woman being *'like a constant dripping on a rainy day'* (Proverbs 27:15). It is like 'acid rain' that destroys trees. Each drip or word by itself, although corrosive, is relatively harmless, but a regular flow over a decade can strip a forest bare! Our words can have the same devastating effect in our lives. They can curse us or bless us, hurt or heal, guide us into God's purpose for our lives or steer us far from it. It is therefore essential that we control them, but before we do that we need to know how they work.

Our words decide the condition of our soul

Prior to becoming a Christian in 1974 I was desperately insecure about my life. I used to learn swear words so that I could protect myself by insulting others! I was rebellious and unforgiven and my heart attitude was expressed in the words of profanity and blasphemy. My church-going mother was often shocked at my language and made it clear that I needed to stop. I agreed with her but found it impossible to change my behaviour. Swearing came naturally. My words clearly indicated the condition of my unclean soul. My 'heart' was in my mouth! Yet on the day that I became a Christian the swearing instantly and miraculously stopped. I cannot remember swearing since. In fact I have often felt nauseous if I even thought of doing so! Why the change? I was encouraged not only to change my faith but also to change my confession. On that day, I read the passage in the Bible which states,

> *'That if you confess with your mouth, "Jesus is Lord," and believe in your heart that God raised him from the dead, you will be saved. For it is with your heart that you believe and are justified, and it is with your mouth that you confess and are saved.'*   (Romans 10:9–10)

The act of not only believing that Jesus died for me but speaking out that He was now the Lord of my life changed me completely. The words that I spoke were a necessary part of deciding the condition of my soul. The tongue, though small, has a great part to play in our lives.

Our words direct the course of our life

The book of James compares taming the tongue with riding a horse! This image doesn't fill me with confidence since I was never very good with horses! My father used to say of them, 'They are dangerous in front, dangerous behind and uncomfortable in the middle!' I tend to share his caution. However, my limited experience taught me that a little movement of the reins can cause a massive and often sudden change of direction! As James says,

> *'When we put bits into the mouths of horses to make them obey us, we can turn the whole animal. Or take ships as an example. Although they*

*are so large and are driven by strong winds, they are steered by a very
small rudder wherever the pilot wants to go.'* (James 3:3–4)

James suggests that our tongue has the same power as a bit or a
rudder. Our lives can be guided by simple, purposeful and gradual
changes of our confession. If we want to win in life and follow the
divine course that is set out for us we need to harness what we say. If,
on the other hand, we want our lives to be shipwrecked we can
deliberately direct our lives accordingly! We speak ourselves onto
the rocks! Whether we like it or not our words will direct the course of
our life.

In the Old Testament, for instance, when God had freed the
Israelites from slavery and was leading them to a land of promise, they
grumbled against their leader Moses and therefore, by default, God's
plan for their lives. At one point they actually said, *'If only we had died
in Egypt! Or in this desert!'* (Numbers 14:2). It seems like a harmless
statement until we realize it indicated their rebellious heart attitude.
The consequences of their self-destructive words were catastrophic.
God responded to them by saying,

> *'So tell them, "As surely as I live, declares the* Lord, **I will do to you the
> very things I heard you say** ... *"'*
> (Numbers 14:28, emphasis mine)

The Israelites had effectively condemned themselves to a life of
needless drudgery in the wilderness. If we continually bring a bad
report about our lives and future we should not be surprised when we
end up living a self-fulfilling prophecy. No wonder a young and
insecure Jeremiah, when commissioned by God, was told, *'Do not
say, "I am only a child"'* (Jeremiah 1:7, emphasis mine). Jesus reiterated
this concept when He taught,

> *'So do not worry, **saying**, "What shall we eat?" or "What shall we
> drink?" or "What shall we wear?"'*
> (Matthew 6:31, emphasis mine)

He was concerned that the slightest shift in our speech slowly but
irrevocably moves us in the right or the wrong direction. Jesus knew
that we can change our life by degrees.

Our words dictate the extent of our success

God did not create humanity to fail. Consequently, we like to focus on success; we tend to record the winners of events and not the losers. It reminds us of our past and inspires us to strive for a better future. Most Bible students, for instance, can name the two successful spies, Joshua and Caleb, and yet cannot name one of the ten Israelite spies who failed to enter the Promised Land, despite the fact that all their names are recorded in the book of Numbers! Unfortunately, the Children of Israel focused on failure instead, believed and repeated the bad report of the ten spies and suffered needlessly until their generation had died out. The good confession of Joshua and Caleb, on the other hand, opened up the entire Promised Land both for them and also the subsequent generation. It was their positive words that played such an integral part in dictating their success. When the land finally stretched out before them God gave them a command:

> *'Do not let this Book of the Law depart from your mouth; meditate on it day and night, so that you may be careful to do everything written in it. Then you will be prosperous and successful.'* (Joshua 1:8)

Their words, thoughts and actions enabled them to enter their blessing and also enabled them to possess it.

It is evident that God also wants us to be prosperous and successful. Jesus Christ desires fruitfulness for His disciples.

> *'If you remain in me, and my words remain in you, ask whatever you wish, and it will be given you. This is to my Father's glory, that you bear much fruit, showing yourselves to be my disciples.'*
> (John 15:7–8)

If we recognized the power of words to access His desire I believe that many of us would be much more fruitful. The book of Revelation tells us that we defeat Satan, the accuser, by Jesus' blood and the word of our testimony (Revelation 12:11). The book of Proverbs reveals that our words have the capacity to fill or empty us, free or ensnare us, defend or destroy us: they pave the way for our blessing.

> *'From the fruit of his lips a man is filled with good things as surely as the work of his hands rewards him.'* (Proverbs 12:14)

We not only choose our path by choosing our words, we also choose the extent of our blessing. Our words set the boundaries. By saying 'I love you' to my wife, 'I am proud of you' to my child and 'I appreciate you' to my friend, I am knowingly building for a prosperous future. If, on the other hand, I tear them down with doubting and 'saprotic' words,[6] then I am deliberately diminishing them and limiting our future together. When God wants to enlarge and stretch us and bring us to a 'spacious place' (Psalm 18:19) it is a tragedy when we consistently let our tongues restrict us.

Our words define the language of our heart

I have travelled to many cities around the world where the traffic conditions are horrendous: not only in volume but also in chaos! There seems to be no rhyme or reason about it and there is definitely no control. Every time you drive or cross the road you take your life into your hands! Even when there are traffic lights, people seem to take no notice. When you challenge the system, they simply shrug and say, 'That's the way we do things around here. Get used to it!' In Rome, for instance, the traffic conditions reflect the passionate culture of the inhabitants! There is a great deal of shouting, horn blowing and hand waving! This is fine until it becomes destructive and then there is a danger of saying, 'We can't change'. Clearly, traffic conditions are indicative but that doesn't mean that we just accept the status quo. If our culture or background is damaging our life we should change it!

When it comes to our verbal traffic, many of us are equally accepting. We tend to be very passive about the way we communicate. We allow our traditions, habits and circumstances to control our speech rather than taking control of it ourselves. Our expressions reflect our attitude and give us away: 'My mother used to say ...'; 'I always say ...'; 'I can't help it, it's just the way I speak ...'! The book of James does warn us that, *no man can tame the tongue. It is a restless evil, full of deadly poison* (James 3:8), but, with God's help, it is controllable. Since our heart determines our language, the first step is to change and guard our heart. However, there is a sense in which our words also define the language of our heart. The Bible describes our heart as a 'tablet' (Proverbs 3:3) on which we can write and our tongues as a 'pen' (Psalm 45:1) with which we can write! I am aware that this is poetic and metaphorical language, but it does suggest that we can change our heart by what we say. Our faith confession can change our heart at conversion and can also change it afterwards. There are many times when I have spoken myself into a position of faith. I choose to speak the word of God until my own heart hears it and believes! It was said of John Wesley that he preached faith until he believed it himself. He wasn't prepared to accept the status quo. We should have the same attitude.

I still have the numerous letters that my wife wrote to me when we were courting. They make great reading! There is no doubt that her words changed my heart toward her. If her words can change me, surely I can pick up the pen of my own tongue and write a note to my own heart every now and again! Talking to oneself is not a sign of madness; it is a mark of sanity. King David upbraided his own soul when he was depressed:

> *'Why are you downcast, O my soul?*
> *Why so disturbed within me?*
> *Put your hope in God,*
> *for I will yet praise him,*
> *my Saviour and my God.'* (Psalm 42:5–6)

Dr Martyn Lloyd-Jones commented on this passage by saying, 'Have you realized that most of your unhappiness in life is due to the fact that you are listening to yourself instead of talking to yourself?'[7] We all should take his advice and take control of our verbal traffic and thereby change our heart language.

Our words determine our eternal destiny
It is becoming obvious that our success on earth is to a large extent dependent on what we say. However, our words also determine our eternal reward and destination. Jesus made it abundantly clear that we will all be held accountable for the words we speak, whether positive or negative:

> *'But I tell you that men will have to give account on the day of judgment*
> *for every careless word they have spoken. For by your words you will be*
> *acquitted, and by your words you will be condemned.'*
> (Matthew 12:36–37)

Since our words flow from our heart it is not unexpected that God should judge them; nonetheless, if we really comprehended their power, I think we would all be a great deal more circumspect in what we say. This was brought forcefully to my attention when I read of an event that took place in England in the eighteenth century that mirrors the story of Ananias and Sapphira (Acts 5:1–11).

In Devizes, a small town in the county of Wiltshire, England, near where I was brought up, there is a monument that bears an inscription which I am recording here in full in order to illustrate my point:

> 'The MAYOR and CORPORATION of Devizes avail themselves of the Stability of this Building to transmit to future Times the Record of an awful Event which occurred in this Market Place in the Year 1753 hoping that such Record may serve as a salutary Warning against the Danger of impiously invoking Divine Vengeance or of calling on the Holy Name of GOD to conceal the Devices of Falsehood and Fraud. On Thursday the 25th of January 1753, Ruth Pierce, of Pottern in this County agreed with three other Women to buy a Sack of Wheat in the Market each paying her due Proportion towards the same. One of these Women in collecting the several Quotas of Money discovered a Deficiency and demanded of Ruth Pierce the Sum, which was wanting to make good the Amount. Ruth Pierce protested that She had paid her Share and said, "She wished She might drop down dead if She had not." She rashly repeated this awful Wish when to the Consternation and Terror of the surrounding Multitude She instantly fell down and expired having the Money concealed in her Hand.'

We are left in no doubt from this story that our words have power to bring us life or death. However, sadly, it is often only after hearing such a story that we are challenged enough to act. We all know that cars are hard, for instance, but it is only after being hit by one that we tend to change our reckless behaviour when crossing a road! Now that we have understood that verbal traffic has power, we should desire to control it, not because it has the power to destroy our lives but because it has the power to heal them.

Traffic must be controlled

Traffic lights vary slightly from country to country but the basic principles are the same. After much research, they are put into position by the authorities in order to benefit the community, despite what we may feel when we are waiting at them! The relevant authorities acknowledge the benefit of traffic but also recognize that uncontrolled traffic brings chaos. Assuming that they are positioned and operating correctly, their effectiveness is determined by the people's willingness to obey them. The green light means 'go'; the red light means 'stop'; the amber light communicates 'caution'. They couldn't really be simpler! Yet most of us, at one time or another, have either seen or been involved in traffic accidents that were caused when the traffic lights were either not seen or ignored. Having already established the link between traffic lights and the necessary controls that we need to put on our words, it shouldn't be difficult to work out how we should behave. There is a time to speak, a time not to speak and a time to think before speaking! Nonetheless, we all know that the practice is often not as easy as the theory and so I am suggesting four steps to controlling our mouths.

The prophet Isaiah describes the first step: repentance. He has had an encounter with the Holy God and has come off second best! He suddenly realizes his fallen condition:

> ' "Woe to me!" I cried. "I am ruined! For I am a man of unclean lips, and I live among a people of unclean lips, and my eyes have seen the King, the Lord Almighty." Then one of the seraphs flew to me with a live coal in his hand, which he had taken with tongs from the altar. With it he touched my mouth and said, "See, this has touched your lips; your guilt is taken away and your sin atoned for." '   (Isaiah 6:5–7)

In grammatical terms, the word 'lips' used here is a synecdoche, a figure of speech in which the 'part describes the whole'. His unclean lips represented his unclean life. Both required cleansing. We can make every New Year's resolution known to humanity but we cannot truly control what we say without repentance. Genuine repentance always produces good fruit and it is it this fruit that is the best gift for a sick relationship.

Asking for and receiving an anointing is the second step toward taming the tongue. In a biblical setting the word 'anointing' literally means 'the rubbing on of oil' but often signifies 'empowerment for a God-given task'. Hence Jesus was anointed for ministry:

> 'The Spirit of the Lord is on me,
>   because he has anointed me
>   to preach good news to the poor.

He has sent me to proclaim freedom for the prisoners
  and recovery of sight for the blind,
to release the oppressed.'　　　　　　　　　　　　　(Luke 4:18)

If Jesus Christ required an anointing in order to speak, then we certainly do! The wedding song which describes the tongue as a pen, from which I have already quoted, also describes the bridegroom:

'You are the most excellent of men
  and your lips have been anointed with grace,
  since God has blessed you forever.'　　　　　　　(Psalm 45:2)

Here is a key from which every marriage will benefit. God's favour not only resulted in excellence but also empowerment. In order to lead in life we need the attribute common to many great leaders and that is 'grace under pressure'. This was a bridegroom who was being praised by his wife for having a spirit of grace. This psalm can be read on two levels. It is both a wedding song and a prophetic conversation between the Bridegroom Christ and His love, the Church. Either way, graceful speech is required and offered. As married couples, we need to make a decision whether we want our tongues to be set on fire by heaven or hell. If we love what is right, the psalm goes on to teach, excellence and empowerment will follow:

'You love righteousness and hate wickedness;
  therefore God, your God, has set you above your companions
  by anointing you with the oil of joy.'　　　　　　(Psalm 45:7)

Many of us, after repenting and receiving the power of the Holy Spirit, seem to think that our house is built whereas all we have done is lay the foundation. We now have to 'work out' our salvation (Philippians 2:12) and be 'transformed' by the renewing of our minds (Romans 12:2). It is only then that we will be able to control the traffic that daily passes through our lips. The Bible uses the image of a door or a gate in a city to describe our mouth:

*'Set a guard over my mouth, O L*ORD*;*
  keep watch over the door of my lips.'　　　　　　(Psalm 141:3)

It is a site of exchange and transaction, an outlet for blessing but also a place of enormous vulnerability. Wisdom demands that we appoint a gatekeeper. This requires consistent and vigilant discipline. Carelessness born out of fatigue or familiarity can not only rob us of potential resource but can inadvertently cause us to curse when we should have blessed. Even as an experienced public speaker I still make monumental blunders! Even after years of happy marriage I still occasionally hurt my family by the words that I use or the way that I use them. As the Bible says so matter of factly,

> *'Out of the same mouth come praise and cursing. My brothers, this should not be.'*   (James 3:10)

So what should we do? We should discipline ourselves daily to remove destructive words from our language; never label people; always try and say something uplifting about someone before anything challenging; never say something about someone if we are not prepared to say it to them; be an encourager; ensure that whenever anyone comes to us they leave a better person. In other words, because Jesus only ever said what He heard His Father say and only spoke in the manner in which the Father spoke (John 12:49–50), we should discipline ourselves to be Christ-like in our speech.

Discipline, however, is not enough. James' statement that we encourage with the same mouth that we condemn with is a huge challenge to most of us, since, with the best will in the world, we still find ourselves saying things that we shouldn't. What is the answer? It seems that the best motivator in life is love. Love encourages us to change our heart and empowers us to guard my lips. If we love people we will do our utmost to protect them which includes shielding them from any harmful speech. If we value our close friendships we will avoid everything that drives us apart. So the final step in reining in our unbroken lips is intimacy.

In many cultures one of the common expressions of intimacy is the kiss. Whichever way you look at it, kissing is a strange custom! In some countries it is actually considered repulsive. For many of us, however, pressing our highly sensitive lips against those of another is a very personal and sometimes sensual activity. It is an expression of commitment, value and vulnerability. After all, we don't just kiss anyone! We keep our lips for those who we love. My own daughter, as a teenager, encouraged me to kiss her on the cheek because she 'was reserving her lips for her husband'! In other words, her lips were governed by a promise of intimacy. If love can control our literal lips it can also control our metaphorical ones: the words we speak. Worship, for instance, is an expression of intimacy and is determined by love. The Greek word used for 'worship' in the New Testament is *proskuneo* suggesting obeisance and, according to Bishop David Pytches, conveys the idea of 'coming towards to kiss'.[8] Our love for God causes us to honour Him with our lips, reserving them for worshipping Him and not others. As David sang,

> 'The sorrows of those will increase
>   who run after other gods.
> I will not pour out their libations of blood
>   or take up their names on my lips.'   (Psalm 16:4)

David's intimacy with God caused him to make a covenant with his own lips. We too can choose whom we want to 'kiss'!

In reality, many of us find it very difficult to take these steps to control what we say. Nonetheless, with God's help, we should set out on the journey. There is no doubt that our relational bridges do require verbal traffic and that traffic must be controlled. It is therefore essential that we have some sort of 'traffic control system' in all of our relationships or somebody is going to get injured! We must persist. The first set of gas-operated traffic lights blew up in London on 2 January 1869 injuring the policeman who was operating them! Today, there are millions of traffic lights around the world controlling the ever-increasing traffic flow. The inventors kept going until they got it right.

Summary and advice

1. **Our words could be described as conversational traffic**. Relationships, like bridges, benefit from smooth traffic flow. We need verbal traffic lights that control what we say.

2. **Traffic is an indicator**. Our verbal traffic reveals our personality, gender and attitudes. Our lips are a gauge for the passions and poisons in each of us.

3. **Traffic has power**. Our words can either build or destroy our relational bridges.

4. **Our words decide the condition of our soul**. A change of confession can change lives.

5. **Our words direct the course of our life.** The Bible describes the tongue as a rudder of a ship. A small adjustment can mean the difference between plain sailing and a shipwreck.
6. **Our words dictate the extent of our success.** Words have the capacity to heal or hurt, fill or empty, free or restrict.
7. **Our words define the language of our heart.** If our tongue is the pen then our heart is the paper on which it writes. Talking to oneself is not a sign of madness but of wisdom.
8. **Our words determine our eternal destiny.** Whether we like it or not we will be held accountable for what we say.
9. **Traffic must be controlled.** There are four steps to controlling our tongue: repentance, anointing, discipline and intimacy.

Notes

1. Judith Dupré, *Bridges* (Könemann, 1998).
2. Martin Luther King Jr, Speech, Washington, DC, 28 August 1963. Quoted in Clayborne Carson & Kris Shepard (eds.), *A Call to Conscience* (Warner Books, 2001).
3. The Holy Bible, The King James Version (Cambridge, 1769).
4. Derek Prince, *Blessings or Curse* (Word (UK) Ltd, 1990).
5. Mattys Levy and Mario Salvadori, *Why Buildings Fall Down* (W.W. Norton & Co., 1992).
6. The word 'saprotic' means 'rotten'. I have coined it from the Greek word *sapros* which is used in Ephesians 4:29 and means 'rotten', 'corrupt' or 'putrefied', as in decaying and mouldy fruit.
7. Dr Martyn Lloyd-Jones, Sermon in Westminster Chapel, London. Quoted in E. Gibbs, *The God Who Communicates* (Hodder & Stoughton, 1985).
8. David Pytches, *Come, Holy Spirit* (Hodder & Stoughton, 1985).

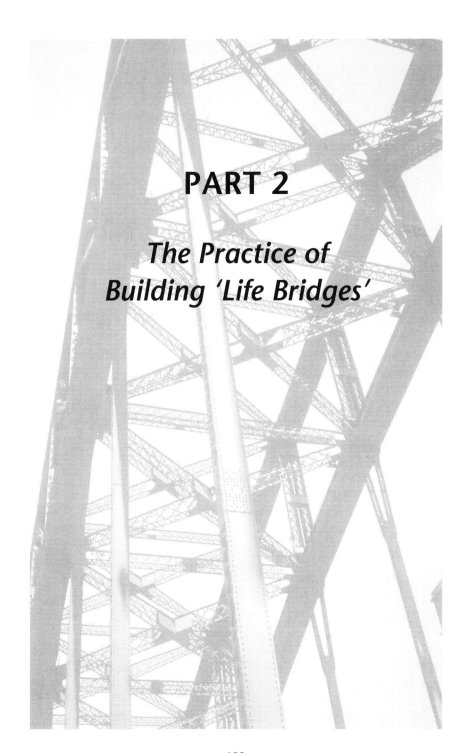

PART 2

The Practice of Building 'Life Bridges'

Chapter 11

Relational Engineering

A Bridge Built

Bridge-builder n. **1.** A person who is involved in the design, construction and/or maintenance of a bridge or bridges. E.g. a civil engineer. **2.** A person who is involved in the design, construction and/or maintenance of something that resembles a bridge either in shape or function. E.g. a relational engineer.

I have only built one bridge in my life. It was a disaster! It lasted about half an hour and then collapsed! It resulted in some bruised and wet friends, some frayed tempers and a lost competition!

The boarding school I attended as a teenager practised a form of conscription. Every Wednesday afternoon we were required to be part of the Cadet Corps. In it we learned to march, polish boots and fire a rifle. The school believed that this discipline and training was a necessary part of our education. The activities included a year-long competition in which we were required to fulfil a variety of team tasks. One of these involved our entire platoon crossing a river on a bridge that we were to build solely with the materials at hand. We were provided with three logs, none of which were long enough to span the river, and some rope. The key to the whole exercise was to learn how to lash the logs together with the rope. We were instructed in a variety of forms of lashing, including what were called 'frapping turns'. Armed with this information we confidently embarked on the project. The practice proved considerably more difficult than the theory. In consequence, the lashings failed and half my colleagues were dumped unceremoniously into the River Kennett! Apparently, the frapping turns were not tight enough. It is one thing reading a book on bridge-building and quite another to build a bridge.

This lesson was drummed home to me in Nottingham, England in 1979. I had been married for nearly three years and now we were expecting our first child. As a result of complications which prevented me from being present at the birth, I paced impatiently outside the door until I heard her first exultant scream and was eventually ushered into the delivery room. No amount of planning, preparation, reading, counsel or instruction could have prepared me for that initial encounter with my baby girl. I was terrified! The awesome responsibility of parenthood fell on me like a concrete blanket. I felt completely inadequate. She lay there helplessly in need of attention and I was unable even to lift her up. The anaesthetic was still wearing off and my wife was only partly conscious, so I couldn't draw strength from her obvious experience in these matters! I prayed for the midwife to return! They didn't tell me about this in the books.

Over the subsequent years, while I learned that I was not as ill-equipped as I thought, I also discovered that practical parenting is enormously different from the theory. John Wilmot, the Earl of Rochester (1647–80), expressed my dilemma when he wrote, 'Before I got married I had six theories about bringing up children; now I have six children and no theories'![1] Most parents know exactly what he was talking about. The key is to learn how to apply what is in the books to our everyday life. We need to marry the theory with the practice. In light of this fact, the second half of this book is about the application of the theory of bridges. However, although it is about the practice of bridge-building, it will also contain numerous principles that I hope you will be able to apply to your lives in your own way. The practical guidelines that I will share from my own life and relationships only serve to show that the principles can be applied effectively. The book is not meant to be a detailed and complete manual for building relationships. I may mention the parent–child bridge, yet I cannot hope to cover even a fraction of the lessons and information that you will need to parent a child effectively!

Three assumptions on which to build

The theory of bridges, as we have seen, is based on the three premises that bridges are necessary, overcome obstacles and provide passage. Similarly, the practice of bridge-building is based on three assumptions.

For a bridge or a relationship to be built successfully, it must be assumed that the civil or relational engineer follows instructions, pays a price and builds for strength. These three assumptions can be applied to the building of all relationships.

Of course, I have met families who have no positive plans for their lives and live independently of external instruction, others who seemingly make no effort at all to help their relationships succeed, and still others who have no concept of investing in the future. They ignore the three fundamentals. Tragically their families will inevitably fail. I am assuming that these people are not reading this book! For those of us who want the best for our relationships, an understanding of the three assumptions will help us immeasurably.

Bridge-builders follow instructions

In 2001, our church in Sydney embarked on a large building pro-gramme. On one visit to the building site, my first required port of call was the site office. In a corner a group of people were poring over the plans of the building that stretched over a large table. The builders were conferring with the overseers and advisors about the interpreta-tion of a particular point in the plan. I was ushered to another corner to sign in and collect my identity tag and hard hat. Suitably protected, I crossed the formless and debris-strewn access to the site itself, trying to connect what I was seeing with the artist's impression of the finished building that I had seen earlier. I passed a sign saying 'Safety boots must be worn on this site'. I needed them! On entering the site itself, I became completely disoriented. Was I at the front or the back, was I inside or out? My companion, Brian Houston, the Senior Minister, seemingly oblivious of the rubble, crowded scaffolding and discarded equipment, gestured with his hand and announced, 'This is the library'! With one act of faith and vision he had transformed a dusty and dangerous building site into a carpeted and fully equipped room. His twenty-year dream was nearing completion.

This image of building and buildings is a common one in the Bible. Both the corporate Church and our individual lives are described as buildings. Although Christ builds both, we are actively involved in the building process and, as the Bible says, *'each one should be careful how he builds'* (1 Corinthians 3:10). My trip to the building site not only illustrates the care that needs to be taken in the building of our lives and relationships but also the principles and instructions that we need to follow.

The builders in question had a 'safety first' policy. Before I even entered the site, I was informed that I had to follow certain safety requirements. This is a common practice in numerous organizations. Pilots in every airline announce to the passengers before take off, 'Safety is our primary concern'. We are then instructed in procedures we hope and pray that we will never need! Yet when we embark on building a relationship we rarely take safety or dangers into consideration. Talking of danger is not an expression of unbelief, it is a confession of wisdom! Jesus Himself taught that when, not if, the wind comes, we need to ensure that we have built the building of our lives with the foundation on the rock (Matthew 7:25) so that we don't fall. The danger of falling and injury is a risk attached to all building work.

Relational bridge-builders need to follow a safety code carefully. There should be a sign over the door of every home saying 'Building in process. Wear a hard hat! In emergency call for help'! Normally, however, there is no such concern or warning. We often enter marriage or friendships with no code. We don't know how to resolve a conflict when it arises. We don't know whom to turn to if things go wrong. Tragically, many relationships fail because simple precautions weren't taken. When my wife and I were married we assumed that we would have some sort of disagreement at some time and therefore decided beforehand on what we were going to do. Had we waited until the heat of the moment we wouldn't have been able to find a solution rationally. People who are saved in house fires are often those who know where the fire exits are and have practised the fire drill! We need to know and practise. In the context of storms threatening our lives, Jesus said,

> 'Therefore everyone who hears these words of mine and puts them into practice is like a wise man who built his house on the rock.'
> (Matthew 7:24)

To know how to prevent injury or disaster and yet fail to implement the procedures is not only unwise, it is selfish and irresponsible (cf. James 4:17).

Despite the fact that safety is a priority, it is not the sole purpose of the building site! As civil engineer Mario Salvadori states, 'The purpose of a building is to perform a function'.[2] Builders do not work in order to demonstrate safety procedures; they work to erect a useful structure.

And although Salvadori continues by saying, 'The function of most buildings is to protect people', they also have numerous other functions. Similarly, we are not here on earth simply to be safe, we are here for a pre-planned purpose. Many of us spend so much of our lives talking about the benefits of safety and protection that we fail to understand what we are saved for! All builders, whether natural or spiritual, must build with this selfless objective in mind. In order to do this they must carefully follow the plans that have been specifically designed to fulfil that objective.

The builders I encountered in the site office were at pains to discover exactly what the plans required so that they could faithfully reproduce the requested specifications. In fact, the skills required on the building site are exactly those needed by anyone constructing a relationship. We need expertise and vision in order to interpret the biblical blueprint correctly. We must have the knowledge, equipment and personnel in order to build effectively and we need faith and resource in order to complete the project successfully. Attempting marriage, parenthood, or even a friendship without reference to the Bible is as ridiculous as a builder starting a twenty-million dollar structure without plans or a cent in the bank. I suspect that the 'architect' would have something to say!

The reality is that the Architect of our souls does have an extraordinary plan for our lives and it would be folly to reject it. He does desire our safety and has purchased a plan for our salvation, yet these are just the outskirts of His favour. He wants to dwell in the buildings we are constructing. He wants to inhabit our lives, homes and relationships and He wants them to reflect His goodness and blessing. He is the Designer of our bridges and the Master of our homes. If we are to be successful builders, we will not only build with safety and the objective in mind but also realize that we are under orders. We are not independent of an outside source. We are the servant of another and not here to please ourselves.

As we begin to look at the more practical aspects of bridge-building, it may be helpful to ask some more questions of ourselves at this stage:

- Do I tend to rebel when given instruction about my relationships?
- Do I have a clear safety code that I adhere to at all times?
- Do I only focus on my own happiness or a higher purpose?
- Am I completely at ease with serving someone else?

Bridge-builders pay a price

My present to myself on my forty-seventh birthday was to climb the Sydney Harbour Bridge. Our guide, aware of those in the party who were scared of heights, insisted on informing us of the dangers of falling off (guides are good like that!) saying that, 'Hitting the water from this height is like hitting concrete'. He went on to tell us that only one man had survived the fall and he had to have his shoes surgically removed from the soles of his feet after the impact! True or not, it certainly made us concentrate! In fact, we discovered that twelve men died in the construction of the bridge. For all the commitment to safety procedures, large engineering projects have invariably resulted in the loss of life. There is a price to be paid in the building of bridges.

When a general goes to war he weighs up the pros and cons of a particular strategy. Though he will attempt to keep the casualties to a minimum he knows that there will always be victims. He will have to decide whether the achieving of the objective is worth the expected loss of life. It is a tough decision to make but it is one that everyone, including himself, knows is expected of him and it is one that he has trained for years to make. Although, thankfully, most of us never have to make such a choice, we do face hard decisions in life. Both the civil and the relational engineer will inevitably face loss in the building and completion of their respective 'projects' and will have to decide whether the goals merit it. Yet curiously we rarely expect to make these sorts of decisions and most of us never train for them.

Many of our relationships fail because we have failed to do some emotional budgeting beforehand. Are we prepared for loss? Can we afford it when it comes? Can we pay the price? Jesus made His position clear from the outset for anyone contemplating a relationship with Him. He said,

> *'If anyone would come after me, he must deny himself and take up his cross daily and follow me. For whoever wants to save his life will lose it, but whoever loses his life for me will save it.'* (Luke 9:23–24)

Dr Jowett comments on this approach by saying, 'I am amazed at the almost audacious candour of the programme. There is no hiding of the sharp flint, no softening of the shadow, no gilding of the cross. The hostilities bristle in naked obtrusiveness. Every garden is a prospective battlefield.'[3] There is no doubt that Jesus established the principle:

good relationships require loss and loss is always accompanied by pain! So, to encourage someone to start a relationship with Jesus, or anyone else for that matter, by saying, 'You have nothing to lose', is deliberate deception! True intimacy demands loss: a loss of independence, a loss of our selfish agenda, a loss of certain rights, in fact, a loss of our life! Of course, we also have everything to gain!

Apparently, in the early days of the ministry of the American preacher and author, David Wilkerson, he would offer a relatively 'pain-free' invitation to follow Christ to the hundreds of young people who came to him until one day a new convert to Christianity accused him of lying. He said that he didn't warn him that he would have to die! The rebuke changed the way that Wilkerson preached. It is a challenge all of us need to hear as we preach, or help others as they prepare for marriage, or as we embark on friendships ourselves. Jesus made no compromise about the cost of fruitful relationship. He said,

> *'I tell you the truth, unless a grain of wheat falls to the ground and dies, it remains only a single seed. But if it dies, it produces many seeds. The man who loves his life will lose it, while the man who hates his life in this world will keep it for eternal life.'* (John 12:24–25)

The death of Jesus, the ultimate sacrifice, paved the way for our relationship with God and provides a model for our relationships on earth. The Bible commands husbands:

> *'Love your wives, just as Christ loved the church and gave himself up for her ...'* (Ephesians 5:25)

Jay Adams interprets this verse by asking two questions, 'Husbands, do you love your wives enough to die for them? Wives, do you love your husbands enough to live for them?'[4] I may think these demands excessive or unrealistic until I remember that lives were lost to build the Sydney Harbour Bridge so that I could get to work more conveniently!

The price of bridge-building, however, is found not only in the loss and sacrifice but also in the time and sheer hard work that it entails: the months of repetitive labour! A staggering six million hand-driven rivets were hammered into the massive steel arch that spans Port Jackson. The building of a marriage is no less arduous, detailed and mundane! In a television interview, when Ruth Graham was asked about the success of her marriage to her evangelist husband Billy, she simply replied, 'Marriage is so daily'! She had evidently unearthed a secret that so many have failed to discover. Good relationships involve a thousand good daily choices and commitment to rectify the few bad ones quickly. The latter is often a confronting and sometimes unpleasant business, but that's life! Life always involves being prepared to get our hands dirty! Progress in life invariably requires us to 'put in the hard yards'!

For those starting a new relationship, the key is a willingness to pay the price. As I said at the beginning of the chapter, there is a great deal of difference between the theory and the practice. Ruth Graham had had over fifty years of practice when she gave the interview. New wives can never share her experiences but they can share her attitude. Expectant fathers have no idea what fatherhood is like but they can train their hearts. Books on parenting fail to prepare us fully for the real thing because they cannot replicate the pain of childbirth or the relief and joy of the first scream. They cannot effectively describe the numbing tiredness of the first few weeks or illustrate the boredom of the routines or capture the smell of a vomit-filled cot or the feel of a baby's neck! So what do we do? Beforehand, we ask the hard questions and make a decision that we will give whatever it takes:

- Am I willing to pay the price of the daily routine of building a relationship?
- Am I prepared to give up my independence to gain intimacy?
- Do I tend to enter a relationship without considering the cost involved?
- Do I avoid the confrontation of resolving problems in my relationships?

Bridge-builders build for strength

In common with most other boys aged ten I loved making things: plastic kits, paper darts and metal toys. Anything! My primary school had a small workshop in which we were allowed to make things in our spare time. Apart from the usual stock of paper, tools and glue, there was always a large supply of balsa wood. Balsa wood is excellent for model making. It is light, soft and easily cut and shaped. It is perfect for model aeroplanes. It is, on the other hand, useless for building bridges! We tried on a number of occasions. The problem, of course, is that bridges are designed and built to carry loads and balsa wood was not strong enough for the loads we wanted to apply! I don't know whether it was then or later that I learned the expression that I have used on numerous occasions when teaching on relationships: 'You can't drive a tank across a balsa wood bridge!'

One of the premises on which a bridge is built is that it provides passage. To provide passage it must carry loads; hence the assumption that all bridge-builders must build for strength. If we are to build a relationship with someone else, it must by definition be strong. There is no point in building it otherwise. My relationship with my wife has to carry huge weights. It encounters great pressures and stresses. We constantly talk about challenges, responsibilities, problems and dreams. In other words, we drive tanks over it on a daily basis. If it were made of modelling wood it would collapse. A mature attitude to all relationships realizes that they are not for play but for passage. Wise people build bridges with good materials, repair them regularly and build them for permanence.

Sometimes a man will come to me for counsel regarding his marriage and will confess during the appointment that he is tempted to have an affair with another woman. What continually surprises me is not that the man is being tempted but, despite years of marriage, he is unable to talk to his wife about his problems. 'She'll kill me if she finds out', is his response. 'I've never been able to tell her about my problem with lust.' Tragically, despite its longevity, it is an immature marriage. The couple has apparently opted for show, not substance. The relationship may look good on the outside but is crumbling within. Lack of passage reveals a lack of strength. In other words, when a couple is frightened to communicate it indicates a deficiency of the love that should undergird the relationship. The man is frightened to tell his wife of his temptation because she might reject him. Where is the uncondi-tional love in that? At the beginning of the relationship, when we are just beginning to build confidence, understanding and trust, we may add too much stress by talking about all our faults and failings but as girders of unconditional love are set in place it must allow for an increasing honesty. Distrust, dishonesty, rejection and fear are not good building materials!

Nevertheless, at least the man in question came for counsel. He was prepared to confront the problem and hopefully resolve it. He exhibited the necessary commitment to repair the damage. It is a commitment that is sadly quite rare. It has been said that when faced with a challenge we have three options, 'to run, to spectate or to commit'. Many run from confrontation or the demands of change. They run from friendships or divorce their partners because the offences destroying the relationship are in the 'too hard basket'. Others choose mediocrity. The problems are real but they can exist with them. Just! They spectate as their interests develop separately and their relationship drifts apart. They spectate as their children choose poor relationships and worse behaviour. The third option is the correct one. We need to commit to reconciliation. We need to commit to a better way of living. We must constantly repair the bridge, not just for our sake, but also for the sake of the children.

Inevitably, this is where my conversation with the tempted man turns. 'What about the kids? What would happen to them?' Some selfish people respond, 'Surely, if I am happy, they will be happy.' They obviously haven't witnessed the aftermath of a divorce close at hand. The trauma of a parental affair runs very deep and often causes lifelong hurt. Others are pulled up short by the responsibility of parenthood. I know of a man who turned to God because his son saw him talking to a prostitute and another who became a Christian at the birth of his daughter. Both realized that their lives were no longer their own. They became aware that they were now influential leaders and had a charge to pass on a godly heritage to the next generation. The civil engineers and builders of the Sydney Harbour Bridge may have had no idea of how important it would become or its iconic significance three or four generations later. Nonetheless, they built it for strength with us in mind. These are not just noble ideals they are practical principles. If I am making a business acquaintance I build with eternity in mind, not just for selfish gain. If I am tempted to contemplate an affair, I think of my grandchildren yet to be born. It is this thinking that saves and strengthens relationships. Model relationships are not made of modelling wood!

- Do I have a model relationship that inspires others?
- Am I prepared to talk about the real issues in my life?
- Do I run, spectate or commit when it comes to confronting problems?
- Do I build relationships with the next generation in mind?

I started this chapter by stating that I had only built one bridge in my life whereas, in fact, I have built hundreds! The first was a wooden bridge and it was a failure. The subsequent ones have been with God and people and many have been very successful. By the grace of God, I am a much better relational engineer than a civil one! The three assumptions to which I have referred and which have been the grounds for much of the fruit, are the foundation for the three sections in the rest of the book.

Summary and advice

1. **We are all relational engineers whether qualified or not**. It is better to be qualified!

2. **The practice of building relational bridges is very different from the theory!** The theory of bridge-building is based on three premises; the practice of bridge-building is based on three assumptions. In our relationships we need to learn to marry theory with practice.

3. **Assumption 1: Bridge-builders follow instructions**. Wise people keep the purpose of the building in mind, regularly consult the blueprint and carefully follow the safety code.

4. **Assumption 2: Bridge-builders pay a price**. Wise people are prepared for the loss, sacrifice and sheer hard work that all relational engineering entails.

5. **Assumption 3: Bridge-builders build for strength**. Wise people build relational bridges with good materials, repair them regularly and build them for permanence.

Notes

1. John Wilmot, the Earl of Rochester. Quoted in Roy L. Stewart, *Quotations with an Attitude* (Sterling Publishing Company Inc., 1995).
2. Mario Salvadori, *Why Buildings Stand Up* (W.W. Norton & Company, Inc., 1980).
3. Dr J.H. Jowett, *Sharing His Sufferings* (James Clarke & Co., 1911).
4. Jay Adams, *Christian Living in the Home* (Baker Book House, 1972).

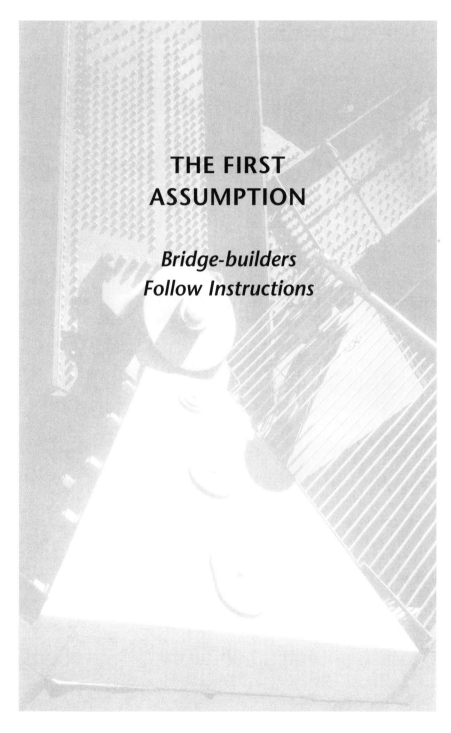

THE FIRST ASSUMPTION

Bridge-builders Follow Instructions

Chapter 12

Structure and Function

Determining the Purpose of a Bridge

Sydney Harbour Bridge is immense. Its presence dominates the harbour. The great ocean liners that dock next to it are dwarfed by its size. With the aid of perspective, the Sydney Opera House appears comparable in photographs but in reality it has to look up to its older and more substantial neighbour. The 'proud arch' seems to be the master of all that it surveys! However, for all its grandeur, it is only a servant! It serves both its designer and the city for which it was built. It was created with a clear and simple purpose in mind and that is essentially all it does. It provides passage across the harbour. Nonetheless, it does serve its purpose breathtakingly well!

I have a slight communication problem with my wife! She regularly ignores me when I talk to her and then just walks away! The reason for this is not that she is not a good listener, quite the contrary; it is because she is not a good hearer. When she was a child, a surgeon attempted to replace her perforated eardrum with a piece of skin from her leg and it's never been quite the same since! On one side, her middle ear no longer works. The cause of the problem: a small bone bridge.

Each one of us has a mechanical device in our ears that connects the outer ear drum with the inner ear membrane. This device consists of three small, carefully connected bones, the hammer, the anvil and the stirrup. It can be described as a bridge because it 'overcomes a barrier and provides communication between two separate entities'. The structure and design of this bone bridge reflects both the creativity and the pragmatism of its Creator. The structure is perfect for its function, which is to act as an amplifier. The three mechanical levers not only transmit sound waves from the outer ear to the inner ear, they also increase the pressure of the sound at the entrance of the inner ear. The inner ear in turn sends the information to the brain. In the case of this biological bridge, the marriage of structure and function is essential for healthy communication. In the case of my wife, the delicate balance between structure and function was damaged and successful communication prevented. It is this balance that I want to address because it is essential in all our relationships.

In my first year of university studying zoology I was continually taught about the importance of structure and function. Every part of the biological world revealed this principle. The theory of evolution, I was told, was 'purpose-driven'. Structures developed to fulfil a particular purpose. This, the lecturers would say, was all a product of chance. I soon discovered that this wasn't exactly true. The principle of structure and function was sound enough, but we are products of design, not chance, with life as the goal, not just survival. Every part of our bodies is designed and made by God with a specific function in mind. Paul uses this image to describe our relationship to each other within the 'Body of Christ', the Church:

> *'Just as each of us has one body with many members, and these members do not all have the same **function**, so in Christ we who are many form one body, and each member belongs to all the others. We have different gifts, according to the grace given us. If a man's gift is prophesying, let him use it in proportion to his faith.'*
>
> (Romans 12:4–6, emphasis mine)

If we are to relate successfully within the Body of Christ or indeed fit comfortably into the world into which God has placed us, we need to realize that we have each been designed with a function in mind and we have been structured, engineered and empowered specifically for that function. We are all graced for a particular purpose.

A failure to discover our God-given function or purpose leads to innumerable frustrations. In the context of relationships, it is vital to understand this. A relationship without purpose will either drift into irrelevancy or pursue an unconscious goal with a godless end. Passage without purpose inevitably ends in disappointment. A failure to determine how relationships are structured can also result in disenchantment. A failure to marry the two effectively is usually disastrous! In the case of natural bridges, for instance, a rail bridge used exclusively for pedestrians is underused: its designed structure ignored. On the other hand, a pedestrian bridge used for trains will be overloaded: its designed function disregarded. In one instance the structure is used too little and in the other the function demands too much. Numerous failed relationships reflect this same problem. They are either underused resulting in frustration or overloaded resulting in stress. Either way, effective communication is the victim. What we have to do is to discover the purpose for our relationships, determine the available relational structures and then marry the two by pairing an appropriate structure with the desired function. And in common with all communicators, purpose must come first.

Of course, this line of argument may seem far too scientific to be applied to the divine mystery of a friendship or the inexpressible passion and emotion of a marriage. However, God made both the stars and the clouds. He is an ordered Mathematician as well as a passionate Artist. In relationships, although we need to receive His grace and appreciate His art, we must also learn His science. This is the emphasis of this chapter.

Discovering relational purpose

Many people have no idea why they start relationships. They just happen! 'Seemed like a good idea at the time.' They often remain directionless throughout. Sadly, if relationships just happen, they can just as easily 'un-happen'. When I proposed to my wife-to-be in 1975, I had a fairly clear idea in my mind of the functions and responsibilities of marriage. So the proposal was more than a simple question, 'Will you marry me?' It was a proposal with purpose. This should be true of all bridges that we build. In 1996, the London *Financial Times* ran a competition for the design of the Millennium Bridge. In his statement of design intent, one of the architects who submitted an entry, Frank Gehry, wrote, 'We propose ... a bridge where sociality becomes the dominant practical purpose, a structure which allows for and suggests the unhurried appreciation of the complexities of views and activities on both sides of the river and on the river itself ...'[1] As we have seen, in common with all designs, the structure had to serve the well-defined function. Evidently, for Frank Gehry and his team, the purpose that best described the proposed footbridge across the Thames River was 'sociality'. In the end, my proposal was accepted and Frank Gehry's was rejected! We cannot always predict the outcome of our proposals. Nonetheless, we both had a clear purpose in mind.

Yet, how do we come to similarly clear understanding about the purpose of a proposed relationship? Assuming we have established that the relationship is necessary, we need to determine whether it will fulfil the two primary purposes of a relational bridge, the overcoming of obstacles and the provision of passage. The best way to do this is once again to ask ourselves some practical questions about these theoretical purposes:

- What quantity of traffic does the bridge need to carry?
- In which direction does the traffic need to flow?
- What needs will the bridge be required to meet?

How do these questions help us as we pursue our various relationships? Let me explain. They relate to the provision of passage. Some relationships require more 'traffic' than others. If I don't know what weight of communication my friendship may need to carry I may not give it the time and energy required to strengthen it. Equally, some relational bridges are one way and others are two way. A teacher–student relationship is more 'one-way' than a close friendship which must be 'two-way'. If I am unaware of what the other party is expecting from the relationship it will inevitably lead to confusion, a traffic jam! Many relationships falter because one person has a completely different expectation from the other, simply because they have not determined together what they want out of the relationship. One side may gain from a relationship, but will both parties benefit from it? One wants a colleague, the other a friend! One looks for a friend, the other a boyfriend! One desires a girlfriend, the other a life partner! I have seen people unnecessarily hurt because they won't ask questions about each other's emotional requirements. When Frank Gehry proposed his design for the Millennium Bridge in London he took the emotional implications into consideration. Before the bridge was built, he knew what it should feel like for the users. Most of us are totally involved with someone before we stop to ponder what this kind of relationship is meant to feel like! By then, it is usually too late to change course.

Another group of questions need to be asked in order to discover more about our relational purpose. These relate to the overcoming of obstacles:

- What is the distance that the bridge will need to span?
- What does the society demand of the bridge?
- What are the safety requirements?

In the case of the Millennium Bridge, before the project could even be contemplated, the size of the river had to be taken into account. If the river had been too wide, the bridge could not have been built. Sometimes, the obstacles are so great that a relational bridge can also never be built; yet some, oblivious to the distance between two people, dream about an impossible relationship. They fantasize about having a great leader as a friend or marrying a film star. Instead of building credible bridges they waste their lives pursuing unattainable ones. When their proposals are rejected they are devastated. Stalking is birthed in this dangerous fantasy. The problem with this kind of reasoning is selfishness. We don't build bridges in a vacuum. Others are also involved! A civil engineer takes into account the demands of the environment, safety considerations and the various needs of all parties concerned. We should do the same. If the 'society' of which I am a part rejects my proposed relationship I cannot hope to succeed if I try and build it. Our bridges must be socially acceptable. Equally, if the proposal for a relationship is not considered 'safe' and will result in someone being damaged or hurt it should not be considered. Honest answers to these questions will not only help us determine the purpose of a relationship, but will also prevent us from embarking on a path of regret.

Determining relational structure

Completed in 1890, the Forth Railway Bridge rises out of the mists and Scottish brine like the body of a vast steel monster. William Morris, Victorian artist and exponent of good design, criticized it as 'the supremest specimen of all ugliness'![2] Yet it wasn't designed by Sir Benjamin Baker for its beauty, but for its efficiency and strength. It is a steel cantilever bridge that is purpose built to transport heavy trains across the Firth of Forth, the wide stretch of water that intersects

Scotland between Edinburgh and Dundee. At the time it was the best structure for that function. The task of the architects and engineers was to find an appropriate structure. In order to do that they had to know what was needed and what was possible or available.

Bridge-makers have only a few structures to choose from. All differ in the way they carry their own weight. According to Judith Dupré there is a fundamental trio: 'Bridges are based on one or more of three basic structures that are derived from forms found in nature: the *beam* from a log fallen across a stream, the *arch* from natural rock formations, and the *suspension* from a hanging vine'.[3] Variations on these three types are seen in the cantilevered bridge, such as the Forth Rail Bridge, and the moveable bridges, such as the bascule Tower Bridge in London. Each of these structures possesses differing qualities and attributes. For instance, a beam is characterized by its simplicity, an arch by its beauty and stability, a cantilever by its efficiency and strength, and a suspension bridge by its length. If we add the flexibility of all the moveable bridges, the architect has a variety of structures and characteristics to choose from and may elect to incorporate one or all of these into the design. All this may seem totally removed from the complexities of human relationships, but whether we are civil or relational engineers we are looking for the same essential qualities. We could easily describe two children holding hands in a playground as: 'Simple; Beautiful' – the very words Frank Gehry used to describe his favourite railway bridge![4]

The reality is that there are not many types of human relationships. Of course, I could describe the intricacies of the parent–child relationship and how it differs from the teacher–pupil relationship. I could also explain our need of mentors, the characteristics of fathers or the levels of friendships. But instead I would like to reduce all of these structures into another fundamental trio. Relationships can be categorized into three basic structures, those above us from which we draw, those beside us with which we share and those below us to which we give. (The words above, beside and below describe position not value. We are all equally valuable.) Those above us should include fathers, mothers, mentors and shepherds or their equivalents. Those beside us should include siblings, friends, colleagues and partners. Those below us should include children (natural and/or spiritual) and disciples. We each require these relational levels in our lives. The primary characteristic of the first level is the drawing of strength. An athlete may have a good friendship with a coach but the focus of the relationship is to gain expertise. It is principally 'one-way'. The second level is very different. Now we are sharing strengths. We draw from each other. It is 'two-way' traffic. The goals, depth of intimacy and emotional needs of each relationship will vary considerably on this level but all involve sharing with each other. The third level is different again. Now the characteristic is the giving of strength to another. Obviously, giving is a quality necessary in all relationships but here it is the heart. Once again, the traffic is 'one-way'! In practice, the realization of these levels of relationships can help us enormously. It tells us not only what bridges we *can* build, but also what we *should* build.

The marriage of structure and function

An honest appraisal of both the function and structure of relationships should give us the answers to these two questions: what do we want and need from a relationship and what relationships are there? Now we need to answer the third question: which relationship will give us what we want and need? In order to illustrate the marriage of structure to function, I would like to show how we can pursue relationships on each of the different levels.

The obvious example of relational success is Jesus Christ. He had rich and positive relationships with young and old, rich and poor, and men and women. These relationships did not just happen. He was motivated by divine purpose. He describes it by saying,

> *'I have come down from heaven not to do my will but to do the will of him who sent me. And this is the will of him who sent me, that I shall lose none of all that he has given me, but raise them up at the last day.'*
> (John 6:38–39)

In order to fulfil this clear function he had to form the three relational structures that I have highlighted. Firstly, He had to maintain a good relationship with His Father through prayer, then develop a network of friends to support Him in His task and finally find a team of disciples in order to pass on the baton. It seems that Jesus actively pursued these necessary relationships. Amidst pressing crowds that drew on His compassion He repeatedly made time to withdraw and pray (Luke 5:16). Even when He was fulfilling His commission to heal the sick, He still spent time with His disciples who would carry on His work. Mark tells us that, *'Jesus did not want anyone to know where they were, because he was teaching his disciples'* (Mark 9:30–31). Despite His totally selfless approach to life He also found time to build friendships. We find Him revealing His heart to His best friend John, sharing His highs and lows with those closest to Him on the Mount of Transfiguration and in the Garden of Gethsemane, and staying for a meal at the house of Lazarus and his sisters.

These friends were not chosen by accident but by design. He knew that *'a companion of fools suffers harm'* (Proverbs 13:20) and so selected them carefully. On top of that His Father evidently instructed Him on the choice of the disciples. After a night of prayer He appointed the disciples (Luke 6:12–16). These were the ones who would enable Him to fulfil His purpose on earth. Additionally, in order to be effective, the depth of the relationship varied among His disciples. He shared the most with Peter, James and John, but He shared more with the twelve than the seventy-two. If we had the same commitment to purpose we would be far more successful in our bridge-building. Some may argue that this is a clinical approach to the building of relationships. Not at all! He was simply choosing the relational structure that best suited the function that He was to perform. For instance, we may choose the relational structure of marriage because we feel we need a life partner. Jesus Christ, on the other hand, chose not to get married *'because of the kingdom of heaven'* (Matthew 19:12). He knew that He was to die and therefore marriage was inappropriate for Him.

I used to be the Principal of our church Bible College in Sydney and during that time I attempted to model my relational patterns on those of Jesus. It seemed like a good idea! Though I was preaching to the crowds at the weekend, my week was taken up with training the students. I considered them to be my 'seventy-two'! I talked to them about issues that I never addressed in the more public arena of a Sunday service. However, of those students there were a few that I singled out for more concentrated discipleship. I spent the most time with one. The reason for this was that I had had a dream about him! Even before I had met him or moved to live in Australia to live, I knew his name! Some time later when I became Principal and he became one of my students, I knew that I should train him to take my place. For a number of years, we would meet every Tuesday for lunch. About twelve years after my dream, he was given the job of Principal! Although this has never happened to me before or since and probably never will, it did teach me that God is vitally interested in purpose-driven relationships.

Incidentally, the reason that we met on Tuesdays was because at the time I had lunch with my wife every Monday and lunch with my boss and mentor every Wednesday! In other words, although I hadn't specifically planned it like that, the first three lunches of the week were based around the three levels of relationships!

I am fully aware that our relationships are not nearly as predictable and unemotional as I am suggesting, nonetheless, what I am arguing for here is a more rational approach to the building of them. If an architect has a clear purpose-driven proposal before he even attempts to build a bridge, it seems reasonable to suggest that we should not rely on luck or fatalism when building life bridges. When we initially build a friendship we may have no idea where the relationship will lead, but at least we should be asking the right questions. For instance, if students ask me to be their mentor I don't immediately say yes! I ask them what they want out of the relationship and then I ask myself whether I have the resources to meet that need; whether I am able to give them the time, energy and gift that will equip them for their God-given destiny. If we cannot marry the structure with the function we don't pursue the relationship and neither of us is hurt. If, on the other hand, we both feel that the relationship could work, we lay down some simple ground rules. How often will we meet? Who will contact whom? What should we expect from each other? When the disciples wanted to follow Jesus, He made it absolutely clear what it would involve from the outset. Some jumped at the opportunity, others like the 'rich young ruler' couldn't pay the price (Mark 10:22). Obviously Jesus was a perfect mentor, but not all have the same attributes. When, at the age of seventeen, my friend wanted to pursue a career as a professional tennis player, he changed his coach. Not because the previous one was unhelpful or unpleasant but because the new one was more modern in his approach and was able to take him further. He knew what he needed and pursued it. It proved to be a fruitful relationship.

At the beginning of this chapter I suggested that the marriage of structure and function was essential for healthy communication. If we don't realize this and act accordingly we will continually build bridges that have no destination, no point. Instead of being places of exchange, outlets of exploration, symbols of a bright future, they become objects of ridicule. A bridge in the North Island of New Zealand is occasionally visited by curious trekkers. Surrounded by thick bush land, the concrete structure arches across the River Wanganui from one uncultivated bank to the other. Aptly named 'The Bridge to Nowhere' it is a testament to a long-abandoned settlement project! There is something tragic and impotent about pointless bridges and pointless relationships.

Summary and advice

1. **Every one of us has been structured for a God-designed function.** We are empowered for this God-given purpose and therefore need to discover it if we are to fit into the world in which God has placed us.

2. **In common with bridges all relationships should be structured for a purpose.** A failure to discover the purpose and determine the appropriate structure will result in communication failure. A relationship without purpose will become obsolete. A relationship without the correct structure will either be overloaded or underused.

3. **We need to discover the purpose of our relationships.** We do this by finding out whether it will provide the necessary communication needs of both parties and whether it will overcome the evident obstacles.

4. **We need to determine the available relational structures.** Relationships can be categorized into three basic structures: those 'above' us such as mentors whom we draw from, those beside us such as 'friends' whom we share with, and those 'below' us such as disciples in whom we invest.

5. **We need to marry the appropriate structure with the agreed function.** Jesus Christ formed fruitful relationships at every level and is the perfect example of how we should have a more rational and purpose-driven approach to the building of our relational bridges.

Notes
1. Frank Gehry. Quoted in Judith Dupré, *Bridges* (Könemann, 1998).
2. William Morris. Quoted in Dupré, *Bridges*.
3. Dupré, *Bridges*.
4. Frank Gehry. Quoted in Dupré, *Bridges*.

Chapter 13
According to the Pattern
Choosing a Design and a Designer

Although assisted by numerous others, the general design and specifications for Sydney Harbour Bridge were drawn up by the chief engineer Dr J.J.C. Bradfield, who is remembered by the Bradfield Highway that crosses it. The design involves a 39,000-tonne steel arch that is 503 metres long and hinged at the base at each side of the harbour. The 300-tonne steel hinges or bearings support the full weight of the bridge; approximately 20,000 tonnes thrust on each bearing under maximum load, and allow for necessary movement. They spread the load of the bridge into concrete foundations or 'skewbacks' set 12.2 metres into the solid sandstone. Bradfield was confident of the accuracy of his design, the quality of the materials and the strength of the foundations. Unconsciously, thousands trust him every day!

On 28 December 1879 a gale blew in Scotland that determined the fate of seventy-five people. A train was crossing the recently completed Tay Bridge when the force of the gusts of wind buckled the bridge. The designer, Sir Thomas Bouch, had been commissioned to build two bridges, of which this was the first. At the time of completion it was described as an 'engineering triumph' and Bouch was knighted for his efforts. After the collapse, his skills were questioned and his reputation ruined. His design for the second of the two bridges, which was to cross the Firth of Forth, was abandoned, and Sir Benjamin Baker and Sir John Fowler were given the project. They completed the magnificent Forth

215

Rail Bridge in 1890, which as I have already noted still stands. This series of events illustrates the challenge that faces anyone planning to build a bridge. Who should design it? Should we choose Brunel or Bradfield, Eade or Eiffel, or in this case Bouch or Baker? Obviously, in the case of the Forth Bridge, Bouch's second design was rejected because of his previous failure. Baker's design, on the other hand, was accepted, not just because of his previous engineering successes, which included part of London's Underground Railway system, but also because the design he proposed was far stronger than the broken Tay Bridge. Nonetheless, the planners still had to put their confidence in their new designer. For a start, he had never built a bridge before!

Once the designer has been chosen we have to trust the design that is proposed, a trust that may prove to be ill-founded. On 15 October 1970 the span of the West Gate Bridge in Melbourne, Australia collapsed. Thirty-two people died that day and five more died later as a result of the catastrophe. There were numerous theories as to the cause of the failure. The Royal Commission Report said that, 'Error begat error ... and the events which led to the disaster moved with the inevitability of a Greek tragedy'.[1] One of the flaws seemed to be in the design: it was a box girder bridge. Part of the evidence that added weight to this theory is that other bridges of similar design failed around the same time. A bridge collapsed in Vienna in November 1969, one in Milford Haven in June 1970 and another in Koblenz in 1971. Apparently, many bridges around the world that were built along the same lines were carefully examined or closed as a result of the West Gate failure. The box girder design was subsequently reworked to prevent further loss.

All of this points to some simple conclusions. If we are surrounded with brokenness and grief, failed designs and flawed designers, we are duty bound to be cautious in our choices. Building bridges of any sort is a risky business and lives are put in danger as a result. We increasingly live in a world where lives are undervalued and many live in a society of failed marriages, backstabbing business colleagues and murmuring teams. In a world of uncertainty we need to be as certain as possible in our bridge-building.

Building according to a foolproof pattern

There are not many building blueprints in the world that are faultless. However brilliant, they will contain some small flaws. The fact is they are put together by imperfect people. Nonetheless, there are two that I would put my complete trust in. They are the tabernacle of Moses and the temple of Solomon. The reason, of course, is that they were conceived by the perfect Architect. With this in mind, God's specific instructions to Moses about His project are understandable. Talking of the Old Testament priests, the writer of the book of Hebrews states that,

> *'They serve at a sanctuary that is a copy and shadow of what is in heaven. This is why Moses was warned when he was about to build the tabernacle: "See to it that you make everything according to the pattern shown you on the mountain."'*   (Hebrews 8:5)

The structure on earth had to be built according to the pattern, not just because the pattern was correct, but because it reflected something of what was in heaven. Moses' obedience, therefore, guaranteed success but also glorified God. His disobedience would not only result in loss but would also be seen as rebellion. On top of this, Moses was required to have a personal revelation of the blueprint. His building success was not based on hearsay or tradition but was birthed in a personal knowledge of God. The building of relationships should have the same parameters. We should each meet God on the mountain to view His proposals and then diligently follow His counsel. We cannot afford to build our families independently of God since they were His idea. As Paul teaches, *'I kneel before the Father, from whom his whole family in heaven and on earth derives its name'* (Ephesians 3:14–15). His pattern is not one of numerous options. It is *the* blueprint for our life and relationships. God holds the patent for all bridge designs!

When God created Adam and Eve and gave one to the other, it wasn't just because He didn't want them to be on their own. When He established the covenant of marriage it wasn't just so that they would enjoy a lifelong companionship. When He invented the sacred and pleasurable sexual union within marriage it wasn't just because He wanted them to enjoy each other and have children. God created Adam and Eve from an eternal template, a heavenly pattern.

> *'So God created man in his own image, in the image of God he created him; male and female he created them.'*   (Genesis 1:27)

The unity of the Godhead, God the Father, God the Son and God the Holy Spirit, needed to be expressed on earth. God was One and He wanted us to be one. Jesus prayed for unity so that the world would see what God was like (John 17:21). For the Kingdom of God to come, its subjects on earth must echo heaven. If there was companionship in heaven, so there should be on earth. If there is intimacy in heaven, it should be reflected among human beings. The reason that a man and a woman becoming 'one flesh' (Ephesians 5:31) in marriage is compared to the connection between Christ and His Church is because it reflects an intimate mystery that is present in heaven. I have heard the preacher and author Allan Meyer, teaching on the potency of sex, state that, 'Intimacy is one of the eternal realities of the Divine Nature'.[2] Sex within the context of a holy marriage was never meant to be unclean as some would have it: it is meant to be God-like: pure, passionate and thoroughly enjoyable! That is why Allan Meyer went on to say that, when we commit adultery, 'Heaven screams'. We are not just ripping up God's pattern, we are tearing at His heart.

If we fully understand that we are created in the image of a holy God and He is our blueprint for life, we are less likely to go our own way. However, there is another pattern that He has drafted for our success and with which we also need to be intimately acquainted: the cross. This was the template for the ministry and message of Paul the apostle. He informed the Corinthian church that he *'resolved to know nothing while I was with you except Jesus Christ and him crucified'* (1 Corinthians 2:2). Christ crucified was the pattern on which he built his life and since the cross itself is the perfect example of a bridge it is the best model for our relationships.

The love demonstrated on the cross surpasses human comprehension, yet at the risk of removing the 'mystery' from something so precious, we can compare the purposes of the cross to those of a normal bridge. In common with all bridges, it overcame obstacles and provided passage; it removed a negative and added a positive! The negative was the naturally impassable gulf of wrongdoing that separated us from God and the positive was the remarkable communion that the cross opened for every one of us. Once on a visit to Venice in Italy I caught a tiny glimpse of what the cross had accomplished for me. One of the most significant landmarks in Venice is a bridge. Lord Byron describes it in his poem 'Childe Harold', 'I stood in Venice, on the Bridge of Sighs: a palace and a prison on each hand'.[3] It is a covered passageway that arches across one of the often putrid canals that intersect the city, connecting the famous Doge's Palace with the old jail. It is so called because it was the thoroughfare for condemned prisoners going from the judgment hall to the place of execution. What struck me was that this was my destination in life until Christ reversed it. I was cramped and condemned until released by a gracious King and given access to His palace. I now stand on 'the Bridge of Laughter', a kingdom and a cell on either hand.

The two components of what I have termed the 'Bridge of Laughter' are mercy and grace. Both are essential for our relationships. The difference between mercy and grace is that mercy prevents us receiving what we do deserve and grace gives us what we do not deserve! Mercy enables the removal of a negative whereas grace makes possible the addition of a positive. Mercy releases us from the prison and grace gives us access to the palace. It is these two ingredients that were so evident in the life of Paul. The pattern of the cross could be clearly seen. He didn't just write epistles, the epistles were written on him. When speaking of his suffering for the cause of Christ he wrote, *'I bear on my body the marks of Jesus'* (Galatians 6:17). These were not religious 'stigmata' but the scars of persecution, the evidence of ownership, a proof that he belonged to Christ. If we are going to share his resolve for Christ we must make the cross our template, and our lives must be marked with grace and mercy. We must go out of our way to be generous in our conversation and attitudes, giving praise when little is due, giving gifts when none are received and continuing to trust when failure is common. In our homes, 'Forgiveness has to be like breathing', as the author Faith Lees put it,[4] a way of life. Since bitterness suffocates the soul, we cannot hope to live if our absolution is stuttering and asthmatic. Of course, this may seem like an impossible pattern to follow until we realize that like Moses on the mountain, a personal revelation of the cross can give us the power to live it.

Alongside the first two patterns, God and the cross, the third blueprint, sound teaching, seems the more obvious since it actually involves the printed page. The challenge is to ensure that we refer to the correct one! There are a myriad of dealers peddling their panaceas in the markets of the world in order to provide answers for our broken relationships: self-help manuals; motivational conferences; the latest meditation techniques. Many have genuine intentions and most contain some common sense, but unless they exalt Christ and the cross, they are powerless and fruitless, without a sound origin or a sound ending. Even books written from a Christian standpoint, including this one, are biased and demand scrutiny! There is only one book that can be relied on to provide a foolproof pattern for our bridge-building and that is the Bible. Sadly, so many of us ignore it or neglect it, choosing rather to access what we consider to be less confrontational. Yet God has entrusted His master plan to us, not to gather dust on a shelf, but to use for building something of beauty, strength and value. Paul commanded Timothy to hold onto this pattern at all costs:

> *'What you heard from me, keep as the pattern of sound teaching, with faith and love in Christ Jesus. Guard the good deposit that was entrusted to you – guard it with the help of the Holy Spirit who lives in us.'*
>
> (2 Timothy 1:13–14)

He also reminded the Roman church that it was through obedience to its tenets that they were set free:

> *'But thanks be to God that, though you used to be slaves to sin, you wholeheartedly obeyed the form of teaching to which you were entrusted.'*
>
> (Romans 6:17)

The expression 'form of teaching' is important. According to W.E. Vine, 'The metaphor is that of a cast or frame into which molten material is poured so as to take its shape. The Gospel is the mould; those who are obedient to its teachings become conformed to Christ, whom it presents'.[5] What God requires of us is that we are transformed by being conformed to His image through the faithful application of His Word.

Following a flawless Designer

By 1876 it had become abundantly clear to the Corporation of London that a new bridge was required in England's ever-growing capital city. A special bridge committee was established to consider the options for a new bridge over the River Thames down river of the existing London Bridge. It initiated a public competition to find the best designer and the most appropriate design. During the ensuing years numerous designs were submitted and considered until in 1886 work finally began on what was to become known as Tower Bridge. The chosen design was a 'bascule' bridge, consisting of moveable sections called 'bascules': a word derived from the French for 'seesaw'. The chosen designers were Sir Horace Jones and Sir John Wolfe Barry.

This concept of a public competition was also employed for the choice of designer for the London Bridge. Sir John Rennie's stone arch bridge replaced the decrepit and crumbling old London Bridge in 1831. As I have already noted, the London Millennium Bridge design and designer, Sir Norman Foster, was chosen in the same manner in the 1990s. In each case, the preferred designer was considered to be the best person at the time to complete the project and the design that was submitted was deemed to be the most suitable in the circumstances. This same competitive approach to bridge-building is also used by many to build their relationships. Yet it contains some fundamental flaws. It may be acceptable when simply transporting goods across the Thames but cannot be applied when connecting the souls of human beings.

The first flaw is that a competition is not a suitable method for choosing a friend! A bridge competition is based on the premise that any architect can enter with any reasonable proposal. In the case of Tower Bridge the Chamber of Commerce in London exhibited fifty such proposals that had been submitted over the years! In other words it is an 'any designer, any design' approach to bridge-building. As long as it fulfils the necessary requirements it is acceptable. As long as it works, it is OK! If we follow this line of thinking in our relational bridge-building, it proves disastrous. We cannot afford to bet on our future as we would a horse race. Life is not a lottery yet millions gamble with their destiny by trying to select a 'winning designer' for their friendships! In the world there are not just fifty such bridge proposals but thousands and everyone wants to 'pick a winner'. One couple commits to marriage whereas another simply 'live together'. One person believes in celibacy, another believes in 'sleeping around'. One follows the philosophy of an Eastern guru, another swears by the teaching of a Western therapist. In our post-modern world, where there is only relative truth, all of these differing views are accepted and acceptable. 'As long as it works for you, it is OK!' 'There is no right or wrong.' I once heard the American theologian Cheryl Bridges-Johns describe post-modernism as 'a carnival of cruelty', equating it to a theme park or a circus. We enter this colourfully plastic world with the aim of trying everything. Every tent invites us in to try a new experience. Every stall tempts us to sample its wares. It's all free. There is no correct path or forbidden encounter. We experiment and move on. There are no boundaries and no answers. Eventually, the heartless Mardi-Gras moves on leaving us exhausted and bankrupt. We lost. We made the wrong choices. We are left to pick up the pieces, not the winnings.

A friend of mine at university typified this reasoning. Her faith placed the teachings of an Indian mystic next to the Bible and the Book of Mormon on her bookshelf. She chose whichever teaching suited her at the time. For her they were all true despite the fact that they contradict one another. Her life was as confused as her library. Jesus Christ didn't allow for these choices and subsequent uncertainty. He didn't want us to have to choose a designer for our lives. He made it clear from the beginning that He was the only Designer. Therefore, the only choice we have is either to accept Him or reject Him. He said,

> *'I am the way and the truth and the life. No-one comes to the Father except through me.'*   (John 14:6)

Simple, clear, absolute: no rivals, no contest and no winner. Jesus is not the best in the field, He is the only entrant. He is the Race. God will not become embroiled in our petty competitions. When Joshua challenged God's 'Captain', the Lord Jesus Christ, with the question, *'Are you for us or for our enemies?'* He simply replied, *'Neither ... but as commander of the army of the Lord I have now come'* (Joshua 5:13–14). In other words, 'I am above your earthly reasoning: Either submit to me or rebel!' Joshua wisely submitted! When it comes to the building of relationships we need the same absolutes and the same response.

The second fatal problem with the Thames competitions is that the designers in question are themselves flawed. Despite the evident expertise of Barry, Rennie and Foster, their bridges have had their problems. Barry's Tower Bridge, though still functional, has been described as 'the most monumental example of extravagance in bridge construction in the world'![6] Rennie's London Bridge began to sink and, no longer necessary, was transported to Arizona in 1968, and Foster's Millennium Bridge was closed as soon as it was opened because it was considered unstable! Each one of these examples of 'competition winners' provides a parable for us. They all insist that we have a perfect designer providing the pattern for our lives. Even if it were acceptable to pick a designer out of the 'hat', wisdom would suggest that we choose one who will not leave our relationships unused and unstable. Jesus Christ is the only flawless Designer. No competition!

The stages of design

There is a sense in which engineering is more godly than pure science! Although, as one who studied pure science at university, I am loathe to say this! The reason that I do is because engineering involves creating something whereas pure science does not. It has been well said that, 'At its core, science is observation'.[7] Engineers, therefore, are more actively involved with the world around them than pure scientists. In simplistic terms, while a pure geneticist observes genetic codes, a genetic engineer tries to change them. According to Theodore von Kármán, 'The scientist explores what is. The engineer creates what has not been'.[8] This may seem to be semantics but it is important because when it comes to forming a relationship many have a passive scientific approach instead of an active engineering one! When we build a friendship we have an opportunity not just to observe its growth but to be actively involved in seeing it take shape. It is a creative process. We work with God to see our dreams become reality. The active process involves clear steps that take the project from a thought to completion and because we need an engineering mindset we must be aware of the stages of design.

Richard White and his colleagues, teachers of structural engineering and design, identified a 'five-step process' in 'the evolution of a structure'. Their case study was the Solleks River Bridge in Washington State, USA. In simple terms, these are: the 'general planning stage' where needs are recognized; the 'idea stage' where alternatives are proposed; the 'analysis stage' where alternatives are evaluated; the 'final design stage' where everything is detailed and refined; and fifthly the 'implementation stage'. In describing this last stage they make a fascinating comment, 'This construction phase is the culmination of the aspirations of the client and the efforts of the engineer; the design documents are transformed into reality'.[9] For us as prospective relational engineers, the parallels are obvious. God's heart and hope for us is that we build bridges. His design documents are available to all. We, therefore, need to make every effort to see His plans take shape in our lives. In order to apply these five design stages to our relationships I am going to convert them, once again, to questions:

- The general planning stage: What is our general plan for our relationships? What do we want to do? What should we do?
- The idea stage: What are the different types of relationship available to us? What can we do?

- The analysis stage: Which of the relational types is best suited or not suited to us and our circumstances? What can't we do? What won't we do?

- The final design stage: What will we do? How will we implement the plan?

- The implementation stage: When do we start?

The challenge for us is this: though a structural engineer plans meticulously when it comes to the building of a fairly mundane concrete bridge, we tend to embark on far more significant relationships with no vision or strategy at all. Of course, the steps of design may seem too theoretical on paper, but in actual fact when we start a friendship we automatically ask ourselves these questions. Let me illustrate this from my own life. I attended boarding school from the age of seven to eighteen. The months away from home necessitated the forming of good friendships. The second boarding school that I attended as a teenager was divided into 'houses' of about sixty boys. In my house, there were two dormitories of thirty boys each. At the beginning of each term there was a rush to find a good bed! The best choice was a bed with a comfortable mattress near the communal bathroom and next to a good friend! There were numerous fights over the mattresses but the most important thing was the person next to you, as it was, among other things, a protection against bullying. During the day, our free time and 'homework' took place in a study room allocated to us in which we kept all our personal belongings and which we shared with one other boy. Once again, it was essential that we chose this study companion well since we spent most of our time with him. With my limited expertise, how did I make these mature choices that were possibly going to affect my life, my education and so, by default, my future drastically?

It was obvious that I wanted and needed a friend so the general planning stage was settled! Of the many acquaintances available to me, four were possible: Mark, Simon, Graham and John (not their real names). I liked them and they liked me. The basis of a good friendship! So much for the ideas stage! Now for the tricky part! The best way to succeed at the analysis stage is by a process of elimination. Mark was always in trouble and I got into trouble with him! Eventually, my teacher suggested that I didn't pursue the relationship! Simon was beginning to choose a life of homosexuality. Sleeping in the bed next to him was proving to be a hazard! His admirers occasionally attempted to turn their attention toward me. I knew what the Bible taught about homosexuality and so I refused to follow him down that track. Graham, on the other hand, proved to be an excellent dormitory companion. His popularity balanced my tendency to be alone and his friends 'protected' me. John, however, was the faithful one. He didn't seem to have as many friends to choose from for a study companion as Graham and so we decided to implement our plan of sharing together. He became a good friend.

Instinctively, without knowing the five-step process of design I had negotiated it correctly. Perhaps more importantly, however, without knowing the Designer or His pattern for my life, I had made good choices. In retrospect, I believe that God was graciously guiding my footsteps before I had consciously invited Him to do so! Nonetheless, in this chapter, I have explained the essentials of design because it is always better to act with foresight than learn from hindsight! Had the builders of the Tay Bridge in Scotland and the West Gate Bridge in Australia known in advance that there was a problem with the competence of the designer or the proposed design, they may have changed their course and thereby averted catastrophe. Most of us, however, plunge into relational projects without giving design a second thought. This kind of blindness tends to be recorded as a date and a disaster: 'On Monday the divorce papers landed on my desk. What am I going to tell the children?' – 'On 28 December 1879 a gale blew in Scotland that determined the fate of seventy-five people.'

Summary and advice

1. **Many bridges have collapsed due to poor design or bad designers**. We are surrounded with relationships that have failed for the same reason. As relational engineers it is therefore imperative that we choose a proven pattern and a faultless designer.

2. **We should build according to a foolproof pattern**. God holds the patent for all relational bridge designs and so it is folly to ignore His blueprint.

3. **God Himself is the pattern on which we should build**. Our relationships on earth should be formed from the template of heaven.

4. **The cross of Christ is a pattern on which we should build.** It is the perfect bridge and exemplifies the components of mercy and grace that are so essential for fruitful relationships. Where mercy prevents us receiving what we do deserve, grace gives us what we do not deserve.

5. **The Bible is a pattern on which we should build.** Our relationships will be transformed if we conform to the divine mould of the gospel.

6. **We should follow a flawless Designer.** Although we live in a world that offers numerous alternative lifestyles, there is only one perfect designer for our relationships: the Lord Jesus Christ.

7. **There are clear stages in bridge design.** The five stages are: general planning, ideas, analysis, final design and implementation. They invite the questions: What should we do? What can we do? What won't we do? What will we do? When do we start? We are required to engineer our relationships actively instead of passively observing them.

Notes

1. Royal Commission Report, 14 July 1971. Quoted in William M. Hitchins, *West Gate* (Outback Press, 1979).
2. Allan Meyer, Victoria State AOG Conference. Message recorded on 2 October 2001.
3. George Gordon Byron (Lord Byron), 'Childe Harold's Pilgrimage', 1816.
4. Faith Lees, *Love is Our Home* (Hodder & Stoughton, 1978).
5. W.E. Vine, *Vine's Expository Dictionary of Old and New Testament Words* (Fleming H. Revell, 1981).
6. Waddell. Quoted in John H. Stephens, *The Guinness Book of Structures* (Guinness Superlatives Ltd, 1976).
7. David Breese, *Seven Men Who Rule the World from the Grave* (Scripture Press, 1991).
8. Theodore von Kármán. Quoted in Richard N. White, Peter Gergely, Robert G. Sexsmith, *Structural Engineering. Vol. 1. Introduction to Design Concepts and Analysis* (John Wiley & Sons, Inc., 1972).
9. White, Gergely, Sexsmith, *Structural Engineering. Vol. 1. Introduction to Design Concepts and Analysis*.

Chapter 14

Failure Sensitivity

Determining Why Bridges Fail

During the month prior to the official opening in March 1932, Sydney Harbour Bridge was subjected to rigorous load testing. For three weeks seventy-two steam locomotives were placed buffer to buffer on the then four rail tracks. They were moved and removed from each side and either end as scrupulous measurements were made. Apparently the bridge passed all the tests and was declared safe to use. The impressive structure had conformed to the designers' and builders' specifications and requirements. Dr Bradfield assured the public that there was no danger of the bridge collapsing during the tests. However, if there is no possibility of failure there is no need for testing!

Lyndon Baines Johnson, thirty-sixth President of the United States, led the American people in a troubled season. His presidency started with the assassination of President John F. Kennedy in 1963 and finished with the assassination of Martin Luther King in 1968. His time in office spanned the muddied waters of the Cold War, race riots and the conflict in Vietnam. In an attempt to resolve the divisiveness that he saw, he addressed the nation in March 1968. He told the people of America that there was a 'division in the American house' and challenged them with the truth that 'a house divided against itself by the spirit of faction, of party, of region, of religion, of race, is a house that cannot stand'.[1] In fact he spoke of the dangers of division and the need for unity in his inaugural address in 1965 and continued the theme in many speeches. His Secretary of Defense, Robert McNamara, describes Johnson as 'building bridges'. Whether successful or not, he did attempt to span divides. However, it wasn't only political and social bridges to which he turned his attention but natural ones. He communicated his evident enthusiasm to John Hopkins University when he said, 'We often say how impressive power is. But I do not find it impressive at all ... A dam built across a river is impressive'.[2] No doubt fuelled by this passion he ordered an inquiry into bridge safety throughout the nation! According to the structural engineers Mattys Levy and Mario Salvadori, 'More than seven hundred thousand bridges were inspected and classified by a president's panel on bridge safety',[3] a panel made necessary by a catastrophic bridge failure.

Early on a cold December evening in 1967, at the height of rush-hour traffic, a crowded bridge over the Ohio River collapsed without warning into the freezing waters below. Apparently, due to the failure of one connection (a steel 'eyebar') in one link of one of the chains on which the bridge was suspended, thirty-seven vehicles plunged into the river, killing forty-six people. The subsequent investigation revealed what is called 'stress corrosion' in the eyebar, the cold temperature adding to the 'failure sensitivity' of the steel. The Silver or Point Pleasant Bridge tragedy led to the dismantling of its 'twin', the St Mary's Bridge, in 1969 in order to prevent another collapse and also to the setting up of President Johnson's bridge safety panel. It was evident that a better understanding of the stresses and loads to which bridges are subjected on a regular basis could only help to build with greater strength and avoid further disaster in the future. The same could be said of our relationships. An investigation into 'bridge failure' and 'bridge safety' is of paramount importance. Furthermore, the recognition of the fact that a relatively small failure can have such vast and devastating consequences should sober us into action.

The primary loads of bridges

Although the exact reasons for the collapse of a building, a bridge or even a marriage may well be highly complex and unique to every situation, some of the principles behind them are fairly simple. Any structure in this world is subjected to various loads, and it is an important part of the design process to ensure that it can withstand them. Its strength is measured by its capacity to do so. If the loads are too great for some reason, the structure will fail. In the case of a bridge, there are three primary loads. As Judith Dupré describes, 'Every bridge, large or small, must withstand and overcome the forces or stresses to which it is subjected. Bridges are designed to carry their own weight, or *dead load*; to carry people and traffic, or *live load*; and to resist natural forces, such as wind and earthquakes, or *environmental load*'.[4] In the case of the Sydney Harbour Bridge, 63 per cent of the steelwork is required for the dead load, 27 per cent for the live load (this includes 2 per cent for the braking of trains) and 10 per cent for the environmental load. I would like to suggest that the same three loads are evident in each of our relationships.

Dead load

Although it doesn't sound very positive, every one of us has a 'dead load'! We are all designed to bear our own burdens, whether they are physical, emotional or spiritual. If we are healthy, our musculoskeletal structure is strong enough to carry our own body weight and our 'emotiospiritual' structure capable of withstanding the normal 'life loads'. Everyone, for instance, has to face the challenges of growth and the pressure of making choices. Our relationships also possess a 'dead load' and they should be able to withstand the normal 'weight' of that relationship, the additional pressure that sharing brings. The Bible teaches that each one of us has a responsibility of carrying this 'dead load': *'for each one should carry his own load'* (Galatians 6:5). In other words, we are meant to stand on our own. This obviously does not mean that we are to live independently of others but simply that we should shoulder our own responsibilities in life. If we collapsed under our own body weight, there would be something seriously wrong with our internal structure. If we are constantly depending on others for our life choices or as a married couple continually turning to others for support and strength, the basic structure of our life and relationships is at fault and needs to be examined carefully. Levy and Salvadori, in their fascinating book *Why Buildings Fall Down* from which I have drawn many illustrations for this chapter, state categorically that, 'The accidental death of a building is always due to the failure of its skeleton, the *structure*'.[5] It is an observation that is worth noting by relational engineers who are building bridges with others.

Of course, there are times when, usually due to our own folly or when subjected to forces beyond our control, we may fall and need someone to carry our load. The passage in Galatians explains this scenario:

> *'Brothers, if someone is caught in a sin, you who are spiritual should restore him gently. But watch yourself, or you also may be tempted. Carry each other's burdens, and in this way you will fulfil the law of Christ.'* (Galatians 6:1–2)

If they are a good friend, however, they will only carry our burden until we are recovered enough to carry it ourselves once again. A trip to the Pyrenees in the south of France illustrated this concept to me with some force. I was walking rapidly down a steep path with a heavy backpack when I came across a sharp bend in the track. Instead of negotiating it successfully I managed to propel myself over a small cliff! When I stopped falling, I found myself on my back, facing head down on a steep rocky slope and unable to move! Thankfully, I was with a friend who climbed down, removed my pack and helped me back to the path. There was nothing broken, so when he had attended to my various cuts and bruises, he placed my burden back on my back and told me to walk more slowly! He had no intention of carrying my burden down the mountain, and anyway it was my stupidity and not my burden that was the problem! Climbing up the Pyrenees did me good! It is a beneficial burden to take responsibility to make decisions. Falling down the Pyrenees proved painful! It is an overbearing burden to make irresponsible decisions, as I discovered to my cost!

Live load
The second primary load, the 'live load' in our relationships, describes the traffic, the communication that crosses the bridge on a daily basis. The term 'live load' is an apt one because it is constantly changing and moving. When a bridge is designed, a great variety of traffic conditions are taken into consideration: the types of vehicle; quantity; speed; the impact of braking and accelerating; and even small accidents. These are the normal working conditions of the bridge. Bridges are designed to withstand the expected 'live load' easily and so each bridge, like each relationship, has a different load capacity. Marriages, for instance, are designed to carry greater traffic than mere acquaintances. These burdens are not only valid but important. We need to carry them in order to fulfil our responsibilities.

The Bible uses the image of an agricultural yoke to describe burden bearing. Oxen, for instance, are required to wear a yoke in order to draw a plough; the burden is necessary for the task. In the same way, every one of us has been given an area of responsibility, a *'field God has assigned to us'* (2 Corinthians 10:13), in which we have authority to act, for which He has empowered us and for which we will be held accountable (cf. Mark 13:34f.). Due to this gift of strength, we should wear our yoke with ease. When my mother worked on a farm in England in her youth, she had a wooden yoke fashioned for her that enabled her to carry large pails of milk. Others may have struggled but the fitted yoke helped her carry the burden easily. In Jesus' day, ruthless landowners would overburden their animals and their workers. It was this situation that He was addressing when He said,

> *'Come to me, all you who are weary and burdened, and I will give you rest. Take my yoke upon you and learn from me, for I am gentle and humble in heart, and you will find rest for your souls. For my yoke is easy and my burden is light.'* (Matthew 11:28–30)

It is evidently good to bear a light yoke but also relatively easy to become overburdened. We become weary, either by carrying too heavy a weight or by working outside our assigned field. If we attempt the latter we work without God's grace, in our own strength and at our own peril! Once again, it tends to be our own folly that overloads us!

We all have a capacity to *'go beyond our limits'* (2 Corinthians 10:15). Sharon was a case in point. She was a godly woman and a committed churchgoer. Her husband, Stephen, on the other hand, though a hard worker, was less reliable in his relationship with God. Sharon was frustrated with his inconsistency and felt that her feelings were completely justified. She believed that Stephen was failing in his duties to be a good role model for the children. She didn't trust him to fulfil his God-given role of headship over the home. So she thought that she would help him out a little! She decided to become the leader in the home: sometimes even making fairly significant decisions without his input. It all seemed innocent enough, even spiritual. After all, she was the godly one and so would make the better decisions! However, it wasn't long before she became very weary, began to shout at the children and complain to her husband. Stephen, after an initial period of retreating into silence, became very angry with her and felt that his feelings were completely justified! He was disempowered by his own wife and blamed the church. Thus the destructive cycle continued and worsened. It was at this point that they came for counsel. What had happened? Sharon had overextended herself by carrying some of Stephen's burden in the leading of the home. Stephen, who should have been trusted to carry his own burden, instead of feeling relieved because of reduced responsibility, felt robbed. In bridge terms, Sharon was overloaded and began to collapse. Stephen, on the other hand, was under-used and began to become redundant. The resultant traffic chaos was enormous! Sharon's side of the bridge was too full and Stephen's too empty. There was imbalance, 'major accidents' and danger of imminent collapse. The simple solution was for Stephen to take on a more active and responsible role in the home, which he was happy to do, and for Sharon to trust him to do so. The bridge not only survived but started carrying its live load with safety and efficiency.

Environmental load

The possible bridge failure in the marriage of Stephen and Sharon was obviously due to their poor choices; however, there are often other forces that endanger our relationships that are outside our control. These are what I would term 'environmental loads'. Sometimes there are extreme conditions that threaten the strongest of structures. Apparently, even steel becomes brittle at very low temperatures and can break suddenly under heavy loads. For instance, on a particularly cold night in Canada a train crossed a steel railroad bridge and the girders snapped 'as if made of glass'![6] Most bridges are designed to stand for over one hundred years and withstand all the predicted environmental catastrophes that could occur in that time, but occasionally freak conditions test their strength. Our relationships are similarly challenged. However, it isn't excessive temperature that can shatter our hopes, but sudden trauma, unforeseen tragedy or spiritual attack. Many relationships falter during the stress of a chronic illness or after a death in the family, and all of them are always open to the temptations of the accuser. Our relationships should stand firm even under these pressures, but it is in these times of great environmental load that we should be aware of those things that make us vulnerable.

The vulnerability of bridges

Some bridges are colossally strong. They are designed to withstand phenomenal loads. Yet even these monsters are at risk and strangely enough they share almost exactly the same threats as every other bridge. It is this realization of their vulnerability that is, in fact, their greatest strength. If we know both the possible weaknesses and the potential threats to our bridges, we can build accordingly.

Regarding our own lives, the Bible warns us about ignoring the possibility of failure,

'So, if you think you are standing firm, be careful that you don't fall!'
(1 Corinthians 10:12)

Paul is saying that we need to realize that we can fall. Most of us, if we are honest, know that we have certain weaknesses that can cause us to self-destruct. However, we are also exposed in the area of our strengths! I didn't always have this realization. I used to believe that, because I had such a strong marriage, it wasn't possible for it to fail. This is a dangerous philosophy. The author Gordon Macdonald describes how he believed that he was at his strongest in the area of his personal relationships, 'And then', he writes, 'my world broke – in the very area I had predicted I was safe'.[7] He became aware of his mistaken belief both from personal experience and also from the insight of Oswald Chambers who had taught him that, 'The Bible characters never fell on their weak points but on their strong ones; unguarded strength is double weakness'.[8] In other words, we need to guard our weaknesses but doubly guard our strengths. I clearly remember when my attitude changed on this point. I was talking to a friend about my relationships. He was nearly ten years older than I was and so I valued his wisdom. At one point in the conversation I said, 'I really love my wife, so I couldn't commit adultery.' I will never forget his reaction. He turned toward me and almost looked straight into my soul. His answer came with a sudden and shocking awareness. 'Oh, yes, you can!' he said. I genuinely believe that, maybe unwittingly, my friend saved my marriage on that day. He taught me that it is stronger and safer to say, 'I can commit adultery but I won't', than 'I can't commit adultery so I won't.'

The fact is that we are vulnerable and our relationships are threatened. As I explained in Chapter 5, the challenges and threats we all face are the same. The Bible states, *'No temptation has seized you except what is common to man'* (1 Corinthians 10:13). The verse then goes on to say that there is a promised solution. *'God is faithful'* and will always provide a *'way out'*. The realization of my 'failure sensitivity' under certain conditions and my knowledge of God's faithfulness at those times has been my salvation on numerous occasions, which is why I want to describe briefly some bridges that are particularly susceptible to falling.

Bridges with the wrong foundations

In 1991 there was a devastating mudslide in Antofagasta in North Chile that swept through the town killing 116 people. I visited the town soon after and was guided through the maze of rubble by a small boy. He wanted to show me the remains of his house and how he had escaped. As I stood with him, shocked and saddened by what I saw, I became painfully aware that I was standing on sand. Immediately Jesus' words came to mind with renewed clarity:

> *'But everyone who hears these words of mine and does not put them into practice is like a foolish man who built his house on sand. The rain came down, the streams rose, and the winds blew and beat against that house, and it fell with a great crash.'*   (Matthew 7:26–27)

If we build on sand and the storms come, which they inevitably will, there will be tragedy. Anyone who has stood on a sandy beach at the edge of the sea will know the experience of having the powerful undertow of the waves remove the sand from beneath their feet. The technical term for this is 'scouring' and it is the cause of numerous bridge collapses across the world. If we fail to build our relationships on the tenets of the Bible we may well find ourselves guiding a sympathetic visitor through the wreckage of our life and showing them where our home used to be.

Bridges that lack redundancy

When my children were younger, I used to lift them up and put them on my shoulders (a feat that would now be virtually impossible!). When I did, my skeleton would behave like the structure of a building or bridge and automatically channel the extra (very) 'live load' through my legs to the ground. If one of my knees gave way, my body would automatically redistribute the load to the other leg so that I wouldn't fall and damage my precious cargo! In engineering terms this is called 'redundancy'. It is an in-built safety mechanism. A structure that is unable to redistribute the load lacks redundancy and will fail. In communication redundancy is equally vital. Our language is struc- tured with safeguards that allow a teacher to fail by missing out words and yet still be understood, for which I am immensely grateful! Relational bridges that lack redundancy will also falter. In fact, lack of redundancy is the one thing that accompanies all bridge failure. We must therefore build bridges with safeguards so that when the tests come we find and take the God-given *'way out'* (1 Corinthians 10:13) and not fail completely.

Bridges that are old

When the original London Bridge was dismantled and replaced in 1831 it was because it was old. It had been started in 1176 and so had 'lived' for over six hundred years. There was sadness but no mystery about it. It was much more of a tragedy when the new bridge had to be replaced in 1968. It had failed before it had grown old. (Thankfully, as I have explained earlier in the book, it was moved, rebuilt and is now 'living' successfully in another city!) If we relate this to lives and relationships, there is no doubt that there is *'a time to be born and a time to die'* (Ecclesiastes 3:2); however, the time for a marriage to die should be considerably longer than the current average in many nations. Celebrating fifty years of fulfilling marriage should be the norm, not the exception. Often, the reason that marriages fail 'before their time' is because the couple believe that the relationship is old. A couple going through a 'mid-life crisis' are vulnerable to temptation because they think the marriage needs replacing after only twenty years! Our mindset is the problem. Our relationships can have the chronological age of twenty but the psychological age of sixty! Although our relational bridges do have a lifespan they should, unlike civil bridges, continue to grow in strength over time so that an established marriage will have a greater capacity than a new one.

Bridges built by people

When the Brooklyn Bridge was being built in New York in 1878 an unscrupulous subcontractor swapped some tested wire with an inferior product apparently to save money. A strand of wires subsequently broke on 14 June, killing one worker and injuring others. The resultant scandal could have jeopardized the project. However, any bridge built by people has the potential to fail! Ever since we picked up a hammer we have been cutting costs and corners! It is likely that 'one third of all the structural failures in the United States in the last fifty years were due to outright human errors'.[9] Nonetheless, this information shouldn't stop us crossing bridges. Our attitude should be the same as the Roeblings, the designers and constructors of the Brooklyn Bridge, who faced the facts and determined to continue with greater strength. Thus, I am saddened when 'bridges' fail but not disheartened. It seems to me that humankind has both an enormous capacity for success and also a great propensity for failure. We can build great bridges, but so often our 'fallen human nature' gets the better of us. As the book of Proverbs teaches,

> *'The wise woman builds her house,*
> *but with her own hands the foolish one tears hers down.'*

(Proverbs 14:1)

It is, therefore, wisdom to conclude that our relationships are vulnerable because we're human and yet also are possible because we are human!

Bridges subjected to resonance

My sister is a campanologist. When thousands of bells rang at the start of the millennium in England, she was one of the culprits! Yet how does one person move a massive iron bell? She uses the same technique as she would if she were pushing her child on a swing. An application of a slight force causes the bell or child to move out and back. The time of this oscillation is called a 'period'. If my sister rhythmically pulls or pushes with the same period as that of the swinging bell or child she is applying a resonant force. This may seem a useless fact until we realize that a building also has a period. If a wind gusts in resonance with the period of the structure, it can collapse! A story is told of how a wooden bridge once fell into a river because a group of soldiers marched across it in exact rhythm with the period of the bridge! It could be said that every relationship has a similar 'period' and therefore is equally vulnerable. If I wanted to destroy a relationship, I would discover its period and push it regularly like a swing! There is a sense in which repeated temptation in an area of vulnerability behaves like a resonant force. Samson's downfall was caused by continuous, repetitive, and increasing sexual temptation. Builders counteract this force: it is a tragedy that Samson didn't.

Bridges that are tired

All of us are aware of the dangers of tiredness. It prevents progress, makes us open to attack and increases the likelihood of a fall. It causes us to make poor judgments at work, at home or when driving, often with devastating consequences. There is also no doubt that tiredness can destroy a relationship. 'Workaholics' who refuse to take a break and work seven days a week, 365 days a year 'for their family' are not only disregarding God's laws of life but are deceiving themselves. Sooner or later their weariness will cause suffering. Their family needs them to be re-created as God requires. A holiday is a holy-day and should be treated as such. One of the reasons why the Point Pleasant Bridge in West Virginia collapsed was because a part of it was tired. Metal fatigues just like human beings. Most of us have bent a paper clip backwards and forwards until it snaps and we behave remarkably like paper clips! The Bible teaches that both doubt and deception pull and push like wind and we are *'tossed us back and forth'* (Ephesians 4:14) like ships on the sea. If we don't neutralize these forces the resultant tiredness will shipwreck our families.

Bridges that are neglected

I once visited a bridge on a Mediterranean beach on the east coast of Israel. It is a Roman aqueduct that is part of what little remains of the glory of Herod's now submerged port of Caesarea. It is no longer connected to the river from which it drew life or to the city for which it was built. It is divorced from both its source and its purpose. It is alone and unused. I have also stood among the crumbling ruins of other old civilizations around the world. I have walked through the jumbled remnants of ancient wonders and broken dreams, now the home of stagnant pools, wild animals and tourists! Some of these temples, streets, and bridges were destroyed by war, earthquake or fire: their finery vanished, their tombs plundered and the mortar that once held them together replaced with weeds. It is somehow tragic to see something of such magnificence reduced to rubble, but what is worse is to know that many were simply neglected and abandoned. It exhibits an apathy that has consistently dashed human hopes. The remains of Laodicea, now in modern Turkey, are testimony to Christ's opinion of indifference and the truth of His judgments:

> *'I know your deeds, that you are neither cold nor hot. I wish you were either one or the other! So, because you are lukewarm – neither hot nor cold – I am about to spit you out of my mouth.'*
> (Revelation 3:15–16)

To a God of care, carelessness is a terrible denial. The abandoned wife, the neglected child and the absentee father, so common in our society, not only reflect our un-concernedness but also invite our ruin.

Bridges in times of war

If you visit the excavations in Jerusalem you can see where two bridges, Robinson's and Wilson's arches, used to connect the city to the old Temple area. These were destroyed by the Romans in AD 70, along with the Temple and the rest of the city. Rome was challenging the faith, heart and values of the nation of Israel. As we have seen, at such times, bridges are particularly vulnerable. They provide points of access and so are often the first and most obvious targets for an enemy. Rome itself had seen its own bridges attacked. The nineteenth-century poet Thomas Babington Macaulay published his *Lays of Ancient Rome* in 1842. In it he tells the traditional story of how 'Horatius' saved Rome from Lars Porsena and his Etruscan armies by defending the narrow bridge over the River Tiber. In an extraordinary display of courage, Horatius and his two companions, Spurius Lartius and Herminius, stood between the mocking enemy and the threatened city and held back the 'red whirlwind'.

> 'With weeping and laughter
> Still is the story told,
> How well Horatius kept the bridge
> In the brave days of old.'[10]

Now, our bridges may not have political aggressors but they do have philosophical and spiritual ones. Our traditional values of faith and family are being undermined. The book of Nehemiah describes the aggressively defensive attitude we need when our homes are threatened. Nehemiah had a vision to rebuild the walls of Jerusalem but his progress was challenged by the mockery, insults and threats of Sanballat and Tobiah. His advice to his followers was characteristically determined:

> *'After I looked things over, I stood up and said to the nobles, the officials and the rest of the people, "Don't be afraid of them. Remember the Lord, who is great and awesome, and fight for your brothers, your sons and your daughters, your wives and your homes." '*   (Nehemiah 4:14)

Bridges that are overstressed

The primary loads that are described above put stress on natural and relational bridges. In fact they both should be stressed, but not overstressed. If the structure is overstressed it breaks down. In simple terms the loads either push (compression) or pull (tension) the structure. Jesus describes Himself as coming under stress:

> *'I have a baptism to undergo, and how distressed I am until it is completed!'* (Luke 12:50)

The original Greek word for 'distress' here means 'pressed in'. Yet there was never any indication of Jesus breaking under the strain! Paul uses the same image:

> *'We are hard pressed on every side, but not crushed; perplexed, but not in despair . . .'* (2 Corinthians 4:8)

Both Jesus and Paul were pressed like olives but not destroyed. A relationship, then, should be pressed and stretched but shouldn't be crushed or snapped! In bridge terms, the way a structure prevents overloading is to channel its loads to its foundations successfully. I have often observed that people who are persistently worried and overstressed are those who attempt to solve everything themselves instead of channelling their 'loads' to Christ. The Bible advisedly tells us to *'Cast all your anxiety on him'* (1 Peter 5:7). He is the unshakeable foundation for our lives.

A panel on bridge safety

If I were to chair a relational engineering panel on bridge safety that was set up to minimize future failure and collapse, it would include three proposals: All bridges must include a sacrificial protection system, all bridges must be designed with a tried and tested structure, and all bridges must be built with a high factor of safety.

Civil engineers are currently researching and improving what are termed 'sacrificial members' in bridges and buildings. In the same way that many cars have impact protection systems where a part of the car is sacrificed in a crash in order to save the occupants and preserve the rest of the car, bridges are being designed with the equivalent of these 'crumple zones'. The simple principle is that it is better to sacrifice one part than to lose the whole. As Caiaphas, the High Priest at the time of Jesus, profoundly revealed: *'it is better for you that one man die for the people than that the whole nation perish'* (John 11:50). The concept of sacrifice has in fact been connected to bridge-building for hundreds of years. When I was a child in England we would often play traditional games and sing 'nursery rhymes'. One of them that I innocently sang was:

> 'London Bridge is falling down,
> Falling down, falling down,
> London Bridge is falling down,
> My fair lady.'

It goes on to describe the bridge continually falling and being rebuilt. Of course, at the time I had no idea what it was about, and later assumed it was written to commemorate an historical event: the decay of London Bridge. However, the truth about its origins is much more sinister. Apparently, the song and game that accompanies it is known in many countries in various forms and they preserve 'the memory of a dark and terrible rite of past times'.[11] The rite grotesquely determined that when a bridge was built a 'sacrifice' needed to be made in order to 'placate the river and preserve the bridge unnaturally set across it'.[12] There are numerous legends and much evidence to suggest that many bridges around the world were therefore built with people imbedded into the foundations! A tradition in London tells that the stones of its great bridge 'were once bespattered with the blood of little children'.[13] These vile practices hardly bear repeating except that they can remind us of a profound truth. Christ, the precious cornerstone bespattered with innocent blood on which the Church and our lives are founded, is the one and only sacrifice that our 'relational bridges' require. He is the sacrificial member who saves the bridge.

The other two proposals need little explanation. If, as we have seen, the collapse of a bridge is invariably related to a failure in the structure, it is essential that we carefully examine the structure of our relationships. If, as engineers tell us, the primary purpose of structure is to channel loads to the foundations, we have an immediate solution to our problems. A couple, for instance, who live together because they don't believe in marriage, are putting their trust in a man-made structure and building on man-made foundations. Sooner or later, something will give way. A structure promoted by Christ and built on Him is more likely to be safe because He is the cornerstone that saves the bridge. I say 'more likely' because many of us face unforeseen tragedy that puts huge strain on a relationship, which brings me to the third and final proposal. All bridges should be built with a high 'factor of safety'. Most engineering structures are built with a factor of safety of three, sometimes five, which means that that they can be over-loaded three or five times before they will collapse. In other words, we shouldn't live our lives at breaking strain. If we constantly push ourselves to the limit, there is no room for error, no opportunity for adjustment, no plan to change. When it comes to sin we should take no risks. Christ's wisdom, however, demands safety; once again He is the 'factor' that saves the bridge.

I suspect that my three proposals will meet with some criticism! 'Sacrifice is an old-fashioned word!' 'We need to be modern in our philosophies.' 'Why do we do need the age-old structures, how about some innovation?' 'I want to live on the edge. I don't want to live a safe life!' These are of course valid observations if we were talking about entrepreneurial business, but I am talking about lifelong rela-tionships. I am trying to teach sensitivity to the possibility of failure in order to prevent further tragedy. If there were no problems we would not need saving. Rescued people live safe lives; unsaved people live unsafe lives and need to be rescued.

Summary and advice

1. **Small failures in a relational bridge can result in huge trage-dies**. It is therefore imperative that we are aware of both the general causes of bridge failure and also our personal 'failure sensitivity'.

2. **Every bridge is subjected to three primary loads**: dead (its own weight), live (traffic) and environmental (natural forces). The strength of a bridge is measured by its capacity to withstand these loads.

3. **Every relationship has a dead load**. Each of us is designed to carry our own weight. We need to learn to take personal respons-ibility. Failure to do so can overburden others.

4. **Every relationship has a live load**. Every relationship is designed to carry traffic but each type of relationship has a different load capacity. We need to determine our individual and joint limits so that we do not go beyond them.

5. **Every relationship has an environmental load**. Even the best of relationships are subjected to sudden trauma, unforeseen tragedy and spiritual attack and can occasionally fail under these condi-tions. It is therefore vital that we know what makes us vulnerable.

6. **All bridges are vulnerable**. We are stronger when we are aware of our weaknesses. Bridges are vulnerable when they are built on the wrong foundations; lack redundancy; when they are old; built by people; subjected to resonance; tired; or simply neglected. They are vulnerable in times of war and when they are overstressed.

7. **There are three proposals that will bring greater bridge safety**. Bridges must include a sacrificial protection system, must be designed with a tried and tested structure and must be built with a high factor of safety.

Notes

1. Lyndon B. Johnson, in an address to the nation, delivered on 31 March 1968. Quoted in *The World's Great Speeches*, ed. Lewis Copeland and Lawrence Lamm (Dover Publications Inc., 1973).
2. Lyndon B. Johnson, in a speech delivered on 7 April 1965 at John Hopkins University, Baltimore. Quoted in *The Penguin Book of Twentieth Century Speeches*, ed. Brian MacArthur (Penguin Books, 1993).
3. Mattys Levy and Mario Salvadori, *Why Buildings Fall Down* (W.W. Norton & Co., 1992).
4. Judith Dupré, *Bridges* (Könemann, 1998).
5. Levy and Salvadori, *Why Buildings Fall Down*.
6. Mario Salvadori, *Why Buildings Stand Up* (W.W. Norton & Co., Inc., 1980).
7. Gordon MacDonald, *Rebuilding Your Broken World* (Oliver Nelson, 1990).
8. Oswald Chambers, *The Place of Help*. Quoted in Gordon MacDonald, *Rebuilding Your Broken World* (Oliver Nelson, 1990).
9. Levy and Salvadori, *Why Buildings Fall Down*.
10. Thomas Babington Macaulay, *Lays of Ancient Rome*, 1842.
11. Peter and Iona Opie, *The Oxford Dictionary of Nursery Rhymes* (Oxford University, 1992).
12. Peter Ackroyd, *London. The Biography* (Chatto and Windus, 2000).
13. Opie, *The Oxford Dictionary of Nursery Rhymes*.

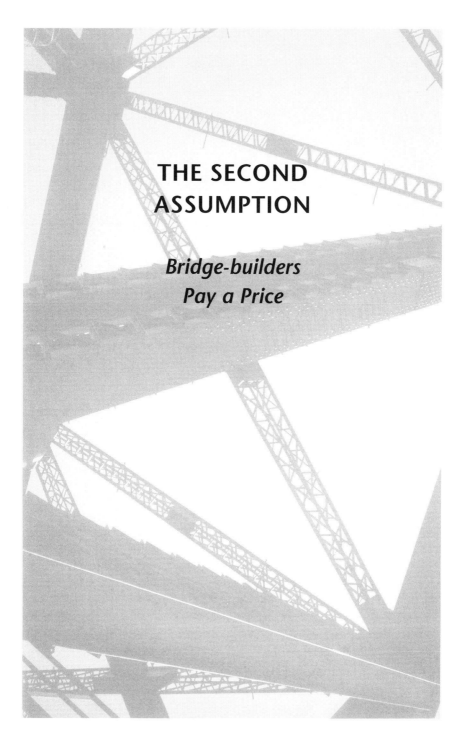

THE SECOND ASSUMPTION

*Bridge-builders
Pay a Price*

Chapter 15

Prepared for Prosperity

Doing the Groundwork

> Although the Sydney Harbour Bridge was officially opened on Saturday 19 March 1932, the ceremony for the 'cutting of the first turf' took place almost nine years previously on 28 July 1923. This followed years of planning, negotiation and acquisition. The first step was to demolish existing properties. In common with many engineering projects, demolition comes before construction, removal before addition and digging down before building up. This groundwork took place before the final design was chosen because much of the necessary excavation for the foundations was common to all designs. Groundwork is foundational!

The history of a bridge is marked by definite times and indeterminate seasons. This is also true of each of our lives. An architect can tell us with certainty the time that a proposal was put forward, a foundation stone was laid or a ribbon cut on opening day. However, if asked about the time it took to conceive, plan or prepare for a project, the eyes become slightly glazed, the answers less exact! There is a timely and a timeless quality to bridge-building. Equally, I can identify significant events in my relationship with my wife – the day that I asked her out, the wedding day, the birthdays of our children – and yet there are numerous hazy periods! I couldn't pinpoint exactly what took place in those and yet they are the fabric of the relationship, the strength that highlights and prepares us for the next memorable event.

The Bible makes a helpful distinction between times and seasons (cf. Acts 1:7). In very general terms, the word 'times' (Gk. *chronos*) is used to refer to measurable moments or periods of time, whereas the word 'seasons' (Gk. *kairos*) is used to emphasize the activities that take place within a period of time. As W.E. Vine puts it, 'Chronos marks quantity, kairos, quality'.[1] Using this idea, the first twenty-four years of my spiritual life can be clearly mapped out. I was born in 1954. The birth was an accurate recorded moment in time! My mother remembered it well! What followed, however, was a season of growth during which I began a journey of discovery about God. This period culminated in my conversion to Christ in 1974. The *chronos* of this period was twenty years but the *kairos* was growth! After this came a year of preparation followed by my 'specific call' into full-time ministry in 1975. A further three-year 'stage of testing' took place before I eventually became a full-time minister in 1978. Of course there have been many other identifiable times and seasons since. This process could be summarized as follows:

- The time of birth (1954) – life starts.
- A season of growth – life unfolds.
- The time of conversion (1974) – the relationship begins.
- A season of preparation – love develops.
- The time of calling (1975) – a seed is planted.
- A season of testing – the vision grows.
- The time of release (1984) – the ministry is birthed.

Many of us prefer to talk about the exact events or definite periods of time rather than the imprecise seasons or stages. They are more easily identified and described. For instance, we know the length of Jesus' ministry and that thirty-five miracles are recorded in the Gospels. They stand out. But what happened in between? What seasons shaped His life? What are the seasons that we all have to go through if we are to be prepared for the next major event? The reality is that it is often these seasons of planning and preparation that are the most challenging. The time of Christ's release into His public ministry was preceded by a tough season in the wilderness. This is the subject of this chapter. We often talk about the challenges of *chronos* but what about the cost of *kairos*? We celebrate the exact day that a bridge was opened, but what about the groundwork that preceded it, the years of preparation that made it possible?

It is a natural and godly principle that all things of excellence or quality need a great deal of preparation. We rightly require architects, teachers and doctors to study for years before we trust them with our houses, children or bodies! In the case of leaders, Christian or otherwise, the principle is the same. The preparation required to produce attributes of greatness often takes a long time. Nelson Mandela's twenty-seven-year imprisonment was not wasted. Yet often gifted individuals rush into positions of responsibility without adequate training. They are not the only ones who suffer the consequences! Every ministry of worth and longevity was tested in the 'wilderness'. Elisha needed ten years of 'washing Elijah's hands' (2 Kings 3:11) before accepting the prophet's mantle. It took Joseph thirteen years of hardship and obscurity to prepare him for his promotion as a ruler in Egypt (Genesis 37:2; 41:46). Moses had to endure forty years in the wilderness before he was allowed to lead the people of Israel out of slavery (Acts 7:23, 30). Paul spent years in relative anonymity before he was released into the full responsibilities of his apostleship (Galatians 1:11–2:1; Acts 9:20–31). The sobering fact is that the three leaders who did not have an equivalent 'wilderness experience', namely Saul, Samson and Solomon, all failed dismally!

I use the word 'wilderness' because it aptly describes a season of preparation before an event. Nowadays, the word 'wilderness' has a negative connotation. We may describe our garden or backyard as a 'wilderness'! It suggests neglect and disorder. Consequently, many argue that God doesn't endorse such a period in our life. However, in the biblical scheme of things, time in a wilderness is not necessarily a negative experience or the Holy Spirit would never have led Jesus Christ into one (Luke 4:1)! It describes the quiet unpredictability and daily challenges of a season as opposed to the fanfare of an event. The biblical wilderness was characterized by a silent uncertainty. Away from the hustle and bustle of a market town, the traveller had to trust God for provision and protection and so was forced to turn to God. When the Israelites left their slavery in Egypt, they needed to journey through such a wilderness before they could cross the River Jordan and enter their land of promise. It was a necessary season in their history. Tragically, their disobedience turned a positive experience into a negative one. Nonetheless, though their rebellion lengthened the *chronos* of the exodus from about two weeks to forty years, they still needed the *kairos*.

This all may seem far removed from our relationships in the twenty-first century, until we realize that God's methodology hasn't changed. He still takes us through positive and life-changing wilderness experiences. He longs for our friendships and marriages to be rich and fruitful, yet He knows that this will not just happen automatically. We need to be prepared for it. In common with bridge-building, every relationship will have its times and seasons and it is often the content of the 'seasons' that shape the success of the 'times'. The choices we make, for instance, in the indeterminate and often difficult period of 'growing up' can enormously influence our ability in forming relationships later on. The lessons learned in the period of an engagement often determine the success of the marriage that follows.

The common theme of the choices and lessons encountered in these 'wilderness seasons' is selflessness! The Israelites had to go God's way and follow His servant Moses, despite the hardships. Even Jesus had to learn to submit to God and His purposes despite the enormous cost. We too have to learn to die to our own agendas, to choose God and others over our selfish desires. Considering our wilfulness and independence, these can be painful episodes in our life. However, any price is vastly overshadowed by the benefits that they introduce. The goal of a 'wilderness season' is to get us ready for the next major blessed event in our lives. Jesus, for instance, was led into the wilderness full of the Holy Spirit, but left it empowered for His ministry (Luke 4:1, 14).

Although, there seems to be only one major wilderness experience in each of the lives of the people of God in the Bible, there are many seasons of preparation, stages of life that equip us for the next growth spurt! There is a sense in which, as I have illustrated above, our life is divided into seasons and events, and doesn't progress gradually but more in a series of steps. In building terms, an indeterminate tread followed by a definite riser! The question that we need to ask ourselves, therefore, is, 'Are we ready for the next step or event in our lives?' The builder, for instance, must determine whether the ground is ready before the first concrete is poured, whether the foundations are ready before the first brick is laid and whether the house is ready before the first occupant moves in. It is a wise person who not only prepares but also knows their state of preparedness.

The Bible gives us a number of images of preparation and examples of people who were prepared by God and I am going to use them to establish whether we are ready to build a bridge. Are we prepared for a fruitful relationship or not? The answer to this question will be found as we answer the following questions honestly. The illustrations I am giving are primarily about our relationship with God but they can be applied to all our life bridges. A person proposing to get married, for instance, would certainly benefit from asking these questions.

Are we prepared to finish?

When Jesus taught His disciples about the cost of pursuing a relationship with Him, He used the example of building a tower:

> *'Suppose one of you wants to build a tower. Will he not first sit down and estimate the cost to see if he has enough money to complete it? For if he lays the foundation and is not able to finish it, everyone who sees it will ridicule him, saying, "This fellow began to build and was not able to finish."'*
> (Luke 14:28–30)

The emphasis of the story here is not the commencement of the project but the completion of it. So before we start a relationship we should ask ourselves whether we can see it through.

Numerous people begin a relationship with no thought of the future. They embark on this potentially wonderful journey in a ship with no compass, map or sail! They have no direction, no destination and no way of getting there. Their life resembles a piece of driftwood. They find themselves washed up, abandoned and alone instead of finishing the race for which they were designed. One of the reasons we often feel so distraught when we fail to complete something is that the God who made us is both a Creator and a Culminator. We all, therefore, have an in-built mechanism both to initiate and complete. In fact, when we fail to do either we feel totally empty. A person who doesn't make friends or cannot keep them will always be unfulfilled.

So what should we do? Jesus Christ is described as an Author and a Finisher and desires and expects us to follow His example:

> *'Looking unto Jesus, the author and finisher of our faith, who for the joy that was set before Him endured the cross, despising the shame, and has sat down at the right hand of the throne of God.'* (Hebrews 12:2)[2]

This, of course, is our problem! In order for Jesus Christ to finish He had to endure the cross. If we are to follow His example, the same is true of us. He preceded His challenge about building and completing a tower by saying,

> *'And anyone who does not carry his cross and follow me cannot be my disciple.'*   (Luke 14:27)

In other words, if we are planning for longevity in our relationships there is a price to be paid. If we want to finish, it is going to cost us! The hope in all of this is that Jesus Christ, who conceives our relationships, offers to empower us to complete them:

> *'being confident of this, that he who began a good work in you will carry it on to completion until the day of Christ Jesus.'*
>
>   (Philippians 1:6)

It is this confidence that helps me plan for the next thirty years of marriage.

Are we prepared for faithfulness?

The latter years of the history of Israel, as recorded in the Old Testament, are a rollercoaster of rebellion, repentance and restoration. According to a brief summary in the book of Nehemiah, God in His compassion *'delivered them time after time'* (Nehemiah 9:28). Their primary sin was idolatry. Instead of continuing to serve the one God who loved and delivered them, in their familiarity and forgetfulness they ran after the numerous gods of the nations that surrounded them. The image used by the prophets in the many attempts to cause them to return was of an 'unfaithful and adulterous wife'. One such prophet was Hosea.

Hosea was prophesying in the years preceding Israel's final defeat at the hands of the Assyrians in the eighth century BC. God used him to assure the Israelites that despite their unfaithfulness He still loved them and wanted them to return to Him. The whole book is an awesome expression of God's love for His people. But how did God woo them back to Himself? He called Israel to the wilderness!

> *'Therefore I am now going to allure her;*
> *I will lead her into the desert and speak tenderly to her.'*
>
>   (Hosea 2:14)

He wanted to prepare her for Himself. But why the desert? In order to understand this we need to paint a picture of Israel's situation.

God's plan for the people of God has always been one of prosperity. He wanted Israel to enjoy a 'land flowing with milk and honey'. During their times of faithfulness to God, this was their experience. Their wine, grain and joy were abundant. However, instead of remaining thankful, they attributed their blessing to the local deities and instead of serving the Lord they sacrificed to the Baals, the gods of fertility and fruitfulness. It was at this point that God, in judgment, removed the vines and fig trees and led Israel to a barren place. It was here in the desert, away from the temptations and trappings of success, that He won her back. Unlike the flood plains adjacent to the River Nile in Egypt or alongside the River Euphrates in Babylon where there is abundance and a million objects to worship, in Israel's wilderness there is One Lord. It was here that He did three things. He firstly removed *'the names of the Baals from her lips'* (Hosea 2:17), the cause of her unfaithfulness, the object of her unholy desire. He then revealed Himself as her tender husband and not her master (Hosea 2:16) and finally promised to restore her to a place of prosperity: *'There I will give her back her vineyards'* (Hosea 2:15).

Whether we are contemplating a closer relationship with God or maybe planning to get married, it is good to ask ourselves in this season if we are genuinely prepared for faithfulness. We need to consider what God said through the prophet Hosea. Am I ready to remove the alternatives, to die to the other desires that will destroy my proposed relationship? Can I commit to a close and tender relationship? Do I believe that this relationship has a great future? These were the issues that faced Israel twenty-eight centuries ago and still face us as individuals today.

Just before I proposed to Amanda I had a strange experience that at the time disturbed me. Unbeknown to her I planned the proposal for months, eventually taking her to a remote and beautiful island in Scotland where I had planned to ask her to marry me. On the set day, as we walked together to the planned destination, I almost unconsciously hung back and watched her. And then, instead of thinking thoughts of romance and admiration, I became immensely critical! I started to paint her in the worst possible light. I instantly saw all her faults and eventually began to voice some of them! My negativity took me by surprise. Amanda seemed somewhat less surprised as she thought that I was getting ready to break up the relationship! She, however, eventually accepted my proposal and left me to ponder my actions. Why had I been so negative? In retrospect, despite my inappropriate actions, I realize now that I was subconsciously preparing myself for my vows: 'For better for worse; for richer for poorer; in sickness and in health'.[3] I was making sure in my mind that I was ready to be faithful to this wonderful woman for the rest of my life, whatever may happen. It was a poor method but a great result!

I had had a similar, yet more positive, experience when I became a Christian and also when God called me into the full-time ministry. Set apart from the obvious benefits of Christianity and away from the glamour of public ministry, God drew me aside and spoke to me. I realized that there were no alternatives and there was no going back. There simply was no one like Jesus and if He never did another thing for me, His love and sacrifice alone demanded my eternal service. As a result, I have not looked back from either decision and nothing that either choice has brought me has shaken my resolve. God, I believe, was preparing me for faithfulness.

Are we prepared for intimacy?

When a couple is engaged to be married there are numerous preparations to be made. The wedding ceremony must be planned to the last detail, the respective families should be entertained and the new home has to be made ready. And then of course there is the honeymoon and more specifically the first night together – an event to which the couple will without doubt give much thought! This thinking is obviously full of expectation, passion and excitement, but also may contain a measure of uncertainty and fear. Whatever the couple's background or experiences, this powerful moment of intimacy on their wedding day requires a great deal of preparation.

I had reason to think about this on a memorable visit to a harem! My daughter and I were guided around the numerous tiled rooms and open courtyards that once housed the wives and concubines of the sultans of the Ottoman Empire. Although hundreds of years old they still maintain the mystery and magnificence of a once opulent rule. However, as we walked among the columns and pools and through the decorated bedrooms, I tried to imagine what it must have been like for one of these women. I thought of Queen Esther who was chosen for King Xerxes but according to Persian custom *'had to complete twelve months of beauty treatments'* (Esther 2:12) before she could go to him.

The whole of her future rested on that initial encounter. After the first night she was taken to another part of the harem reserved for the concubines and couldn't return to the king unless *'he was pleased with her and summoned her by name'* (Esther 2:14). Imagine the possible fear of rejection, the nervousness about the way she looked and the almost terrifying vulnerability. Yet, as we know, she entered gracefully, won the king's favour and became his queen in accordance with God's will. How did she do this with such confidence? Because she had been prepared for intimacy.

During the twelve months under the care of the maids and eunuchs it wasn't only her body that was being cleansed and perfumed it was her mind and soul. She came to understand that she was attractive, chosen, favoured and gifted. She had to learn to trust God for her future. This all took place in the season of preparation. In the book of Hosea, the image is not Esther the virgin but rather Israel the adulteress, used and exposed by her lovers. She had already been rejected by her suitors and hurt by her choices. Yet she too was taken aside by God to be healed of her rejection and prepared for betrothal:

> *'I will betroth you to me forever;*
> *I will betroth you in righteousness and justice,*
> *in love and compassion.'* (Hosea 2:19)

Whatever our background, we need to be prepared for relationships. We need a season to die to our self-consciousness or self-hatred and learn that we have been cleansed and made beautiful for God or the one to whom we are engaged.

In the Old Testament one image used in connection with betrothal is the act of 'covering with a garment'. Ruth made such a request to Boaz when she asked that he marry her (Ruth 3:9). This same picture is alluded to by both the prophets Hosea and Ezekiel. Israel's sin and judgment for her spiritual prostitution had left her exposed, ashamed and vulnerable to her so-called lovers (Ezekiel 16:35–39; Hosea 2:10) but God's heart was to cover her nakedness in an act of betrothal (Hosea 2:9; Ezekiel 16:8). Although this picture may seem old-fashioned, the truth it contains is wonderfully liberating. Many of us have been exposed by our sin and as a result carry an immense weight of shame. God, however, wants to cover and clothe us in an act of mercy and acceptance. *'Love'*, after all, *'covers over a multitude of sins'* (1 Peter 4:8). As God makes us ready for Himself and we make ourselves ready for another it is God's covering that heals us and prepares us for intimacy.

Are we prepared for responsibility?

Bridges are not built solely for decoration, they are built for purpose. Relationships are not formed simply for companionship and connection but for responsibility. We have a responsibility to the God we serve, the society in which we live and the future generation we conceive. If we become Christians only for the obvious benefits and blessings that it affords us, we will create a heartless and self-centred society. If we make friends and get married just for the personal satisfaction and sexual gratification, our 'world' and families will be disempowered by rejection. If, on the other hand, we can grasp that we relate for a reason, then we understand that we are blessed to be a blessing, forgiven to be forgiving and made holy to make whole. This selfless approach to life, however, doesn't come easily. Most of us do start our relationships for what we can get out of them. Like a baby intent on suckling, we have one thing on our small minds: what we can draw from others for our benefit! With maturity, however, comes responsibility and we need to be prepared for it.

The lives of two men in the Bible, Moses and Peter, give us a very clear idea of how God trains people for responsibility and leadership. Both men's lives can be divided into clear times and seasons, events and stages. In both cases there was a 'death process' that took place in a 'wilderness season'.

Moses lived for 120 years. The first forty, when Moses was a prince in Egypt, were marked by natural success. According to Stephen's account,

> *'Moses was educated in all the wisdom of the Egyptians and was* **powerful in speech** *and action.'*   (Acts 7:22, emphasis mine)

Apparently, he was assertive, decisive and proactive. Many people would have chosen him as their leader but he was not yet ready to be God's ambassador. The second forty-year period finds him living as a shepherd in the desert, in silence and anonymity, forgotten by his people and seemingly neglected by God. At the end of what the Bible simply describes as a 'long period' (Exodus 2:23), God appears to Moses and asks him to be His representative, to which Moses gives a remarkable reply:

'Moses said to the LORD, "O Lord, I have never been eloquent, neither in the past nor since you have spoken to your servant. I am slow of speech and tongue."' (Exodus 4:10, emphasis mine)

What is Moses doing? Is he being ignorant, deceptive or just rebellious?! Or has the wilderness been at work? Has he died to his selfish ambitions and simply lost his self-belief in his natural ability? Certainly in the next forty years we see a remarkable change: bold and powerful once again but this time with God's authority and mantle; no longer self-assured and secure in his own abilities but now supremely confident in his calling and God-given gift. I personally believe that he had been prepared for responsibility, to be a spokesman. His life could be summarized as follows:

- The time of birth – 'no ordinary child'.
- A season of education – a prince of Egypt.
- The time of crisis – 'Moses fled'.
- A season of preparation – a shepherd in the wilderness.
- The time of calling – 'the burning bush'.
- A season of leadership – a prophet of God.

Peter's life takes a similar turn. He was a natural leader: a passionate enthusiast. He always seemed to be the first: the first to be picked by Jesus, the first to walk on water, the first to get to the tomb and later the first to jump out of the boat! It was obvious that he was the premier disciple. So self-confident was he that he made the presumptuous claim, *'I will lay down my life for you'* (John 13:37). But afterwards came the curses and the awful denial. He abandoned the One whom he had been first to recognize. Devastated and broken he returns to the boat that he had left with such self-certainty a few short months before. Then the risen Christ appears on the shore and asks, *'Simon, son of John, do you truly love me?'* (John 21:16). It was a powerfully restorative and yet challenging question to which Peter falteringly replies, *'Yes, Lord, you know that I love you'* (John 21:16). I say falteringly because the dialogue in the original text reveals that each of them was using a different word for love. Whereas Jesus uses the Greek word *agapao* twice and *phileo* once, Peter uses *phileo* every time. It seems to me that Peter, after his failure, couldn't bring himself to use the more 'unconditional' of the two words. His was a tender and affectionate response but with none of his original bravado. Peter's self-confidence had been replaced by self-examination. It was now that Jesus prophesied about the final season of Peter's life in which he *would* eventually lay down his life. Peter was ready to be an apostle. Part of his life could be summarized as follows:

- The time of calling – 'Come, follow me'.
- A season of self-confidence – Peter the rock!
- The time of denial – 'I don't know the man'.
- A season of self-examination – Peter the fisherman.
- The time of restoration – 'Do you love me?'
- A season of self-sacrifice – Peter the apostle.

I identify with Peter. When I started in full-time evangelism, I had too great an opinion of my own importance. There was a part of me that secretly believed that Jesus was lucky to have me on His side! I cringe now at my arrogance. It wasn't long before Jesus led me into a series of wilderness experiences that left my self-confidence in tatters. I then wondered whether I could achieve anything for God. The turning point came one day in a Yugoslavian hotel room! I was resting on my bed when God clearly and unexpectedly spoke to my spirit. He asked, as He had to Peter all those years before, 'Do you love Me?' I immediately replied, 'Yes, You know that I love You.' I will never forget the blinding glare of His response. It cut through all the pretence and challenged the depths of my soul. '*Do you*, Robert? *Do you* love Me?' I instantly thought of the times that I had failed Him and the verse in the Bible that says, *'And this is love: that we walk in obedience to his commands'* (2 John 6). I therefore hesitatingly replied, 'Well, I *want* to love You.' To which He lovingly and disarmingly responded, 'Do you *want* to love Me?' I thought briefly and eventually concluded, 'I *want to* want to love You!' It was the best that I could do! The conversation finished as abruptly as it had started. I felt empty but strangely expectant. I felt empowered rather than condemned. It was as though I had passed a test. I was ready for the next stage.

This process of change is not only evident in the lives of Moses and Peter but is also observed in most of the great biblical leaders who were prepared by God for a future challenge. Joseph, for instance, was transformed from an egotistical dreamer, through a variety of self-denying tests, to a life of fulfilling service. Paul summarizes the goal of all these experiences. He had had his own arrogance problems and his own wilderness experience and concluded,

> '*I have been crucified with Christ and I no longer live, but Christ lives in me.*' (Galatians 2:20, emphasis mine)

For Jesus Christ to be revealed in him, the selfish '*I*' needed to die, but the '*me*' needed to live. Paul the Pharisee was gone but Paul the apostle was here to stay. He was now prepared for anything!

Are we prepared for blessing?

We have established that one of our responsibilities in life is to be a blessing to others. However, we cannot give to others if we have nothing to offer them; we cannot be a blessing if we ourselves are not blessed. Many people are frightened by the term 'blessing' or 'prosperity'. They feel somehow that it doesn't fit with the Christian ethos. Yet it is abundantly clear that God planned for Abraham to be blessed in every way (Genesis 12:1–3) and Christians are his heirs:

> '*So those who have faith are blessed along with Abraham, the man of faith.*' (Galatians 3:9)

It is also evident that God made provision for Israel to be blessed in all aspects of the nation's life (Deuteronomy 28:1–14). Since Christians have a better covenant (Hebrews 8:6), there is no doubt in my mind that God desires to bless us both spiritually and naturally. He wants each one of us to have wonderfully successful lives and fruitful relationships. He wants to bless our companionship, our children and our finances. Since it is what God wants, it should be our desire as well. Many Christians refuse this blessing believing that they are choosing a life of holiness. Yet how can we arrogantly reject what He has already purchased for us and convince ourselves that it is God's will? The problem for us, it seems, is not having prosperity but handling it! This is why He needs to prepare us for it.

As we have already noted, it was in the desert that God prepared the children of Israel. The book of Deuteronomy clearly tells us why God took them through the wilderness before their entry into the Promised Land. He wanted to test them in order to know what was in their heart (Deuteronomy 8:2). He wanted to see whether they would crave His presence and purposes rather than their daily bread or the dubious benefits of their life in Egypt. He longed for them to realize that *'man does not live on bread alone but on every word that comes from the mouth of the* Lord' (Deuteronomy 8:3). His initial purpose was not to punish them but to humble them *'so that in the end it might go well'* (Deuteronomy 8:16). He was preparing them for prosperity. He had to teach them the lessons that were necessary for them to enjoy the blessing of the Promised Land. He knew that otherwise the abundance of their inheritance might cause them to forget the God who gave it. Tragically, they misinterpreted His heart and rebelled. What happened to them is recorded as an example and a warning for us (1 Corinthians 10:11).

Israel's failure in the desert has led many Christians today to argue against the necessity of these wilderness seasons in our life. They are happy with the destination but not the route. They want the blessing but not the preparation. However, as Jamie Buckingham argues, 'To bypass the wilderness in our journey to the Promised Land is to bypass God. And what is the use of occupying a land of promise unless the God of promise goes with us'.[4] What these desert-free critics have failed to grasp is the true significance of these periods in our life.

In reality, the wilderness is a test of sonship. God was training Israel as a son prior to receiving the inheritance:

> *'Know then in your heart that as a man disciplines his son, so the* Lord *your God disciplines you.'*   (Deuteronomy 8:5)

In the case of Jesus Christ, after His sonship had been revealed at His baptism, He was led by the Spirit into the wilderness before He was released into His public ministry. It was this sonship that Satan questioned in the wilderness and it was this same passage in Deuteronomy that Jesus used to refute him:

> *'The tempter came to him and said, "If you are the Son of God, tell these stones to become bread." Jesus answered, "It is written: 'Man does not live on bread alone, but on every word that comes from the mouth of God.'"'*   (Matthew 4:3–4)

How does this affect us? God is also our Father and therefore as His sons we can expect a time of testing before we are released into a prosperous future.

In our own case, at the beginning of our marriage, which was also the outset of our ministry, we were seriously low in funds! This is common to many newly married couples and so seemed insignificant until it became desperate! I questioned God's faithfulness until I realized that it was my faithfulness that was in question! God was testing us to see if we would trust Him. He wanted me to know that He was my Father and so would always provide. But He also wanted to know if the relationship was more important to me than the provision. It took me six years to learn the lesson! Then one day, after I had been praying for money as usual, a man of God gave me an envelope. I ripped it open excitedly only to find a £10 note! Surprisingly, I was immediately disappointed. I had wanted a word from God and all I received was money. It might not seem a momentous event but it changed my life. It was as though God looked on approvingly and I had passed a test. I didn't want to live on bread alone. Within a few days I was offered a vastly increased salary. God wanted me to be blessed but knew that I had to be prepared for it. Since that defining moment, I have handled thousands of dollars gratefully but lightly.

Are we prepared for change?

It is one thing to know that blessing is ahead, but quite another to comprehend fully the change that it brings. Joshua and Caleb must have been desperate to enter their inheritance. Held back for forty years by the small-mindedness of their compatriots, they were now on the edge of the Promised Land. They must have been convinced that they were prepared for blessing, yet I suspect that they had no idea about the challenges that faced them. They knew that the land was theirs for the taking but it still needed taking! They had known the guidance, miraculous provision and protection of God for years and yet now God was going to let them explore, cultivate the land and fight for themselves. Even with their faithful perseverance through the trials of the wilderness, as they approached the River Jordan, their future must have appeared vast and daunting. No wonder God told Joshua to be strong and courageous at least five times! Most of us, at one time or another in our lives, have had similar experiences. I clearly remember thinking on the last night before our first child was born that the next day our lives were going to be changed irrevocably and there was nothing we could do about it! I said to my wife, 'Let's go out.

It's the last time for about fifteen years that we can do so without making special arrangements beforehand!' The fact is we will never feel completely prepared for the future. It will always take us by surprise. It is always a step of faith. What we must do therefore is to be as ready as we can by submitting to God's dealings in our lives. When, as our Shepherd, He leads us into a wilderness, we should learn from it and not fight it. When He makes us *'lie down in green pastures'* (Psalm 23:2) we should not run on ahead! It just may be that He knows what He is doing, that He understands the times and the seasons of our lives and is preparing us for a momentous event, a challenging season or a time of transition! Whatever the future holds, we need to be as prepared for it as possible.

Summary and advice

1. **Our lives are marked by definite times and indeterminate seasons**. It is often the lessons we learn in the seasons that prepare us for the events. The lessons learned in the season of engagement will often determine the success of the marriage that follows.

2. **Seasons of preparation can be described as a 'wilderness'**. A wilderness season should not be a negative experience. It is a season in which we are tested and its goal is to prepare us for the next blessed event.

3. **We need to be prepared to finish**. A season of testing gives us the time to determine whether we can complete what we have started.

4. **We need to be prepared for faithfulness**. As we get ready for a committed relationship, a wilderness season removes the alternatives.

5. **We need to be prepared for intimacy**. In common with Esther, prior to the intimacy of a marriage relationship we need to cleansed and healed if our relationship is to be fruitful.

6. **We need to be prepared for responsibility**. Moses, Peter and Paul all had a wilderness season in which their 'self-life' was crucified. It was this that equipped them for the great responsibilities of their calling.

7. **We need to be prepared for blessing**. God wants to prosper us but unless our hearts are tested beforehand we will not be able to handle it.

8. **We need to be prepared for change**. When God as a Shepherd leads us into a wilderness we should learn from it and not fight it. It may be that He is preparing us for a momentous event that we haven't foreseen.

Notes

1. W.E. Vine, *Vine's Expository Dictionary of Old and New Testament Words* (Fleming H. Revell, 1981).
2. The Holy Bible, New King James Version (Thomas Nelson, Inc., 1982).
3. *Book of Common Prayer*, Solemnization of Holy Matrimony (1662).
4. Jamie Buckingham, *A Way Through the Wilderness* (Kingsway, 1984).

Chapter 16

Just Passing Through

The Trauma of Transition

Despite the severe conditions of the 'Depression', Sydney Harbour Bridge was officially opened with great ceremony and pageant. One report suggested that one million people witnessed the transition. There were balls, exhibitions, fireworks, regattas, carnivals and of course dignitaries and their speeches. The proceedings commenced on the southern approach to the bridge where the Premier, the Hon. J.T. Lang, was officially to declare the bridge open. However, in common with many rites of passage, not everything went as smoothly as planned. Before Lang had an opportunity to cut the ribbon, a disenchanted Irishman called Francis De Groot rode forward and slashed it with his sword declaring the bridge open in the name of 'the decent citizens of New South Wales'! De Groot was fined, the ribbon re-tied and the ceremony continued! Transition tends to invite confrontation.

In 1830 the artist Edward William Cooke attempted to portray the chaos of the building of John Rennie's new London Bridge. On one side of the etching is the old bridge, still being used and almost intact: smoking, crumbling and congested. On the other side the new clean design is taking shape. It is equally crowded but infested with ropes, cranes and pulleys. A church tower stands tall in the distance and a young man sits in the foreground among the debris: a discarded can, a disused rope and an upturned and empty basket. It cannot possibly capture the loss and hope of the event itself, but it is a wonderful depiction of the new replacing the old, the need for progress and the cost of transition.

In common with all architects, John Rennie was a visionary and as such would have craved progress. Yet he would have known that it comes with a price tag! Whether we are building a bridge or a relationship we have to embrace progress and face the pitfalls of transition. The formation of a new friendship, the rite of marriage, the signing of divorce papers or the hopeful uncertainty of remarriage all require transition and it is the manner in which we negotiate the process that will determine the success or failure of our relationships.

Progress is a biblical word. In the Old Testament, the story of Abraham is one of pilgrimage and progress and the narrative of the Children of Israel reveals a journey toward promised blessing. The New Testament promotes the advancement of the Church. Paul the Apostle told the Philippians that his ministry on earth was for their development,

> *'Convinced of this, I know that I will remain, and I will continue with all of you for your progress and joy in the faith.'*   (Philippians 1:25)

As well as this the Bible is also concerned that the growth of individual Christians is evident to all. As Paul explained to his son in the faith Timothy,

> *'Be diligent in these matters; give yourself wholly to them, so that everyone may see your progress.'*   (1 Timothy 4:15)

The reality is that, 'God never changes but He is always on the move'. This was how a friend of mine used to try to describe the tension between God's eternal constancy on the one hand and His enormous vitality on the other. However, it is the latter characteristic that probably creates the greater challenge for us. God moves and has created a world of progress and change. Movement and growth are, in fact, two of the biological signs of life. All living things grow and can move by themselves. If we are alive we should develop without constant external stimuli. If we apply this principle in a spiritual context, it is questionable whether a person who is not progressing positively without constant encouragement is exhibiting the necessary signs of life! Equally, it could be said that if a church is not growing it is not a great advertisement for a living God!

These signs of life can be interpreted in a number of ways, but there is no doubt that God wants us to progress: to move from strength to strength. The psalmist makes it clear:

> *'Blessed are those whose strength is in you,*
>   *who have set their hearts on pilgrimage.*
> *As they pass through the Valley of Baca,*
>   *they make it a place of springs;*
>   *the autumn rains also cover it with pools.*
> *They go from strength to strength,*
>   *till each appears before God in Zion.'*   (Psalm 84:5–7)

The phrase 'just passing through' can be associated with purposeless vagrants and drifters but here it is the language of faith, the heritage of the pilgrim, the pioneer and the apostle. What is also evident is that if we are going to be pilgrims, sooner or later we will have to pass through a valley. However, a valley is transitional, something we enter and leave. It is not for dwelling. The waddies of the Negev Desert, for instance, are subject to severe and sudden flooding and are therefore a particularly hazardous place to pitch a tent! In this case the valley is called Baca, the Valley of Weeping. In the shepherd's psalm it is *'the valley of the shadow of death'* (Psalm 23:4). Both demand that we pass through. William Shakespeare reiterates the same theme when he writes, 'All that live must die, passing through nature to eternity'.[1] However, though we simply pass through, these transitional experiences can be painful. We must first accept this before we can learn to navigate them successfully.

There is a small but fascinating science museum in Florence, Italy. Every room takes you on a journey of discovery past telescopes and astrolabes, globes and quadrants. One of the rooms is devoted to surgery and surgical instruments: tidy lines of scissors, scalpels and forceps. Beside them, a bizarre collection of wax and terracotta models of babies and wombs illustrate every stage of childbirth and every possible problem: twins, a breach birth, a tangled cord. It is a record of transition, the painful and priceless journey of a child leaving the womb and entering the world. As you move from room to room, pointing, smiling and questioning you become aware of an absence common to all museums. This is a record but it is not an accurate one. There is no noise, no life and no disorder. It is a reminder of the past but it isn't real. There are no screams of pain or cries of joy. There is no blood anywhere! Everything is on neat shelves and enclosed in glass cases. There is a smell of dust and old leather but not of surgical spirit or fear. Real transition is often much more traumatic. I distinctly remember my daughter's face when she first saw a lamb being born. Her face was shocked and her eyes were transfixed on the shepherd as he gently eased the precious life onto the straw. Her one comment, as she turned to her mother in consternation, was, 'Was it as messy for you?'

The Bible indicates that where there is life there is transition and where there is transition there is muck!

> *'Where there are no oxen, the manger is empty,*
> *but from the strength of an ox comes an abundant harvest.'*
> (Proverbs 14:4)

In other words if we want food it comes with dirt, and if we want a harvest it comes with sweat! If, as well as this, we want to progress in life, if we want to give birth, if we want to grow or change in any way, the price will get higher! We will need to move from one place to another or convert from one lifestyle to another and conversion always costs. As Edwin Louis Cole argues, 'The first thing you need to understand is that crisis is normal to life. Whenever you are in transition from one situation of life to another, you will go through a crisis. The only way to go from a transient state to a more permanent state of life is by way of crisis'.[2] This is a necessary truth to face if we are to embark on the building of bridges.

The process of transition

I have already established that life demands progress, progress requires transition and transition is often messy! If this is the case, we need to explore the workings of transition in order to progress in our relationships as painlessly as possible. Transition can best be described as walking through a doorway. First, we have to decide to leave our old position and approach the door with hope. Second, we have to open the door and walk through the doorway with love and, finally, we have to close the door behind us and enter the new position with faith. When we build a bridge or start a relationship, whether it is a temporary acquaintance or a marriage, we have to negotiate the same three distinct stages. Each one of these three stages has its own principles to apply and challenges to face.

Approaching the door

The first stage of transition takes place before the bridge-building. In it we have to face the possibility of change. Imagine the arguments behind closed doors in the early part of the nineteenth century as it became clear that something radical had to be done about the old London Bridge. Those who hated change, the traditionalists, would have opposed its replacement: 'Let's repair the old bridge, as we always have. We should appreciate our heritage.' One of the reasons that many cling to their traditions is that they are fearful of loss. They don't want to lose what they already have. They don't want to leave the 'room' in which they are comfortable or at least familiar. However, as we have already seen, all new things demand a loss of the old. To enter a new school, a new job or a new house it is necessary to leave the old one. If we start a new relationship we are bound to lose something in the process. A single person contemplating marriage, for instance, will lose their singleness! If we start a new relation with Christ we are required to lose our old life. The Bible says,

> *'if anyone is in Christ, he is a new creation; the old has gone, the new has come!'*   (2 Corinthians 5:17)

The traditional Pharisees objected not just because they were rejecting Christ but because they were resistant to any sort of change. On top of this, since birth, growth, maturity and indeed life itself necessitate transition, it is in Satan's interests to promote tradition.

If we are to overcome the Pharisee in all of us and move on into something new and better, we have to grasp the principle of 'gain through loss'. The Bible tells us to leave 'elementary teachings' (Hebrews 6:1) and 'childish ways' (1 Corinthians 13:11) but only so we can gain the benefits of maturity. The curious but compelling truth is that if we give we will gain (Proverbs 11:24); if we lose we will find (Matthew 10:39); if we sell we will obtain (Matthew 19:21); if we leave we will receive (Matthew 19:29); if we choose last we will come first (Mark 9:35); if we sow we will reap (2 Corinthians 9:6); if we are weak we will become strong (2 Corinthians 12:10); and if we die we will live (John 12:24–25)! In each case there is a requirement to lose but a destiny to win. For instance, by sacrificing Isaac to God, Abraham saved Israel; by dedicating Samuel to God, Hannah gained a prophet; by giving Moses to God, his mother kept a deliverer.

Of course, this is all well and good in theory but much more painful in practice! How do we do it? By simply looking where we are going! If we are to go through the door and negotiate the doorway without injury, our focus needs to be on the room we are entering and not the one that we are leaving! Abraham had to leave his home but he was looking forward to the Promised Land with confidence and expectation. An engaged couple have to leave their father and mother but they only have eyes for each other. Jesus Christ Himself gave us the example by enduring great loss *'for the joy set before him'* (Hebrews 12:2).

In common with many fathers I have had the privilege and felt the pain of giving my daughter away at her wedding. I consider my children to be gifts from God, and the concept of giving away such a gift to someone else is a difficult one! She and her husband had also invited me to speak at the ceremony and so I spoke about the principle of 'giving away'. The Bible says,

> *'A man will leave his father and mother and be united to his wife, and the two will become one flesh.'*   (Matthew 19:5)

With emotion I told them that numerous marriages had failed because the mother and father had continued to be in authority, make decisions and interfere with the new couple's future, and so if they were to have a successful marriage they had to leave us. By leaving us they would gain each other and by giving my daughter I would gain a son. As the book of Proverbs teaches,

> *'One man gives freely, yet gains even more;*
> *   another withholds unduly, but comes to poverty.'*   (Proverbs 11:24)

Once again, by concentrating on the gain we can cope with the loss. The principle is dramatically illustrated in the life of the missionary Jim Elliot who lost his life for the gospel. He was able to live a life of sacrifice because his focus was on the prize. As he said, 'He is no fool who gives what he cannot keep to gain what he cannot lose'.[3]

Walking through the doorway

Once the intransigent Pharisee is silenced and the decision is made to enter a new room or to build a bridge, another group of antagonists bar the way! The indecisive philosophers! Their role is to argue interminably about how the transition is to be made! If we go back to the discussion about John Rennie's proposed new bridge, we can hear the cautious with their delaying tactics, 'We have plenty of time. We mustn't offend the "lovers of the old" ', to which the impetuous reply, 'Who cares about the traditionalists? The old bridge is falling down. Let's get on with it.' Which is right: caution or impetuosity? The prudent action embraces both, a sort of reckless vigilance. In the context of forming a relationship, this stage is like an engagement before marriage. A very short engagement is probably ill-advised as it leaves little time to catch a breath before the wedding, whereas an unnecessarily long wait puts immense pressure on the couple. My view tends to be, 'If you have decided to get married, get on with it!' Doorways are not there to hang around, they are there to pass through!

However, there is a truth that must be applied at this stage and that is: 'A successful entry is dependent on a successful exit.' This biblical principle is fundamental to success in life. It can be applied in almost any context of departure: when leaving a job, home, relationship, country or even leaving this life. It was highlighted to me a number of years ago when I read a small booklet about transition by Edwin Louis Cole in which he wrote, 'How we leave childhood determines how we enter adolescence. How we leave determines how we enter'.[4] I have seen many people ignore this principle to their detriment. A rebellious child leaves home without the blessing of his parents and finds himself in debt. An embittered wife leaves her uncaring husband for another in order to start again and finds her nightmare is recurring. A disloyal employee changes jobs only to find an equally domineering boss! In each case these people consistently find themselves 'at the scene of the accident' but of course it is always 'someone else's fault'! Instead of resolving their rebellion, bitterness and disloyalty, they take it with them 'into another room'. Changing rooms doesn't change our character. Tragically, this is a concept that is ignored in many churches. I have seen independent and un-reconciled Christians leave their church against advice, join another and fully expect that their life and ministry will prosper. I have personally counselled many in this situation to deal with the problem first and then a change of character may result in a change of room. In my own life, a change of room involved moving to Australia! However, I refused to go without the blessing of the local church. I wanted to be sent and not just released. I preached the same sermon about leaving and entering correctly on my last Sunday in England and my first in Australia. I wanted to enter with blessing and so I left in unity.

Once again, the practice is more difficult than the principle. However, there are a few truths that have helped me pass through numerous doorways successfully. For me, transitions are like the grout on a tiled wall! The owner of an expensive bathroom wants people to admire the tiles and not the grout in between them! Yet without the grout the tiles would look terrible. Passing through a transitional stage in our life is a very small part of the whole and yet if we do it poorly it affects our entire life. Good transition, like grout, needs to be clean, clear, short and smooth! Correct attitudes, clear communication, appropriate timing and consistent behaviour are all critical for good transition. When my family left England we had to ensure that our attitudes and relationships were exemplary. I didn't want there to be any 'skeletons in the cupboard'. We set a definite date to say goodbye to the church where we had been members for fifteen years. Our farewell was purposely 'short and sweet'.

The primary reason why we make inappropriate transitions is selfishness. We seek our own path and possess our own agenda. That is why love is the key to successful entry. When we enter a new phase of our life or start a new relationship we should remind ourselves of the Jewish declaration of faith: the 'Shema'. The Shema is the name given to the passage in the Bible that includes the words:

> *'Hear, O Israel: The* LORD *our God, the* LORD *is one. Love the* LORD *your God with all your heart and with all your soul and with all your strength.'*   (Deuteronomy 6:4–5)

It is this passage that Jesus identified as the first commandment (Mark 12:29–30) and also the one that Israelites were commanded to write on their doorposts (Deuteronomy 6:9). In Judaism the Hebrew word *mezuzah* meaning 'doorpost' also came to mean the small receptacle containing this and other verses that are fixed to the doorposts of Jewish homes, a continuous reminder, no doubt, of the Passover where the blood smeared on the doorposts saved their ancestors. The *mezuzah* is traditionally touched as people pass through as a sign of their faith. Thus every 'doorway' has to pass the test of faith, love and forgiveness. If we genuinely applied this test to the beginning and end of our relationships we would be recipients of God's blessing,

> *'You will be blessed when you come in and blessed when you go out.'*
>   (Deuteronomy 28:6)

Closing the door behind you

Well after the new London Bridge was finally completed, I bet there were still people who crossed it muttering, 'The old one was better'! The reason that it is so easy to imagine is because it is a voice that has echoed through history. Whenever we start a project or begin a relationship a small voice of doubt creeps in, 'Have you made the right decision?' While the Pharisees attempt to prevent change and the philosophers try to delay it, the pessimists endeavour to make us regret it. They seek to rob us of its blessing. Whereas optimists looks forward, pessimists look back. They are like Lot's wife who looked back to Sodom or the unfaithful Israelites who looked back to Egypt. Neither inherited the promise. If we are going to defeat this final member of the triad that opposes positive transition we need to realize that a doorway is not only a point of entry, it is a moment of closure. Once we have made the decision to pass through we need to close the door behind us. When, for instance, we commit ourselves to a successful marriage we need to close the door to the alternatives. One of the reasons that Amanda and I have a good marriage is that we have not looked back. Neither divorce nor failure is an option. Like Abraham and his descendants, we constantly look forward. The Bible tells us,

> *'If they had been thinking of the country they had left, they would have had opportunity to return.'*   (Hebrews 11:15)

Many married couples are tempted to return to their previous life because they insist on wondering whether they should have left it.

Once we have moved into a new stage and closed the door behind us a new principle must come into operation. We need to forget in order to win. Paul told the church at Philippi that he had found a secret to pursuing his calling:

> *'Brothers, I do not consider myself yet to have taken hold of it. But one thing I do: Forgetting what is behind and straining toward what is ahead, I press on toward the goal to win the prize for which God has called me heavenward in Christ Jesus.'*   (Philippians 3:13–14)

He didn't, of course, forget what he had already attained, as he goes on to explain, but he knew that he had to close the door on the past and walk confidently into the future. He realized that any unforgiven sin would destroy him, any unresolved conflict would torment him and any unsubmitted failure would discourage him. He therefore chose to put certain things behind him. When it comes to the often painful progress of transition we too need to forget the despair behind and set our course on the hope ahead. The prophet Jeremiah illustrates this counsel:

> *'I remember my affliction and my wandering,*
> *the bitterness and the gall.*
> *I well remember them,*
> *and my soul is downcast within me.*
> *Yet this I call to mind and therefore I have hope:*
>
> *Because of the LORD's great love we are not consumed,*
> *for his compassions never fail.*
> *They are new every morning;*
> *great is your faithfulness.*
> *I say to myself, "The LORD is my portion;*
> *therefore I will wait for him."'*   (Lamentations 3:19–24)

Had Jeremiah failed to forget the past, he would have abandoned his prophetic calling in despair and his winning words would never have been recorded.

Transition in practice

There are many films and fairy tales that highlight the significance of passing through doorways. For instance, doors are entry points into other worlds in C.S. Lewis's Narnia Chronicles, Lewis Carroll's *Alice in Wonderland* and, more recently, Disney's *Monsters Inc.* In each case they emphasize the excitement, uncertainty and resultant transformation but rarely the difficulty of the actual transition. Life is often a little less 'fantastic'. Yet transition doesn't have to be as traumatic as some have made it. Marriage, divorce and remarriage all involve transition and all involve different measures of pain, but if they are approached biblically the outcome is blessed. There is a time to build, dismantle and rebuild bridges, but when the time comes God equips us with the grace for change. We simply need to access the grace by doing the right thing.

When we build a bridge we have an opening ceremony; when we get married we choose a day on which to have the covenant witnessed; when someone dies we have a formal funeral. These symbolic rituals are important for both the individuals concerned and the community as a whole. Dr William A. Haviland, a Professor of Anthropology, described their significance, 'Religious ritual is the means through which persons relate to the sacred; it is religion in action. Not only is ritual the means by which the social bonds of a group are reinforced and tensions relieved; it is also one way that many important events are celebrated and crises, such as death, made less socially disruptive and less difficult for the individuals to bear'.[5] In anthropological terms, the ritual that takes place in many cultural groups at the time of crucial stages of our life cycle is termed a 'rite of passage'. These rites of passage guide us through the transitional doorways of our lives such as birth, puberty, marriage, promotion and death and help us face the crises associated with them. However, what has happened in some circles of our 'correct', contemporary and clinical Western society is that these rites, which are often associated with more primitive tribal customs, are dispensed with: circumcision is considered barbaric, 'coming of age' old-fashioned, the covenant of marriage unnecessary and formal mourning overemotional. In so doing, we have ignored our Creator, relegated ritual to a museum and sanitized transition. In our desire to be humanistic we are in danger of being dehumanized. The denial of pain doesn't remove it so much as prolong it. The truth is we are created and graced for crisis. What we should do when we are building a bridge is to embrace and celebrate the transition both individually and corporately. The accompanying ceremony will equip us to face the inevitable hardships.

The change associated with the demolishing of a bridge or the dismantling of a relationship, however, is often more painful and other factors need to be taken into consideration. In a previous chapter, I have referred to the ancient Roman legend of Horatius defending the bridge over the River Tiber against the invading Etruscans. However, there comes a point in the story when the only way to save Rome is to destroy the bridge. The poet Macaulay describes the scene:

> 'Out spake the Consul roundly:
> ' "The bridge must go straight down;
> For, since Janiculum is lost,
> Nought else can save the town".'[6]

The officials destroyed the lesser in order to save the greater. The biblical story of Abraham and his nephew Lot describes the relational equivalent. The Bible says that, because of the inability of the land to support their combined possessions, *'they were not able to stay together'* (Genesis 13:6). However, further reading reveals that Abraham and Lot had vastly different motives and desires and therefore opposing interests. It is apparent that whereas Lot was self-absorbed, Abraham had eyes only for the covenant, his future seed and the blessing of the earth. Lot was holding Abraham back. They had to go their separate ways in order for Abraham to fulfil his destiny. Abraham knew that his choice of companion would forecast his future. But, how did they separate? Not with the 'sharp disagreement' (Acts 15:39) with which Paul and Barnabas parted company generations later, but with an amicable agreement. Abraham trusted God enough with his own welfare to give Lot the pick of the land and, despite Lot's self-destructive choices, Abraham continued to help him as best he could although they never travelled together again. In other words, though Abraham was strong enough to choose separation, he made the transition gracefully and thereby preserved his own future.

I have been in pastoral work for long enough to have witnessed the breakdown of scores of relationships, but perhaps the greatest transitional pain is reserved for those relationships that are either destroyed through our own folly or are lost through circumstances beyond our control. Divorce and death come into this category. Both involve a terrible loss that needs to be 'passed through' before new bridges are built. It is not my intention here to discuss the theology of death or the biblical requirements for divorce. That is the subject of other books. I just want to highlight some guidelines that will help us negotiate these dark and familiar doorways. Of course, each person has their own story, but there are always common solutions. The first solution is to face the fact of loss. Many deny it and cannot move on. I once had a man come to my office in order to obtain permission to grieve for his father! His friends considered his deep sadness abnormal and their disapproval had trapped him in denial. But as Gary Collins says, 'Grief is a normal response to the loss of any significant person, object, or opportunity'.[7] If we cannot let one relationship go we will not be able to form another correctly. But before we even think of new relationships we need to know what it is like in this valley we are passing through: what are the normal responses to grief? Grief is a valley filled with waves of unpredictable emotions such as numbness, anger, tiredness, distraction, fear, guilt and irritability. Some people suggest that we go through stages of grief whereas others suggest that we accomplish tasks. I agree with psychologist Dr Bruce Stevens who favours the latter approach to grief because, as he writes, 'Stages or phases of grief imply a measure of passivity'.[8] I believe that we need actively to choose a way through loss. We need to take clear steps to traverse the valley. For instance, if we are going to handle loss successfully, we should carefully prepare for it, take time to walk though it, bring God into it, confess the promises of God in it, talk about it, see a way out of it and leave it! It is only then, as Stevens and others teach, we can 'reinvest in other relationships'.

As we have clearly seen, bridge-building demands progress. All vital relationships grow and so require the trauma of transition, but then, as I heard a preacher once say, 'Revival is always dependent on the fact that we are looking down the road'. If we don't relish change and accept the cost, we will inevitably stagnate or be enslaved. Edward Gibbon describes how the nomadic nations in the second century chose to abandon their lifestyle of movement and settle down and consequently 'soon became subjects of the Roman Empire'.[9] We, like them, should be pioneers, not settlers, or we too will become enslaved.

Summary and advice

1. **Movement and growth are both signs of life**. Progress, however, invariably involves transition and transition is often painful. The Bible describes this process as passing through a valley.

2. **All relationships require us to experience transitions**. They are equivalent to walking through a doorway. We have to approach these doorways in our life appropriately, negotiate them carefully and close the door behind us before we move on.

3. **We should approach 'transitional doorways' with confident expectation**. The principle operating at this stage is 'gain through loss'. Tradition and pharisaism will attempt to prevent us making these beneficial changes in our lives.

4. **We should walk through 'transitional doorways' with love**. Indecision, selfishness and unforgiveness all work against us. A successful entry is dependent on a successful exit.

5. **We should firmly close the 'transitional doorways' behind us**. A doorway is not only a point of entry, it is a moment of closure. Although pessimism tempts us to look back, it is only as we forget what is behind that we will press on and win.

6. **Transition requires grace for change.** We need to access this grace by understanding the significance of 'rites of passage', accepting necessary separation amicably and inviting God into our inevitable losses.

Notes

1. William Shakespeare, *Hamlet*, Act 1, Scene 1, line 68.
2. Edwin Louis Cole, *Entering Crisis and Leaving* (Honor Books).
3. Jim Elliot. Quoted in John F. Walvoord and Roy B. Zuck, *The Bible Knowledge Commentary* (Scripture Press Publications, Inc., 1983, 1985).
4. Cole, *Entering Crisis and Leaving*.
5. William A. Haviland, *Cultural Anthropology* (Holt, Rinehart & Winston, Inc., 1985).
6. Thomas Babington Macaulay, *Lays of Ancient Rome*, 1842.
7. Gary R. Collins, *Christian Counselling* (Word (UK) Ltd, 1989).
8. Bruce A. Stevens, *Setting Captives Free* (HarperCollins, 1994).
9. Edward Gibbon, *The Empire of Rome*. AD 98–180. (Phoenix).

Chapter 17

The Price They Paid

The Cost of Construction

Sydney Harbour Bridge cost a great deal! However, although the average weekly wage in Australia in the 1930s was only £4 6s 10d (four pounds, six shillings and ten pence), the building of Sydney Harbour Bridge was relatively inexpensive by today's standards. The accepted tender price of Dorman Long & Co. Ltd in 1924 for a two-hinged steel arch bridge was £4,217,721 11s 10d! Of course, the actual outlay was considerably more. The original capital cost of the bridge was nearer £10 million. However, the families of the twelve men who died in its construction may have viewed the price a little differently.

'How much does a bridge cost?' This was the question on the mind of every prospective buyer when the Corporation of the City of London put London Bridge on the market in 1968. How can you accurately value such an important icon? As its eventual buyer Robert McCulloch said, 'Nobody ever bought London Bridge before'.[1] In the end the dollar price that McCulloch paid was totally arbitrary. He doubled the estimate of a city engineer, added $60,000, a thousand dollars for every year of his life, and so offered $2.46 million dollars, the bid that was eventually accepted! On one of the 10,276 blocks of granite that he purchased, however, there was a more sobering record of the cost of the bridge. The letters R.I.P. were written in chalk to commemorate the forty men who died during its construction. But are human lives lost an accurate record of the price of a bridge? If that is the case, the bridge over the River Kwai must be one of the costliest bridges ever to be built.

In 1942, during the Second World War, what became known as the 'Railway of Death' was built between Bangkok and Rangoon. The film *The Bridge on the River Kwai*, made in 1957 and based on Pierre Boulle's book, attempted to tell the story of its construction. Although the movie is inaccurate in many details including the type of bridge built, it is accurate in the tragedy it records. Of the sixty thousand prisoners of war who were forced to work on the railway and the bridge, at least sixteen thousand died of disease, malnutrition or exhaustion at the site. However, even these awful statistics do not give the full picture. How can we measure the loss, pain, anger and determination that it really took to build it? The fact is, we cannot begin to estimate the cost of a bridge any more than we can put a price on a life. Of course, accountants and historians want precise figures, but life is often less exact.

The visionary Joseph P. Strauss, the builder of the Golden Gate Bridge in San Francisco, has been variously described not only as a competent structural engineer and a builder of hundreds of bridges but also a seer and a poet. He completed the bridge in 1937 despite the scores of critics who said that it could never be done because of the unpredictable weather and the strong currents in the area. It took four and a half years to build and eleven men lost their lives in its construction. The recorded price tag was $35 million. Joseph Strauss himself, however, attempted a more accurate assessment in a poem entitled 'The mighty task is done'. A part of it reads:

> 'Launched midst a thousand hopes and fears,
> Damned by a thousand hostile sneers.
> Yet ne'er its course was stayed.
> But ask of those who met the foe,
> Who stood alone when faith was low,
> Ask them the price they paid.'[2]

The task for Strauss had begun twenty years earlier in 1917 when he was invited to consider the project. At the time the estimated cost was between $25 and 30 million. In common with all building in my experience, the reality was completely different. After having an extension built on my house in England I learned a number of very valuable lessons about construction! The builder sat in my living room before he started and told me the price and the time that it would take. He said that he would have to dig some foundations but that it shouldn't be difficult and that he would ensure that the workmen didn't carry mud into the house! He was an honest person and good friend and meant every word sincerely! However, not one of his predictions came to pass. When the extension was complete and we moved in, we didn't regret anything. It was worth every penny. Nonetheless, it had taken longer, been more difficult, cost more, gone deeper and produced more dirt than we could possibly have imagined!

If this is true of building a house, building a home throws up even more surprises. People ask me how much it costs to bring up a child or how much it takes to make a marriage work. The simple answer is 'everything'; however, it is a totally unsatisfactory and unanswerable question. It always saddens me to read in a newspaper how a teacher has attempted to evaluate the cost of a child's education or to hear on the radio how a lawyer has agreed to a figure to compensate for a parent's loss. It seems so cheap, so dehumanizing and so wholly inaccurate. How can you possibly reduce life and time to a sum of money? How can we quantify beauty? With this in mind, I want to attempt to establish some principles and lessons I have learned in building relationships. But I am warning you now, each one is costly. I am not going to take you to the local mall where the bargains are marked clearly for all the passers-by, I am going to take you to an expensive designer shop where there are no price tags to be seen!

General building requirements

Any of us who have had the joy of buying a house will also have had the pain of discovering how poorly it was built or maintained in the past! We regularly find broken pipes, cracks plastered over, loose boards and dangerously exposed wires. We once rented one such 'house from hell' when we lived in Spain. The walls were paper thin and combined with the ill-fitting windows managed to allow everything into the house including the elements and the local wildlife! The electrical circuitry was highly suspect; we had sockets blow out of the wall, fireworks inside and out and an unpredictable fridge. This was 'live' and so gave a small electric shock when opened but once flung my wife across the kitchen! Water used to cascade down the bedroom walls. In answer to our complaints, the house owner came and taped the wallpaper back to the wall! We moved! We, of course, can laugh about this in retrospect and were genuinely grateful to have a roof over our head at all. However, tragically there are many relationships as uncomfortable and dangerous as this and the people in them can't just move! The reason for the state of these houses and homes is because some essential principles of building have been neglected. These are the foundations on which we build. There can be no half measures or short cuts here. Whether we are a building a house, a bridge or a home there are at least four fundamental requirements that will enable us to succeed: authority, wisdom, excellence and trust. Each of them may cost us dearly!

Permission granted

The first step to take when building a house or an extension to an existing house is to get permission from the relevant authorities. In our often honour-free, independent world this may seem to be unnecessary, but quite the reverse is true. Although in many countries there may seem to be some ridiculous building regulations, submission to the law of the land is integral to an ordered world. If we build outside the law we are jeopardizing the security of the property and neglecting our responsibilities to the society in which we live. We may lose the property completely and we will almost certainly lose friends among the neighbours! Assuming a righteous legal system, the law of the land is established under God to protect the rights of the individual. If we neglect it we forfeit our rights. In relational terms, that is exactly what happens when people reject God's ways and choose to live lawless lives. We need both God's authority and power to build our lives and homes. Authority is the right to do something, whereas power is the ability to do it. Yet many today are attempting to build bridges with others without God's permission and without His power. For instance, they sleep together outside of the covenant of marriage. They rarely, if ever, call on Him for help, preferring to trust their own counsel and judgment. No wonder they end up with devastation. If we want a home that is not going to crumble, we must obtain God's permission and authority through submission to His Word, and His power through the reception of His Spirit.

It is not in the devil's interests for you and me to have successful homes. It doesn't play into his hands. It is not a good advertisement for his strategies! Our homes, therefore, will come under attack. The attack may come in various forms. He may foster discord between the parents or dishonour from the children. Either way he will attempt to undermine the home in order for it to collapse. This is where authority and power are so essential. When everything is going well, we may be able to get away with our lawlessness, but when our backs are against the wall, we need to know the rights on which we are standing and the power we are wielding. Jesus offered His disciples both authority and power to live. They would have been fools to refuse it. The Bible says:

> *'When Jesus had called the Twelve together, he gave them power and authority to drive out all demons and to cure diseases.'* (Luke 9:1)

> *'I have given you authority to trample on snakes and scorpions and to overcome all the power of the enemy; nothing will harm you.'*
> (Luke 10:19)

Make no mistake, Satan does have power and will use it against us but because I have built my home with God's permission I have the ability to resist him and I am not harmed. As the great Baptist preacher C.H. Spurgeon wrote, 'If indeed the name of the Eternal God is named upon us, we are secure; for as of old, a Roman had but to say *"Romanus sum"*, "I am a Roman", and he could claim the protection of all the legions of the vast empire, so everyone who is a man of God has omnipotence as his guardian, and God will sooner empty heaven of angels than leave a saint without defense. Be braver than lions for the right, for God is with you.'[3]

A quality supplier

A number of years ago we were having difficulty with our heating system in our house. As a result I had to get under the floorboards of the house in order to look for a faulty pipe. I was shocked by what I found! The whole area was festooned with pipes of every conceivable length and girth. Some were painted and some were bare metal. There were unnecessary bends and useless taps and not one of the joints and connectors matched! The plumber who accompanied me under the house in order to fix the problem shook his head in despair. It was obvious it would be really difficult to find the problem, let alone mend it. Apparently, a previous owner had done his own plumbing. Instead of buying standard supplies he had tried to save money and used any materials that he found lying around. Obviously he had access to a factory of sorts because many of the fittings were industrial rather than domestic. Instead of going to a reputable supplier, purchasing new materials appropriate to the job in hand, he had gone to a scrap yard and bought cheap rejects. Of course, my plumbing problems are irrelevant in the scheme of things until one realizes that this is exactly how some people run their lives. They are equally careless and indifferent, except the consequences are greater than a burst pipe.

People form friendships and build their homes with a scrap yard mentality. Instead of going to the Word of God, some seek counsel in the local bar, talking to people who will understand because they share the same problems. Their friends may be empathetic but they will hardly be instructive. All they manage to do is gather failed ideas in order to fix their problems. Others do the same with books, magazines and seminars. At least they are attempting to resolve the issues, but they take this philosophy and that concept and try to weld it together, wondering why it doesn't work. Worse still, others look to science. Surely doctors and scientists are the 'gods in white coats' who will lead us into all truth! However, most of them seem to believe that humans are just complex animals and therefore they simply apply the lessons of behaviourism to our divinely instituted marriages. As a zoologist, I am passionately interested in animal behaviour: we can learn a great deal from rats, but they are unable to help me bring up my children! Rather, we need to follow Solomon's example who learned from creation but drew wisdom from the Creator. As he taught,

> 'By wisdom a house is built,
>   and through understanding it is established;
> through knowledge its rooms are filled
>   with rare and beautiful treasures.'   (Proverbs 24:3–4)

God is our quality supplier and His Words are our materials.

An expert builder

In one of the episodes of the famous British television comedy series *Fawlty Towers*, the hotelier, Basil Fawlty, is instructed by his wife Sybil to organize some building work. Unbeknown to her, he hires O'Reilly the builder to do the job. A decision that nearly costs him his hotel and his marriage! O'Reilly, who is famous for his shoddy but cheap workmanship, nearly manages to destroy the hotel. In his attempt to save time, effort and money Fawlty nearly loses everything! The episode is hilarious but can also be alarmingly true to life. Many of us are tempted to take short cuts and suffer the consequences. Though most of us are completely unqualified we attempt to mend our own cars, build our own houses and, more expensively, construct our own bridges, and then we wonder why they fail. We wouldn't dream of trying our hand at surgery without years of training and yet we tend to embark on marriage or parenting or even friendship without the least idea of what we are doing! Many people, including myself, got married without any sort of formal counselling or intensive instruction. We simply assume that it will be all right. We end up paying for our lack of foresight later. In retrospect, it seems better to pay the price beforehand.

Of course, price is the problem. To obtain the necessary permission, discover the quality supplier and become an expert builder all takes considerable time and effort. It will cost us a great deal to have excellent homes. Yet, it is always worth it in the end. The Bible encourages us to *'excel in everything'* (2 Corinthians 8:7), including love. Why? It is because excellence glorifies an excellent God. We are His workmanship and there is nothing cut-price or second-rate about His creation. We should, therefore, lift our standards when it comes to our relationships. The Greek word *huperbole*, which is translated 'excellent' in the Bible, means 'a throwing beyond'.[4] It is akin to a javelin thrower throwing a centimetre further than any other competitor in order to win the gold medal at the Olympics. Yet it is that extra centimetre that costs the most and separates the winner from the losers, the excellent from the good.

The way we become an expert builder and achieve excellence in our relationships is not only to pay the price of good instruction but also to draw from God's expertise as a Builder! He wants to equip us with excellence which, as we have seen in an earlier chapter, comes from His anointing and empowerment (Psalm 45:2). However, He also wants to gift us for whatever relationship we embark on. We may not think that it requires a divine skill to make a friend or be successfully married but the Bible says that, whether single or married, *'each man has his own gift from God; one has this gift, another has that'* (1 Corinthians 7:7). We can receive this grace gift by faith. It certainly seems a better option than phoning O'Reilly!

A team of character

Some time ago I watched a documentary on the building of the Empire State Building in New York. It was built in the 'Depression' and yet was finished in record time with the vast steel beams still warm from the foundry as they were placed in position. Like the Sydney Harbour Bridge, one of the many reasons for this success was the teams of riveters who worked on the project. The teams consisted of highly skilled workmen, each with a specific role. One of the team would literally throw the red-hot rivets across the scaffolding to the designated catcher who would carefully capture the dangerous projectile before it could plummet to the street below. It was then hammered into position and another rivet was thrown. This extremely hazardous and skilful procedure was accurately repeated thousands of times. It was teamwork based on mutual respect. Each was so reliant on the other that if one worker was sick the entire team refused to work with a replacement. What the riveters had created were teams of character that were founded on experience, reliability, unity and, above all, trust. This last characteristic of trust is vital to building anything, especially good relationships.

In any team, including a family, trust is essential, not only for survival but also for success. If I commit my life to God I have to trust that He rewards those that seek Him. If I confide in a friend I have to trust that he won't tell the world. If I am intimate with a partner I have to trust that she won't exploit my vulnerability. If I share a discovery with my colleagues I have to trust that they will not steal my idea. If I follow a leader I have to trust that he has my best interests at heart. In each case trust is the basis of a committed relationship and results in honesty, integrity, confidence and ultimately fruitfulness. It is therefore imperative that we foster trust in our relationships. However, in order to do so, we have to understand two aspects of this essential quality.

Firstly, we obviously have to create trust by being trustworthy. We have to be faithful, consistent, honest and, perhaps above all, keep our word. If we say, 'I'll be there', we will be. If we say, 'I'll do that', we will do it. This kind of trust is based on a proven track record. It is like a bank account that accumulates over time. The Antarctic explorer Sir Ernest Shackleton showed himself faithful to his fellow travellers so that they could trust him with their lives. One of his team recorded, 'Shackleton had that personality that imbued you with trust – you felt that if he led you everything was going to be all right'.[5] One of the great problems with this aspect of trust is that, although it takes time to build, it can take a moment to destroy. One major failure can empty the trust account. This is where the second and less talked about aspect of trust comes in. We have to choose to trust. The God kind of love that we all need is not a nebulous, inconsistent feeling, it is an active, willing sacrificial choice to give to another. This love, the Bible says, *'always trusts'* (1 Corinthians 13:7). In other words, we are challenged both to trust our friends and our enemies, the trustworthy and the untrustworthy! The latter, of course, seems totally unreasonable. How can we trust a friend who has continually let us down? How can we trust an unfaithful partner? It seems wrong until we think of how Jesus Christ trusts us. Even though we fail Him, He readily trusts us with His Word, His ministry and His reputation. He trusted Peter with His precious 'lambs' just after Peter had publicly denied Him! The American preacher David Wilkerson, whose story is portrayed in the film *The Cross and the Switchblade*, was challenged to trust the normally untrustworthy Nicki Cruz with the responsibility of taking the collection! No one had trusted him like that before and it was this act of unconditional love that began to turn his life around. We need this kind of costly and 'unreasonable' trust in our relationships if we are going to rescue them from mediocrity.

Building a home

Bridges are often prohibitively expensive. The much criticized Humber Bridge in England cost $250 million in 1981. However, this pales into insignificance in comparison with the Akashi Kaikyo Bridge in Japan, which in 2002 cost $4.3 billion! Although this cost may seem astronomical, the price of a bridge is irrelevant in comparison to its immeasurable worth to the community. The effort and expense required to build a relationship is equally incalculable. A good marriage, like a great bridge, is beyond price and its secrets unfathomable. Nonetheless, there are some simple and quantifiable steps I want to describe that hopefully will help us build such a priceless and measureless marriage.

Get our priorities right
Maybe only a farmer would fully grasp the significance of one of Solomon's proverbs which says,

> *'Finish your outdoor work and get your fields ready;*
> *after that, build your house.'*   (Proverbs 24:27)

It is pointless for a farmer to seek shelter before sustenance. His entire livelihood depends on his ability to prepare the field, sow the seed and eventually reap the crop. His success in this area will determine what he can then build with the fruit of his labour. The farmer knows that we must first sow for the future and then build for the present. In relational terms we need to follow this advice and get our priorities right. If we are to produce long-term fruit in our relationships we need to do the first things first. As Jesus taught in the Gospel of Matthew, we need *first* to be reconciled, *first* to seek God, *first* to point the finger at ourselves and *first* to deal with the internal issues that make us unclean (Matthew 5:24; 6:33; 7:5; 23:26). These are our priorities. It is only then that we are able to be effective givers, be prosperous, successfully help others, and be attractive and exemplary in the world in which God has placed us.

Follow God's creative plans
Once we have our priorities right we need to know the general plans that God has for each one of us. We need to believe the promise given through the prophet Jeremiah that God wants to bless us,

> ' *"For I know the plans I have for you," declares the* LORD, *"plans to prosper you and not to harm you, plans to give you hope and a future."* '
> (Jeremiah 29:11)

However, we also need to understand that every family has a pattern. It is from this that we, with God's help, are going to build our unique homes. No two are the same. Every one has its individual flavour, character and purpose. I once lived in a street in England where the houses were identical. The only way that you could tell the homes apart was from the different coloured doors! Our lives should not be like this. God is creative and wants us to reflect His creativity. In the same way that God personally revealed a 'pattern' to Moses from which he built (Hebrews 8:5), he wants to do the same for us. My wife and I don't relate exactly the same as other couples. Neither do we bring up our children exactly the same as anyone else. However, we are both confident that the manner and methods that we are using are wise and God-given and therefore will bring good fruit.

Use materials that last
There are parts of Australia that are subject to bush fires. We cannot avoid them. They are part of the distinctiveness of the nation. To live in these areas without any knowledge of the dangers, or build houses

without any form of fire resistance is asking for trouble. A good home needs to be built with fire retardant materials. As we will see in the next chapter, relationships must also be built with imperishable materials because they too will be subjected to 'fire'. As the Bible says, *'Fire will test the quality of each man's work'* (1 Corinthians 3:13, see verses 9–15). As a relational builder we need be aware that love is fire resistant and has an eternal guarantee, whereas lust is temporary and invites destruction! Of course, fire resistant materials are usually more expensive!

Commit to a lifetime of giving

Quality building work has always cost a great deal. Three thousand years ago King David wanted his son Solomon to build a temple *'of great magnificence and fame and splendour'* (1 Chronicles 22:5) and so took pains to provide *'a hundred thousand talents of gold, a million talents of silver, quantities of bronze and iron too great to be weighed, and wood and stone'* (1 Chronicles 22:14). That is 3,450 tonnes of gold alone! This generosity would have required sacrifice and extensive preparation. He loved God's House and was prepared to give to it. If we love our marriage partner we will be equally sacrificial, knowing that true love, by definition, demands acts of giving. A good marriage is not built with one act of love but many. Neither Rome nor a relationship is built in a day!

Don't despise small things

Zerubbabel was one of a party of Jews who returned from exile in Babylon to Jerusalem in 537 BC in order to rebuild the temple. In the context of the restoration of the temple, the prophet Zechariah said,

> *'Who despises the day of small things? Men will rejoice when they see the plumb-line in the hand of Zerubbabel.'*   (Zechariah 4:10)

Whatever the exact prophetic interpretation of this passage, it is clear that we mustn't assume that little things are unimportant. A large building, for instance, may be built with a plumbline and held together by nails, screws, bolts and rivets. Although an apocryphal book, Ecclesiasticus, the Wisdom of Jesus the son of Sirach, reiterates the thought when it states,

> *'A workman who is a drunkard will not become rich; he who despises small things will fail little by little.'*   (Sirach 19:1)[6]

In marriage building, the nuts and bolts consist of 'I love you', 'Thank you', 'See you tonight', 'I am on my way home' and 'You look good'! If we are too distracted or lazy to be conscientious about these small things we will also fail 'little by little'.

Recognize that the neighbours are watching

A building site always attracts its fair share of inquisitive onlookers. Every passer-by wants to record and comment on the progress! We should not be surprised that our relational building is also under scrutiny. Jesus taught that if we failed to complete the 'tower' that we are building, *'everyone who sees it'* (Luke 14:29) will mock us. Whether we like it or not, the neighbours are watching! Isaiah the prophet recognized that it wasn't only his words that communicated God's message to the nation but his entire family:

> *'Here am I, and the children the* LORD *has given me. We are signs and symbols in Israel from the* LORD *Almighty, who dwells on Mount Zion.'*
> (Isaiah 8:18)

My children also silently testify to an observant world. They are a testimony to the faithfulness and favour of God. Like an architect I have learned that I am building my home for the good of both the household and the community.

Give attention to the exits and the entrances

As we have seen in the previous chapter, the Bible has a great deal to say about 'coming in and going out' or as William Shakespeare puts it, our 'exits' and 'entrances'.[7] When we are building a house they become focal points both for us and our neighbours! They are also the places where a building inspector can readily identify structural weakness. When building a home, the manner with which we say 'hello' and 'goodbye' as we enter and leave can affect the atmosphere enormously. The people who are allowed in either create an environment of peace and blessing or an unwanted alternative. Jesus made it clear that our presence and our greetings make a huge difference:

> *'As you enter the home, give it your greeting. If the home is deserving, let your peace rest on it; if it is not, let your peace return to you.'*
> (Matthew 10:13–14)

King David evidently recognized this and wouldn't allow deceivers to live in his house (Psalm 101:7). As both a leader and a shepherd he would have understood the significance of a 'gateway'. Under the guidance of a shepherd, sheep are led out to the provision of the field and in to the protection of the fold. Moses also used this image in his prayer to God,

> '*May the* LORD, *the God of the spirits of all mankind, appoint a man over this community to go out and come in before them, one who will lead them out and bring them in, so the* LORD'*s people will not be like sheep without a shepherd.*'   (Numbers 27:16–17)

In light of this, Jesus' teaching gives us a guideline for our homes. He said,

> '*I am the gate; whoever enters through me will be saved. He will come in and go out, and find pasture.*'   (John 10:9)

If we want salvation in our homes we need to allow Jesus Christ to be the example and filter for all our exits and entrances.

Write the vision on the fabric of the house

The Jews, as we have noted, write their 'mission statement' on the doorframes of their homes. It is this that they impress on their children (Deuteronomy 6:4–9). Many Christians have a similar plaque displayed in a prominent position. We used to have an Armenian tile above our door simply inscribed with the word 'Jesus' in Aramaic. Not many could read it but it reminded us of His pre-eminence in our lives! It recently fell off but anyone who enters our home still knows what we believe! It is reflected in our conversation, books, music and mindsets. In fact, in my view, the very fabric of our homes should reflect our vision. In his disturbing short story, *The Rocking Horse Winner*, D.H. Lawrence wrote about a house in which the walls whispered words of fear to the boy who lived there. He was driven by the values of the home that seemed to be contained in the plaster itself. Although a tragic narrative, it illustrates the power of our environment. There have been occasions when I have totally failed to understand why someone behaved in a particular way, until I visited their home and then it became abundantly clear. Children, for instance, not only have to hear their parents say, 'I love you', they have to feel it in the home.

Prepare places of meeting

One of the ways to create a positive atmosphere in a home is to prepare a place of meeting. This can be a significant room, a regular event or the celebration of a family tradition. In the case of the classic Australian film *The Castle*, it was a weekly TV programme! In our case it has always been dinner time. The conversations are inspirational, provocative, eccentric, educational and fun. The table is a place of unity, thanksgiving and redemption. I don't think that it is insignificant that Jesus ate a Passover meal with His disciples just before He died and subsequently established the regular habit of 'breaking bread' in the Church, or that it was only when He was 'at the table' (Luke 24:30) that two of the disciples recognized Him after He had risen. These were places of encounter and can be created purposefully and deliberately in our homes. The Danish writer Isak Dinesen's remarkable story, *Babette's Feast*, describes how a French cook brought reconciliation and healing to a small, religious and divided community through a sumptuous meal. Philip Yancey concluded that 'Babette's Feast opened the gate and grace stole in'.[8] However, it is not just grace that this 'Agape' or 'love feast' allowed in, but a myriad of other qualities that homes can ill afford to lose.

Invite salvation into the house

When Zacchaeus allowed Jesus into his life he probably had no idea of the immediate change that it would bring. The sense of acceptance, the power of forgiveness and the compelling desire to repent came flooding over his threshold the moment the Stranger from Nazareth stepped into his wealthy home. Jesus responded to his hunger and evident faith by saying, *'Today salvation has come to this house'* (Luke 19:9). It is a simple statement but it is the key to all the other principles I have just described. The word 'salvation' here encompasses wholeness, healing and deliverance and without it we are powerless to effect change in our homes. However, if we are going to invite salvation into our homes we need to understand that it will cost us everything. Jesus demanded change of Zacchaeus and expects the same of us.

Building a friendship

There is an expression in building circles that defines an engineer as 'someone who can do for one dollar what any fool can do for three'! This economical attitude seeks to build what is called a 'minimum cost bridge'. Although completely understandable for civil engineers it is disastrous for relational engineers. Yet it is the attitude that many employ when building friendships. In our frenetic world many opt for minimum cost, low maintenance, high turnover relationships. It is a shallow alternative to the rich adventure and high price of a lifelong friendship. I can't possibly deal here with all the necessary building blocks of a quality friendship, but in the context of the cost of building I want to highlight just three for which we do need to be prepared to sacrifice: honesty, loyalty and care.

Give wounds that can be trusted

A number of years ago a friend of mine strongly criticized me. He basically told me that I was an opinionated know-all! Of course, I didn't immediately agree! The Bible says that a fool *'delights in airing his own opinions'* (Proverbs 18:2), and so I wasn't readily going to admit that I was a fool! However, I apologized for my attitude, as did he for his manner. But the comment hurt for some time. Why? It was because he was a good friend and the Bible says, *'Wounds from a friend can be trusted'* (Proverbs 27:6). He was on my side and was trying to help me. It was really the truth that hurt me and not my friend. I came away a better person. We are still good friends! Some, of course, would say, 'Who need friends like that?' To which I would reply, 'Everyone!' We all need friends who will challenge, stretch and, if necessary, criticize us. What is the benefit of friendships that simply ensnare us with flattery? I thrive on encouragement, but ultimately it is the truth that sets me free, not adulation. Of course, it takes a great deal of moral courage to confront someone with the truth and yet the alternative is deceptive and tragic. If we genuinely want to change for the better, we all need friends who love and know us well enough to see what we don't see and tell us what we don't want to hear!

Stick closer than a brother

If it takes courage to tell someone the truth it also takes courage to stand with someone who is being criticized. When a person is genuinely or falsely accused his friends are caught in the line of fire. When the flak comes, as it inevitably will, it is always interesting to see who runs for cover and who stands up to protect their friend. We all know that when a leader fails there are few who visit them in prison! Of course, there are times when a friend continues in his or her folly and remains unrepentant, in which case pulling out of the friendship may be the wise course of action. However, distancing ourselves from a troubled friend is often promoted by self-interest and not love. Self-protection may desire withdrawal but a covenant of friendship requires loyalty and commitment. I once had dinner with a colleague in a restaurant whose past lifestyle had attracted immense disapproval. He told me that that the friends whom he honoured were those who stayed with him even when their own reputations were tainted. Even as he spoke I noticed people glancing at us and making judgments. The book of Proverbs tells us,

> *'A friend loves at all times,*
> *   and a brother is born for adversity.'*   (Proverbs 17:17)

and,

> *'A man of many companions may come to ruin,*
> *   but there is a friend who sticks closer than a brother.'*
>   (Proverbs 18:24)

I have certainly been immensely grateful for those who have stood beside me when I have been accused and spoken for me when I have been spoken against.

Go to your friends in the desert and leave them there

One of the great stories of friendship in the Bible is that between David and Jonathan. There was no immoral physical relationship as some have suggested, but there was an emotional commitment and also a spiritual connection between the two of them: *'Jonathan became one in spirit with David, and he loved him as himself'* (1 Samuel 18:1). Consequently, when David was in trouble, Jonathan's care for his friend motivated him to help. He found him *'at Horesh in the Desert of Ziph'* (1 Samuel 23:15). Of course, there is a cost involved in seeking out friends in need and being with them in a crisis. However, perhaps Jonathan's greatest act of care was that after he encouraged David he left his friend in the desert to make his own choices and prove God for himself. The Bible simply states,

> *'The two of them made a covenant before the LORD. Then Jonathan went home, but David remained at Horesh.'*   (1 Samuel 23:18)

It was the last time that they met! Theirs was not a 'minimum cost bridge'.

Of course, we cannot ask David and Jonathan the price they paid for their friendship. Nor can we ask any exemplary bridge-builder the real cost of construction. It is immeasurable. However, we all know that if we want something of quality and longevity, the likelihood is that we will have to pay a great deal for it.

Summary and advice

1. **It is impossible to gauge accurately the real price of a bridge.** It is pointless, unhelpful and dehumanizing to reduce the cost of bringing up a child to a sum of money.

2. **There are necessary requirements for building relationships.** A home is built with authority, wisdom, excellence and trust.

3. **We need God's permission.** Christ's disciples needed both His authority and power. We are foolish if we think we can do without them.

4. **We need a quality supplier.** Good relationships are not built with a scrap yard mentality.

5. **We need an expert builder.** Excellence in our relationships glorifies the excellent God who designed them.

6. **We need a team of character.** We need two kinds of trust to build a home: reasonable and unreasonable!

7. **Building a home is a costly experience!** We need to get our priorities right, follow God's creative plans, use materials that last, commit to a lifetime of giving, and not despise small things. We need to recognize that the neighbours are watching, give attention to exits and entrances, write the vision on the fabric of the house, prepare places of meeting and finally invite salvation into the house.

8. **When building a friendship we mustn't choose a 'minimum cost bridge'.** We should learn to give faithful wounds, stick closer than a brother and find our friends in the desert and leave them there!

Notes
1. Robert McCulloch. Quoted in Terry Gwynn-Jones, 'The Town London Bridge Built', *The Australian Way*, Qantas (April 1997).

2. The poem can be found on the website www.sfmuseum.org/hist9/mcgloin/html

3. C.H. Spurgeon, *Cheque Book of the Bank of Faith* (Marshall, Morgan & Scott).

4. *Enhanced Strong's Lexicon* (Logos Research Systems, Inc., 1995).

5. The Holy Bible, The Revised Standard Version (Oxford University Press, 1973, 1977).

6. William Shakespeare, *As You Like It*, Act 2, Scene 7.

7. Philip Yancey, *What's So Amazing about Grace?* (Zondervan, 1997).

THE THIRD
ASSUMPTION

Bridge-builders
Build for Strength

Chapter 18
Fire, Flood, Air and Time
The Permanence of Relationships

The Sydney Harbour Bridge was intended for longevity. Its designers bore a century of adverse conditions in mind. Its steel and stone are both flexible and stable. It can resist winds of up to 200 kilometres an hour. It can safely handle temperature variations of 49°C though it may rise or fall 18 centimetres during temperature extremes. It was designed to cope with the loading associated with totally congested roads, railways and footpaths: an estimated 160 trains, 6,000 vehicles and 40,000 pedestrians an hour. It was built for our grandparents and will, barring an unforeseen tragedy, serve our grandchildren.

London Bridge has had a chequered history. It has evolved like the Irish axe! (The head and handle have been replaced many times but, 'It's been in the family over a hundred years'!) Although the bridge's foundations, materials, structure and appearance have changed constantly over hundreds of years, it still retains its name and stature at the heart of the divided city.

It was first built by the Romans almost two thousand years ago: probably a relatively fragile structure and yet with a mystical strength. The writer Peter Ackroyd describes it aptly: 'Half the legends of London arose upon its foundations; miracles were performed, and visions seen, upon the new wooden thoroughfare'.[1] Hundreds of years of building, destruction and reconstruction followed. It has been ravaged by fire, flood, air and time. After being pulled down by the invading Norsemen's ships in 1014, it was rebuilt only to be washed away by floods in

1090 and destroyed by fire in 1136. Stone superseded wood as its building material in 1176 and houses were constructed on it. Many of these were damaged by fire in 1632 and more fell victim to what the diarist Samuel Pepys describes as the 'horrid, malicious and bloody flame'[2] in the Great Fire of London in 1666. This great bridge, removed and replaced time and again, has stood in virtually the same spot for a thousand generations. It has a strength and permanence that challenges the transience of our brief lives.

It is this concept of permanence that I want to explore and explain as it relates to our life bridges. Our view of the world is often so myopic that we tend only to look at the eighty or so years that we have the privilege of being on this earth, rather than seeing our lives as a part of a long chain of relationships. However, God has a much longer view of things. Godly covenants have a long life span! His love for those who respond to it extends to a thousand generations:

> 'Know therefore that the LORD your God is God; he is the faithful God, keeping his covenant of love to a thousand generations of those who love him and keep his commands.'   (Deuteronomy 7:9)

His word to Abraham possesses the same longevity:

> 'He remembers his covenant for ever,
>   the word he commanded, for a thousand generations,
> the covenant he made with Abraham,
>   the oath he swore to Isaac.'   (Psalm 105:8–9)

The institution of marriage, though only designed to last a lifetime, is a God-ordained covenant and therefore has both a history and a future. We all have both a heritage and a destiny. If we are to live effectively in the window in-between the two, we need to be aware of them both and build our lives accordingly. In order to instil this permanence into our lives and relationships we have to start with good materials, be prepared to repair and rebuild, and learn to live inter-generationally.

Start with good materials

It is painful when relationships fail. The more it happens, the more reticent we are to embark on them. We need to believe that the next partner will not leave or the next friend will not reject us. We therefore tend to check people out carefully in order to see what they are made of before we commit to the relationships. A complete lack of trust is, of course, very negative and can prevent us taking the sort of faith steps that all relationships require. However, there is nothing wrong with taking care. Most of us are, in fact, automatically cautious when we cross a bridge. A basic bridge, as we have seen, could be described as 'a plank across a stream' and all of us have walked across such a plank at some time in our life. We tend to take a good hard look at it beforehand in order to establish if it is safe. If it is made of rotten wood we will not cross it. If, on the other hand, it looks solid, we may choose to use it. If we are going to trust our life to it we need to know that it is made of good materials. But what exactly are the properties that the bridge needs to enable it to carry our weight? What are we looking for?

To put it simply, when we walk across the wooden plank, the plank will bend under our weight. As it does so, the top will be pushed together (compression) and the bottom will be pulled apart (tension). The ability of the wood to be pulled and pushed is its *strength*. When we have crossed the stream, the plank will automatically bounce back to its original position like a rubber band; this property is called *elasticity*. If a very heavy person has crossed before us the plank may have developed a permanent sag in which case the material is behaving plastically. This *plasticity* is helpful since it acts as a warning to us that the plank is about to fail! There is also a less obvious factor about which we need to be aware. Wood is perishable, as the Romans discovered in London. Good building materials need to be as *imperishable* as possible. We may never have given these qualities a second thought but we do rely on them every time we cross a bridge!

In essence, our relationships must possess all of these four qualities. They need to have the strength to stand up under all manner of loads and pressures that beset them each day. They need the ability to bounce back after carrying loads. They need to have an in-built warning mechanism that tells them when they are overloaded or when they require strengthening or repair, and they also need to build with imperishable materials. It is this latter necessity that I want to emphasize.

The Bible tells that sooner or later, like London Bridge, our lives and relationships will be tested by fire:

'For we are God's fellow-workers; you are God's field, God's building. By the grace God has given me, I laid a foundation as an expert builder, and someone else is building on it. But each one should be careful how he builds. For no one can lay any foundation other than the one already laid, which is Jesus Christ. If any man builds on this foundation using gold, silver, costly stones, wood, hay or straw, his work will be shown for what it is, because the Day will bring it to light. It will be revealed with fire, and the fire will test the quality of each man's work.'

(1 Corinthians 3:9–13)

Basically, the building materials mentioned by Paul are divided into two categories: perishable (wood, hay and straw) and imperishable (gold, silver and costly stones). The imagery is teaching us to build our lives with eternal rather than temporal materials if we are to achieve reward in heaven. However, the principle also holds true if we are to achieve success on earth. Sadly, many people still build with wood, hay and straw.

Wood is dead and not living. A living relationship with a living God transforms and strengthens us but if we bring dead idols or dead religion into our homes we jeopardize the security of our families. According to the Law of Moses, idols defiled a home (Deuteronomy 7:26) and in his day Paul the apostle challenged the believers in Ephesus to burn any writings they possessed that were associated with their former sorcery (Acts 19:19). In more recent times, missionaries have recorded that many families who have turned to Christ and yet who refused to rid themselves of their household idols eventually turned their backs on Him to the detriment of their future. I can personally testify to seeing scores of families who have been healed as a result of removing some sort of idol from their home. However, it is not the dead wooden objects that are as insidious as dead philosophies and dead words. As the book of Proverbs warns,

*'There is a way that seems right to a man,
    but in the end it leads to death.'*   (Proverbs 16:25)

*'The tongue has the power of life and death,
    and those who love it will eat its fruit.'*   (Proverbs 18:21)

We evidently have a choice either to build our homes with our words or tear them down.

Hay is equally impermanent. It is food, not flesh. While it remains hay it is cattle food that has not been eaten and assimilated. It is only when it is eaten that it becomes flesh. In our relationships, God's word not obeyed is food not assimilated. We can have the Bible on our shelves, but unless we do what it says we are in danger of building vulnerable bridges. We may even preach on forgiveness but if we constantly record and recall offences that have taken place among our family, we are asking for trouble. The final consumable material is straw: the litter after harvest, mere remnants, not substance. A home built with leftovers is unlikely to stand. If we only give our children the last seconds of our day or only give God the change in our pockets our families are unlikely to pass the test of fire.

The three imperishable building materials, on the other hand, give us insight into how we can develop permanence in our relationships: gold is valuable, silver beautiful and costly stones durable. A friendship built on value and beauty will endure long after a careless relationship cheapened by casual sex. Even the word 'affair' highlights its brevity. However, the Bible makes it clear that, if these three qualities are to change our homes, they must be primarily internal and not just external. Submission, for instance, is an inner quality that is described as, *'the unfading beauty of a gentle and quiet spirit, which is of great worth in God's sight'* (1 Peter 3:4). Notice the permanent trilogy again: durability, beauty and value. A similarly undying trio is mentioned by Paul,

> *'And now these three remain: **faith, hope** and **love**. But the greatest of these is love.'*　　　　(1 Corinthians 13:13, emphasis mine)

The natural resilience of precious metals and diamonds cannot begin to compare with all of these eternal resources which we have at our disposal. A natural slave may be redeemed by silver and gold but we are eternally redeemed by the blood of Christ. We are born again of the imperishable seed of the word of God (1 Peter 1:18–23). However, starting with good materials is not good enough. We have to learn to build with them.

Prepared to build, repair and rebuild

Stephen Citron, author and composer, used to have a large sign on the wall of his Carnegie Hall studio with a quote from Alan and Marilyn Bergman which read: 'Songs are not written they're re-written'.[3] It is an apothegm that could also be applied to bridges: 'A bridge is not built, it is rebuilt'. The history of London Bridge bears testament to that fact. We could also learn from this idea in our relationships. A long-term relationship evolves through crisis. This may come across as a negative observation since it suggests repeated failure, but a good relationship is one that negotiates the inevitable difficulties and grows stronger as a result. Any couple striving for excellence in their marriage, for instance, must know the benefits of conflict resolution and the principles of successful progression.

Bridge-building takes time and effort

Good relationships like great bridges do not appear overnight. They are constructed and improved over a considerable period of time. This was illustrated to me during a conversation I had with a fellow preacher when he made a very simple and yet profound observation. 'You know, Robert,' he said matter-of-factly, 'the reason that I have plenty of money is that I have been married to the same woman for thirty years!' In other words, there was no hidden expense account, no divided inheritance and no alimony! He had kept making wise daily choices. He had kept doing the right things. It is a lesson that numerous young couples need to hear. They expect all the benefits and blessings of a long-term relationship without the time and effort they require. The reality is that the strength and security that accompanies a lifelong relationship only comes with consistent commitment. It cannot be enjoyed at the outset. The same is also true of a sexual relationship within marriage. To suggest that the honeymoon is the highlight as many seem to do is as ridiculous as it is ill informed. It is a myth that is perpetrated by the immoral world in which we live. Despite the many celebrated lovers, infamous for their sexual exploits, it takes a much greater lover to learn to fulfil a marriage partner for fifty years than it does to have a series of 'one night stands'.

A bridge requires a lifetime of daily repairs

All of us are dangerous individuals! We tend to have hard heads, sharp edges and abrasive personalities that have the capacity to harm the people around us. However, perhaps worst of all, our uncontrolled tongues have the ability to pull down our life bridges as swiftly and completely as the Norsemen pulled down London Bridge in the eleventh century. As the Bible says,

> *'Reckless words pierce like a sword,*
>   *but the tongue of the wise brings healing.'*   (Proverbs 12:18)

> *'The tongue that brings healing is a tree of life,*
>   *but a deceitful tongue crushes the spirit.'*   (Proverbs 15:4)

We all know that we have the capacity to crush people with our words. Most of us can remember unkind and hurtful comments that were made about us when we were younger, which goes to show the power and stamina of a curse. However, as we have seen, it is often the daily repetitive negative remarks that cause the most damage: 'You are so selfish'; 'I won't love you if you do that'; 'You have always been lazy'; 'You will never amount to anything'; 'You will end up in a doss-house'. The last comment was actually said to a friend of mine by his father. It pursued and haunted him until he found himself hopeless and discarded in a refuge. His father's words had both predicted and partially caused his demise. Thankfully, at this point, he found God and started afresh.

Since we are fully aware of the capacity of words to hurt and to heal, we must not only choose to replace the negative with the positive but also regularly repair the damage already done. Paul explains both of these requirements to the church at Ephesus. Firstly,

> *'Do not let any unwholesome talk come out of your mouths, but only what is helpful for building others up according to their needs, that it may benefit those who listen.'*   (Ephesians 4:29)

Secondly,

> *' "In your anger do not sin": Do not let the sun go down while you are still angry . . . '*   (Ephesians 4:26)

He recognizes the likelihood that we will get angry on occasion, but challenges us to address the injury immediately. This is because otherwise it will give Satan an opportunity to gain a foothold in our lives, and also because anger increases exponentially. The Bible warns us about the consequences of ignoring this advice when it says,

> *'Starting a quarrel is like breaching a dam;*
>   *so drop the matter before a dispute breaks out.'*   (Proverbs 17:14)

An unattended crack in a seemingly impregnable wall can develop quickly with devastating results.

Conflict is inevitable
When the single stone arch of the Mostar Bridge in Bosnia and Herzegovina was shelled to oblivion on 9 November 1993 after standing for 400 years at the centre of the multicultural town, it was reported with disbelief: 'How could this happen? How could anyone attack such an important and historic landmark?' Of course, the loss of such a beautiful bridge was tragic but we shouldn't be surprised that war broke out, especially in such an unpredictable part of the world. Some sort of conflict was inevitable and the obvious target was the bridge that united the community. Many people react with a similar 'head in the sand' attitude when it comes to their relationships. They assume every hope will be realized and every desire unchallenged. I remember preaching at a wedding in which I told the couple that because of their respective personalities I would predict some fairly major differences of opinion in the forthcoming marriage! During the reception afterwards I was rebuked by the father of the bridegroom who told me that I had maligned his apparently perfect son! I think that he wanted a 'fantasy' day and I had ruined it with reality. In fact, despite the predicted differences and inevitable conflict the couple has remained happily married as I expected.

We shouldn't be fearful of conflict; rather, we should plan for it. We are all independent, sinful people with our own personalities and agendas and sooner or later we will clash with someone else. Though I now very rarely argue with my wife, it has been known in the past! The way we have dealt with these differences of opinion is to have an agreed strategy that was decided by both of us *before* the conflict developed. We openly recognized our points of weakness so that we would be forewarned and therefore forearmed when the problems arose. We also learned to pick our battles. There are some things that simply are not worth fighting over! My eternal destiny and my temporal sanity should not rest on whether I regularly wash the dishes or whether my wife drives the children to school! There are more important things to fight for!

Respect maintains strong bridges
Tragically, there are many communities around the world that are characterized by devalued people, un-maintained services, neglected

buildings and crumbling bridges. The common denominator in all these places is not just a lack of resources but a lack of respect. Respect is one of the cornerstones of an ordered and prosperous society and one of the fundamental ingredients of a successful home. A husband should respect his wife and vice versa. Children should respect their parents. This respect is birthed in value. If we value each other we will respect each other's opinions. If we value our homes we will respect their sanctity. If we value our friends we will respect their feelings. If we value a friendship we will respect its parameters. In fact, if we value anything, we will do our best not only to respect it but also to maintain and protect it. We will only attack something we do not value. The Ponte Vecchio in Florence was not destroyed in the Second World War because it was considered too valuable to lose. The Mostar Bridge, on the other hand, was destroyed because it wasn't respected. Respect, therefore, must be at the heart of bridge-building, bridge maintenance and resolving conflict.

A number of years ago, a decorator friend of mine was painting a ceiling when a chip of paint fell into his eye. Although it hurt he wanted to finish the job and so failed to remove the problem. By the end of the day his eye was so inflamed that, had it not been for the efforts of the hospital, he would have lost his eyesight permanently. Had he respected his sight more he would have been quicker to act. We can very easily criticize his folly but we all do the same in our relationships. We allow 'sinful splinters' to fester and poison our system instead of stopping, identifying the irritation and dealing with it. Our relationships can be destroyed through disrespect. When and if we do respond we tend to blame everything and everyone except ourselves. Jesus rebuked those who did this,

> *'You hypocrite, first take the plank out of your own eye, and then you will see clearly to remove the speck from your brother's eye.'*
>
> (Matthew 7:5)

The truth is, if we respected ourselves and our friends, we would be honest enough first to remove our problems and gentle enough to help them remove theirs. When helping others, respect should once again be our guide. We should attack the problem and not the person. When my wife is blinded by something, it doesn't help if I poke her eye out! We are not meant to be fighting one another. We should respect one another enough to join forces against a common threat.

Flexibility is necessary for longevity

There are few glass bridges in the world! They don't last. Though glass is immensely strong, stronger than steel in certain circumstances, it is unsuitable as a structural building material since it is too brittle. As we have seen, for a bridge to withstand centuries of storms it must remain relatively flexible. A healthy bridge moves all the time. It responds to the loads placed on it. A steel suspension bridge, for instance, sways in the wind and creaks and groans as it expands and contracts throughout the day. A useful bridge will also change with the times. Traffic flow, roadways and decorations will have to change from decade to decade in order for the bridge to continue to serve the community for which it was built. The tramways were removed from Sydney Harbour Bridge in 1958 because the trams became redundant. For a bridge to remain relevant it must constantly change or it will become obsolete. In a relationship this flexibility is essential. People change over time and so for a relationship to last both parties must move forward. I am a completely different person from the uncertain teenager who first set eyes on his future wife. As we grew together, any rigidity or stubbornness on my part would have inevitably jeopardized our fruitful relationship. Both my wife and I have to change every day. It is tragic to see a person who is *set in their ways* become increasing irrelevant to the changing world around them. Their character, like their bones, becomes brittle and they get hurt easily and best avoided. Mid-life affairs are usually brought on by one party refusing to change. Successful grandparents, on the other hand, are those who have maintained an eye for the future, learning to compromise in order to build another bridge to another generation.

Learn to live inter-generationally

Most of us plan our lives around our allotted number of years, but a life bridge, as I have said, should have a much longer effect than this. If correctly maintained a bridge should not only 'last a lifetime' but span many generations. One of the many London Bridges lasted six hundred years before it was replaced. Of the Sydney Harbour Bridge, the Roads and Traffic Authority have stated, 'With the right care and attention, the Bridge has an indefinite life'.[4] If we are going to build the kind of testimony we desire to and be as influential as we should, our lives and relationships will have to bridge the gap effectively between the previous generation and the next one. We have to live inter-generationally. Although it is often fashionable to 'live for the moment', we cannot pretend that we are not affected by the past and we cannot divorce ourselves from our responsibility to the future. One of the reasons that Jesus Christ built a powerful testimony was because He knew where He came from, who He was and where He was going (John 8:12–14). He is the example for all life bridges.

The Jews are very conscious of their inheritance. They are very aware whom they are descended from. There is a curious story in the Old Testament where the people with no family records, no proof of their past, were excluded from the priesthood until another priest came and overruled the law (Ezra 2:62–63). All of us, in point of fact, want to know where we came from. It is a basic instinct of human nature. We feel as though we cannot properly build for the future without knowing the past. Millions of people search through their family records in order to discover their roots. There are so many orphans and disconnected families, however, that this task is often impossible. Thankfully, another Priest *has* come in the form of Jesus Christ and enabled us to forget our broken past and move on. Nonetheless, that doesn't mean our past is irrelevant. In my own family I have scores of photographs of ancestors going back for many generations. Many of them were ministers. To suggest that this has had no effect on me and my family and friendships is a denial of the power of generational blessing and faithful prayer. I know that my great-great-grandfather blessed me and my great-grandmother prayed for me. Timothy was encouraged by his mentor Paul to build on his past as he had himself done:

> *'I thank God, whom I serve, **as my forefathers did**, with a clear conscience, as night and day I constantly remember you in my prayers. Recalling your tears, I long to see you, so that I may be filled with joy. I have been reminded of your sincere faith, **which first lived in your grandmother Lois and in your mother Eunice** and, I am persuaded, now lives in you also. For this reason I remind you to fan into flame the gift of God, which is in you through the laying on of my hands.'*
>
> (2 Timothy 1:3–6, emphasis mine)

In order to progress successfully into the future Timothy had to draw from the blessings of the past, and so should we.

However, Timothy, although a product of the past, was not a victim of it. He was taught by Paul to be himself and to be confident of his calling. He had his own gift and he needed to learn to use it effectively for the glory of God. He became his own man, serving the purpose of God in his own generation. In this way he became an effective channel between generations:

> 'You then, my son, be strong in the grace that is in Christ Jesus. And the things you have heard me say in the presence of many witnesses entrust to reliable men who will also be qualified to teach others.'
>
> (2 Timothy 2:1–2)

Like a bridge that 'finds its place' in the community, every person is unique, and it is this freedom that enables us to learn from the past without copying it and give to the future without dominating it. Sydney Harbour Bridge is modelled on others and gave birth to others, yet remains distinctive. This appreciation of distinctiveness helped Timothy run his own race, but then trust his followers enough to pass on the baton. When we build for the future and so build permanence into our relationships, we are to disciple people, not clone them.

Paul encouraged Timothy to bring up a new generation of believers because he already knew the power and influence of mentoring. Paul himself had been discipled by Barnabas who through his 'son' Paul and 'grandson' Timothy was changing the known world. As Howard and William Hendricks observe, 'By mentoring Paul, Barnabas had a profound impact on numerous cities and countless people throughout the ancient world. His legacy shows that a mentor's influence affects not only the protégé's life, but every life touched by the protégé.'[5] Personally, I see every student I teach as a million people. I look past their faces to the countries they are going to visit and the crowds they are going to reach. I have even received correspondence from ex-students telling me the places I have visited through them. It is one way by which I can perpetuate my life and message. As the Hendricks go on to say, 'Mentoring is a ministry of multiplication. Every time you build into the life of another man, you launch a process that ideally will never end'.[6] Mentoring and discipleship, however, are only two of the numerous ways that we can build for permanence. Perhaps the most fulfilling way is by parenting children. As Churchill succinctly put it, 'There is no finer investment for any community than putting milk into babies'![7]

It is ultimately through my own children, spiritual as well as natural, that I am going to have the greatest impact on the world. Long after my marriage is forgotten its influence will never die. Hardly any of us have heard of Peter of Colechurch, a humble parish priest who died in 1205, and yet it was his design of London Bridge that spanned six centuries. His vision continues in perpetuity. No wonder the prophet Malachi insists that one of the primary purposes of the covenant of marriage is that God *'was seeking godly offspring'* (Malachi 2:15). God wants our brief lives to go on for ever and has provided a glorious means by which they can do so. It is through my children that the message of my transient life bridge will live on. The prophet Isaiah told Israel how this happens:

> ' "As for me, this is my covenant with them," says the LORD. "My Spirit, who is on you, and my words that I have put in your mouth will not depart from your mouth, or from the mouths of your children, or from the mouths of their descendants from this time on and forever," says the LORD.'
> (Isaiah 59:21)

Whenever I teach my children or stand in a pulpit I am empowered by the Word and the Spirit to live inter-generationally. I am drawing from my past, being myself and investing into my future.

I started this chapter by explaining how London Bridge, having been built of the right materials and constantly repaired and rebuilt, has managed to serve London through many lifetimes. Despite its patch-work history, its destruction and evolution, it is still spoken of with affection. Yet it is sad that somehow in our contemporary world it has lost a part of the magic and mystery that it contained at its outset. London is now more famous for its commerce than its bridges: it is more material than mystical. However, at the start of the book I also spoke of the London Millennium Bridge reaching into the future with renewed hope. I am hoping that this is a sign of things to come. Although the fortunes of our landmark bridges may wax and wane through the generations, the importance of our life bridges never diminishes. Our relationships must retain their central and godly position at the heart of our communities. Life bridges are, and must always be our lifeline.

Summary and advice

1. **All relationships, like bridges, are built to span the generations**. Every relationship has a history and future and so we should build with both our heritage and destiny in mind.

2. **Relationships of permanence are built with good materials**. Our relationships should be strong, have an ability to bounce back, give us a warning when overloaded and be built from imperishable materials.

3. **A strong relationship needs to be built, repaired and rebuilt**. A long-term relationship evolves through crisis. We have to learn that bridge-building takes time and effort, requires a lifetime of daily repairs, will experience conflict, is maintained by respect and must remain flexible.

4. **Everyone needs to live inter-generationally**. We are a product of the past but not a victim of it. If we learn to be ourselves we will be better equipped to pass on what we know to another generation.

5. **Life bridges are our lifeline**. Biblical relationships must retain their position at the heart of our communities if we are to look forward with hope.

Notes

1. Peter Ackroyd, *London. The Biography* (Chatto & Windus, 2000).
2. Samuel Pepys, *The Great Fire of London* (Phoenix, 1996).
3. Alan and Marilyn Bergman. Quoted in Stephen Citron, *The Musical from the Inside Out* (Hodder & Stoughton, 1991).
4. *The Story of the Sydney Harbour Bridge*, NSW Roads and Traffic Authority (1989).
5. Howard and William Hendricks, *As Iron Sharpens Iron* (Campus Crusade Asia Ltd, 1995).
6. Ibid.
7. Winston Churchill, broadcast 21 March 1943. Quoted in J.A. Sutcliffe (ed.), *The Sayings of Winston Churchill* (Duckworth, 1992).

Postscript

Soon after the completion of the first stone bridge over the River Thames, the Magna Carta, a charter of freedom, was drawn up by the English Barons in 1215 in order to counteract the king's oppression. It states, 'No town or person shall be *forced* to build bridges over rivers except those with an *ancient obligation* to do so'.[1] Obviously where freedom was the desired aim, no one was coerced to build bridges. Nonetheless, people were challenged to fulfil their obligations. Equally, my desire is not to force anyone to build life bridges. Nor can I make anyone follow biblical wisdom in the forming of them. However, I do believe we all have a God-given obligation to do so, not only for our sake, but also for the sake of society. Therefore, I have had no hesitation in quoting the Bible throughout because it is eternally true and consistently challenges us. It was Jesus Christ Himself who said, *'the truth will set you free'* (John 8:32). The Bible is the ultimate charter of freedom, and freedom is the goal of this book. I have also had no hesitation in writing that a relationship with Christ is foundational to all other relationships. Jesus continued by saying, *'If the Son sets you free, you will be free indeed'* (John 8:36). These two statements filled me with confidence as I wrote and yet I have written this book with some trepidation! Why? Because I am reminded of the power of books to enslave or free and the unsettling observation of an eighteenth-century king who said that books, 'Never die'.[2] Alongside the eternal truths of God's Word contained in the text, I have placed my less certain and often changeable opinions. I would ask you, therefore, to measure these carefully against the Scriptures. Luke, the writer of the Acts of the Apostles, commended the noble Bereans because they *'examined the Scriptures every day to see if what Paul said was true'* (Acts 17:11). Nevertheless, I have written this book in good faith, attempting to highlight some timeless principles and give some practical guidelines in order for us all to discover the success in our relationships that God so earnestly desires. I hope it has achieved its aim.

I would like to conclude by telling the story of a bridge-builder that encapsulates the parable that runs through the book. Saint Gonsalvo is represented in portrait and statue holding in his hand a model of a bridge. Although he lived in the middle of the thirteenth century, the story of his bridge is known to us over seven centuries later. But what was so significant about the bridge that he built that it continues to be remembered after so many uncertain years? According to the legend, Gonsalvo lived in Portugal next to a ford on the River Tamego. Many travellers had lost their lives in their attempt to cross and so Gonsalvo resolved to build a bridge. He approached a wealthy nobleman for money for the project. In response, the nobleman cynically passed his wife a note which read, 'Give him the weight of this paper in coin'! The wife duly placed the paper on one side of the scales and a small coin on the other. To her astonishment, the scales did not move. It was only when the entire amount of money required for the bridge was placed on the balance that the scales shifted. Gonsalvo returned to the river with a grateful heart. Strengthened by faith in the miraculous, empowered by a sacrificial gift and compelled by a love for people Gonsalvo completed his bridge. A simple faith enabled him to build more than a bridge. He built a testimony. My prayer is that this will also be our experience.

Notes

1. Magna Carta: Section 23. Translation in John McIlwain, *Magna Carta in Salisbury* (Pitkin Unichrome Ltd, 1999). Emphasis mine.
2. The King of Dahomey. Quoted in Kwesi J. Anquandah, *Castles and Forts of Ghana* (Paris: Atalante, 1999).

Personal notes

Personal notes

Personal notes

Personal notes

Personal notes

Personal notes

Personal notes

If you have enjoyed this book and would like to help us to send a copy of it and many other titles to needy pastors in the **Third World**, please write for further information
or send your gift to:

**Sovereign World Trust
PO Box 777, Tonbridge
Kent TN11 0ZS
United Kingdom**

or to the **'Sovereign World'** distributor in your country.

Visit our website at **www.sovereign-world.org**
for a full range of Sovereign World books.